PENGUIN BOOKS
THE PENGUIN BOOK OF GARDENIN

Meera Uberoi paints, writes haiku, and is an expert gardener. Her ⌐   ⌐
The Mahabharata, a management title, *Leadership Secrets from the Mahabh*   ⌐ for children,
Tales from the Panchatantra, *Stories from the Mahabharata* and *The Puffin Bo*   *ssic Indian Tales for Children*.

Meera Uberoi lives in Delhi.

THE
PENGUIN
BOOK OF
GARDENING
IN INDIA

Meera Uberoi

PENGUIN BOOKS

Penguin Books India (P) Ltd., 11 Community Centre, Panchsheel Park, New Delhi 110 017, India
Penguin Books Ltd., 80 Strand, London WC2R 0RL, UK
Penguin Group Inc., 375 Hudson Street, New York, NY 10014, USA
Penguin Books Australia Ltd., 250 Camberwell Road, Camberwell, Victoria 3124, Australia
Penguin Books Canada Ltd., 10 Alcorn Avenue, Suite 300, Toronto, Ontario, M4V 3B2, Canada
Penguin Books (NZ) Ltd., Cnr Rosedale & Airborne Roads, Albany, Auckland, New Zealand
Penguin Books (South Africa) (Pty) Ltd., 24 Sturdee Avenue, Rosebank 2196, South Africa

First published by Penguin Books India 2002

Copyright © Meera Uberoi 2002

The author and publishers gratefully acknowledge the following for permission to reproduce copyright material:

Osman Streater and Fahir Iz for poems by Melih Cevdet, Ahmet Hasim, Pir Sultan Adbal, Yahya Kemal Beyaltli, Ahmedi, Karacaoglan and Ahmed Pasha from *The Book of Turkish Verse* ed. Nermin Menemencioglu in collaboration with Fahir Iz.

Penguin Books Ltd., UK for poems by Bhavabuti and Anon, translated by John Brough from *Poems from the Sanskrit* (1968); poems by Emperor Meiji and Cheng Ssu-hsiao translated by Thwaite & Bownas from *The Penguin Book of Japanese Verse*; poem by Yevtushenko from *Yevtushenko: Selected Poems*; poem by Ammianus, translated by Peter Jay from *The Greek Anthology* (1973).

Penguin Books India for extracts from *The Loom of Time* (1989) by Kalidasa, translated by Chandra Rajan.

All illustrations by Anwar except those on pages 137, 139, 156, 157, 158, 211, 212, 225, 229, 236, 237 by Meera Uberoi.

Photographs by Dibakar Sarkar

Typeset in Lapidary 333BT by Eleven Arts, Delhi 110 035
Printed at International Print-o-Pack, New Delhi

Flower in the crannied wall,
I pluck you out of the crannies,
I hold you here, root and all, in my hand,
Little flower—but if I could understand
What you are, root and all, and all in all,
I should know what God and man is.

—Tennyson

Contents

A Brief History of Gardening

Tradition says that the Garden of Eden lay in the land between the Euphrates and the Tigris and that Eden was divided by the four rivers of life. This should scarcely come as a surprise, considering the earliest civilization, that of Sumer, dawned in Mesopotamia, and gardens, surely the hallmark of any civilization, are first mentioned in a Sumerian cuneiform clay tablet, as early as 3000 BC. Among their creation myths there is one that begins in a garden and a primitive sort of biological language is used to describe it.

Gardens are the direct outcome of leisure and time to appreciate the beauty of nature, which can only occur when there is political and economic stability. The Sumerians rapidly made great strides and by 3000 BC, had developed writing, agriculture, irrigation, architecture and with it the art of gardening. Irrigation was vital in this dry and arid land, and the engineers constructed intricate systems of canals, dykes, weirs and reservoirs. When gardens were laid out, these pools and canals became an integral part of the garden design, as did symmetry and regularity. Criss-crossing waterways, central pools, symmetrical rows of trees and shrubs, and geometric patterns were all necessary to facilitate watering, the primary consideration when planning the garden. The garden design was also determined by geographical conditions—not only were the canals and pools essential but the whole was enclosed within high walls to keep out the harsh desert winds. The natural landscape was shut out, kept beyond the walls. Within lay paradise.

The word 'paradise' is a transliteration of the Persian '*pairideza*': *pairi* (around) and *deza* (wall). It was Cyrus the Great who first used the word to describe his gardens when he laid them out after his Babylonian conquest, almost 2000 years after the Sumerians had laid out their first gardens. His gardens were modelled on the Babylonian gardens he had seen, which in turn had been influenced by those of Sumer-Akkad. It is said that Saragon—the Semetic emperor of Sumer-Akkad—sent roses to his capital after he had conquered western Persia, around 2800 BC. Courtyard gardens too probably originated in Mesopotamia where houses were built around a central courtyard, a permanent feature of most Middle Eastern gardens up to the present day. Thousands of years later, the cloister gardens of medieval Europe based their gardens on those of the Spanish Moors who were responsible for taking the traditional Middle Eastern garden design to Spain.

Around 3000 BC, independent civilizations rose in Egypt and China, and the latter is reputed to have had gardens unrivalled at the time. The knowledge of plants and gardening developed very early in China. The first work on plants may have been the herbal of Shen Nung, who reigned around 2800 BC, though it was not put down in writing until much later, in the 1st century AD.

The earliest extant painting of a garden is a fresco from the tomb of Nebanum. Built around 1400 BC in Egypt. It depicts an exquisite garden dominated by a central pool filled with lotuses and water-lilies. The main entrance is aligned on a pergola walk of vines leading directly to the dwelling. The rest of the garden is laid out with tree-lined avenues, four rectangular ponds containing waterfowl and two garden pavilions. Rigidly symmetrical, the garden is divided

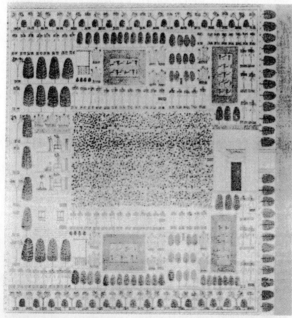

into separate walled enclosures so that the overlying symmetry is not apparent to the viewer. Such a highly developed pattern argues a long period of stability in design implying that gardens were in existence long before the fresco. It is very likely that similar pleasure gardens existed in Egypt as early as 2800 BC. The plants in the garden were irrigated from the pools, like the gardens of Sumer. As in Mesopotamia, Egypt too needed irrigation for agriculture and her gardens, and here too the garden was enclosed within walls to shut out the stark, pitiless landscape. Whether the Egyptian garden design was adopted from Sumer or developed independently is not certain.

Earliest surviving detailed garden plan, the estate of an Egyptian official, c. 1400 BC. From Ippolito Rosellini, *I monument dell Egitto e della Nubia*. In the New York Public Library.

In faraway China, gardens evolved on totally different lines. The beautiful landscapes with their mountains, lakes, streams, cascades and forests filled with amazingly diverse flora inspired the people to imitate nature rather than keep her out, resulting in the most hauntingly beautiful gardens. The Mesopotamians, whether the people of Sumer-Akkad or Babylon, the Egyptians, and later the Persians, all shut out their environs to create a world of fantasy

The Chinese garden

with sparkling waters, scented flowers and fruiting trees. The Chinese, on the other hand, brought the landscape into the garden. At the beginning of Chinese history, their religion was animist in form. All of nature—sky, mountains, lakes, rivers, rocks, trees, had their residing spirits, and this belief made good manners towards nature as important as they were in the crowded human world. With the rise of Taoism, the Chinese began to take great pleasure in the calm landscapes of the remote countryside. Since people in the cities lived far from the country, they made likenesses nearer home, in their gardens. The gardens were a tribute to nature and the guidelines came from the world around them. The dominating influence was the rich flora of the land—peonies, day lilies, camellias, peach and plum, azaleas and roses are

among the numerous flowers native to China. As in nature, there was no rigidity in the design, rather, it flowed like a gentle stream. These gardens were masterpieces of man-made naturalness and studied informality. Hard lines and symmetry were not considered aesthetically pleasing.

The earliest Chinese gardens are said to date back to the legendary Hsia dynasty

The Chinese garden
'The Ambassador's residence at Canton'.

around 2200 BC. By 1763 BC, Jie Gui, the last ruler of the Hsia dynasty, built parkland gardens which bordered on decadence. There were huge lakes, grottoes, streams, hills, cascades and every other garden feature of the time. It is said he filled the ponds with wine and hung large chunks of meat on trees to make the hunt easy for his depraved nobles. But Zhou—the last ruler of the Shang dynasty which fell around 1122 BC—outdid Jie Gui. He squandered the entire imperial treasury on parks and gardens in which highly imaginative orgies are said to have taken place! These deplorable excesses however, are indicative of a sound knowledge of plants, their propagation, landscape design and garden aesthetics. By Confucius' time, the library in Peking had 500 books on roses alone. The Chinese were the first to transplant fully grown trees; and they developed the techniques of air-layering and creating bonsai. They were also the first to invent a pesticide. By 100 AD, they had discovered that dry chrysanthemum flowers kept insects away and developed a powder which was widely used as an insecticide.

> **King Alcinous' Garden**
>
> *From outside the court, by its entry, extends a great garden of four acres, fenced each way. In it flourish tall trees: pears or pomegranates, stone fruits gaudy with their ripening load, also sweet figs and heavy-bearing olives . . . Pear grows old upon pear and apple upon apple, with bunch after bunch of grapes and fig after fig . . . Beyond the last row of trees, well-laid garden plots have been arranged, blooming all the year with flowers. And there are two springs, one led throughout the orchard-ground, whilst the other dives beneathe the sill of the great court to gush out beside the stately house.*
>
> —The Odyssey

The Minoans of Crete, whose civilization ended around 1600 BC were famous throughout the Greek islands for their rose cultivation. Rhodes, which gets its name from the roses growing on the island, was so heavily scented by the flowers, that sailors could smell the land before they sighted it. The six-petalled rose in a fresco in the palace at Knossos is probably the earliest picture of a rose. Roses were a popular motif— gold hairpins, each topped with a full-blown rose, and a chalice with sprays of roses were found in a tomb dating from around 1600 BC. Other frescoes in the palace show lilies, irises, rock roses and what is possibly the saffron crocus. The fabulous garden of Alcinous (the king of Phaeacia who is praised for his love of agriculture and whose daughter Nausicca fell in love with the shipwrecked Odysseus), was probably located near modern Corfu. Odysseus too nostalgically describes the enclosed gardens, vineyards and fruit-trees in *The Odyssey*. He also describes gardens on the island of Ithaca, which may date as far back as 1250 BC.

In India gardens began, as far as we know, with the advent of the Aryans who came to the subcontinent around 1500 BC. Whether the people of Harappa and Mohenjodaro (2600-

1500 BC) had gardens in their utilitarians cities, we don't
know for certain. But we do know that trees and plants were
of great significance, for numerous seals depicting them have
been found, and a people who revered plants almost certainly
grew them around their dwellings. It is also known that there
were trade links between the Harappan and Sumerian
civilizations. Surely the gardens of Mesopotamia were known
to the people of the Indus Valley. The Aryans, as we know

*I live in pellucid Ithaca, the island
of Mount Neriton, whose upstanding
slopes are all a quiver with the wind-
blown leaves.*

—The Odyssey

from the ancient texts, built fabulous palace gardens. There are records of them in the *Ramayana*
and the *Mahabharata*—the garden of Ravana of Lanka and the magnificent palace and garden
that Maya, the *asura*, built for the Pandavas. The Mahabharata says that there were gardens both
within and without the palace. Illusion and artifice were used with such panache and style that
even the Pandavas' most bitter enemy, Duryodhana, had to admit that his palace could boast of
nothing so marvellous. With the use of what could be lapis tiles and quartz, artificial ponds
were made, complete with lotuses and waterfowl, and murky still ponds were used to create an
illusion of dry land. Whether fact or fiction, the tale clearly shows that the ancient Indians
knew how to employ artifice and illusion in their garden design, a concept most consider
modern. But in general, design, whether formal or informal, was not imposed upon gardens.
Ancient Indians lived in communion with nature and saw no reason for strict order and form
in their gardens. In the tropics, nature is bountiful and there is an abundance of flora and
water. This precluded the need for artificial water ways and symmetry in planting. Ponds and
tanks were built not so much for irrigating the gardens but because they were considered
auspicious and as catchment areas. Enclosed gardens with a definite plan and structure such as
the Persian garden simply did not exist in ancient India.

The earliest known gardens were those built around temple complexes. The priests
maintained large groves of flowering trees and shrubs as flowers were an essential part of
religious rituals. Flowers were also grown extensively for their perfume oils which were used
both by men and women. The famed 'Perfumes of Arabia' actually came from India; the Arab
traders simply took them westward. Secluded hermitages had gardens around them filled with
flowering creepers and shrubs, but there was no definite structural form and the gardens
merged into the surrounding forests in a seamless fashion. It was in such a garden that Dushyanta,
father of Bharata (from whom India gets her name), met Shakuntala. Kalidasa, the poet-
dramatist, describes the garden vividly in his play *Abhigyan Shakuntalam*.

South America is very rich in flora; nature is more than bountiful here. Many of the
flowers and fruits familiar to us come from there. The Mayas, whose civilization ended before

the Spaniards arrived, were an astonishing people who had the zero a thousand years before European mathematics acquired it from India via the Arabs. They were also monumental builders, superb craftsmen and excellent astronomers. Whether this great civilization had gardens we can't be sure, since Diego de Landa, a zealous Franciscan monk, deemed it his mission to destroy most of the scientific, religious and historical writings of the Mayas. But ornamentation of buildings was a common practice and this agrarian civilization surely had vast gardens around its citadels and temples. The Yucatan is home to many flowers: cosmos, orchids, flowering cacti, marigolds, zinnias, sunflowers, dahlias and a number of flowering trees like the jacaranda. The Mayans undoubtedly grew them. The Spanish did however, record the elaborate gardens laid out by the later Aztecs of Mexico and the Incas of Peru. The hillsides were terraced, and there were groves of flowering trees, fountains and ornamental ponds.

By fifth century BC, all the known civilizations of the Old World could boast of gardens, the most famous of which were the Hanging Gardens of Babylon. Nebuchadnezzar built this garden for his wife who was homesick for the flowers of her homeland. His technically skilled gardeners grew trees, shrubs and vines in porous earthenware containers and troughs on a series of artificial terraces. Water was carried up by means of pipes, right to the top of the pyramid which was 150 ft high and 1200 ft wide. Flowering and fruiting plants covered it from top to bottom, making it one of the Seven Wonders of the Ancient World. Around this time, gardens of western Asia and Egypt were extremely formal but the Greeks were about to change that. They began to group plants informally in containers of varying sizes which were strategically placed in the garden. By the fifth century BC, Xenophon of Athens and Lysander of Sparta had both separately visited the court of Cyrus the Younger, in Persia, and were greatly impressed by the gardens surrounding the royal palace, which were much like the gardens laid out by Cyrus the Great, more than a hundred years before.

Cyrus the Great's garden design followed the gardening principles of the Babylonians. His garden at Pasargadae, laid out around

The Indian garden
The Mughal *chaarbagh* incorporated in an Indian setting, 1653.

546 BC, was designed to complement and unite the official and residential palaces. Geometric in plan, the garden had features which included carved-stone water courses, symmetrically arranged trees and shrubs within well-defined plots, and straight, tree-lined avenues. All later Islamic gardens right up to the twentieth century, include these essential elements. The Persians are a conventional people in many ways and once the garden design had been perfected to suit their needs and taste, it was seldom altered. Cyrus the Great would have been quite at home in Shah Jahan's garden in Agra which was laid out almost 3000 years later, for the basic design had not changed.

When Xenophon returned to Greece, he laid out a garden in Scillus following the design of the Persian garden. The style was eminently suited to the Greek climate where the summers are hot and dry. Xenophon set the trend of Middle Eastern garden design in Greece, and his garden was to influence all the gardens of Greece for centuries to come, and later, those of Rome. About a hundred years after Xenophon laid out his garden, the Greek traveller Megasthenes visited Chandragupta Maurya's court and was fascinated by the verdant gardens which were quite unlike anything seen in Greece. His record is the oldest Western description of an Indian garden: 'In the parks tame peacocks are kept, and pheasants which have been domesticated, and among cultivated plants there are some to which the king's servants attend to with special care . . . there are shady groves and pasture ground planted with trees . . . some native to the soil while others are with circumspect care brought from other parts . . . . There are also artificial ponds of great beauty.' These gardens extant in the fourth century BC, were almost certainly influenced by Persian garden design, for the western provinces of India, as far back as the sixth century BC, had closer connections with the Persian Empire than with the rest of India, and were politically a part of the Achaemenidian Empire established

Persian-style garden
The Mughal Emperor Babur's *Bagh-i Vafa* (Garden of Fidelity) at Kabul, illustrated in a late 16th-century chronicle of Babur's life.

by Cyrus the Great. Trade routes were well-developed and garden design could very well have travelled from Persia to India, along with the traders and their goods. On the other hand, the gardens described in the Vedas (1500 BC) and other ancient texts bear no resemblance to Middle Eastern gardens. Their setting is sylvan, with trees and creepers growing in great profusion and ponds filled with lotuses and water-lilies, much as they are seen in nature. Groves are mentioned as are trees entwined with creepers but nothing is said of rows or geometric design.

Gardens of first century Rome were Greek in design, as was much else in the empire. The Hellenistic design, which had its roots in the Babylonian garden, was seen in most Roman cities, especially the seaside resorts of Pompeii and Herculaneum. These small town gardens however, had one difference: they were in harmony with the landscape though they retained many of the Eastern elements. Italy is mild in spring and autumn, with hot and dry summers, as is Greece and Persia. Thus the essentials of the Persian garden—shady walks, open-air pavilions and water—were eminently suited to the climate. But as the climate was not as harsh, there was no effort to keep the landscape at bay. In imperial Rome, gardens were more lavish, and sites for villas were chosen not for defence as in earlier times, but for climate and vista. The emphasis in these gardens was on waterworks, sculpture and topiary. Like their Greek counterparts, few flowers played an important role; the exceptions being the rose and the lily. The most ambitious garden was that of Nero's Golden House. This elaborate garden lay in the middle of Rome and covered 300 acres. There was an artificial lake, ornamental pastoral fields, marble pavilions, a vineyard and woods. As the empire expanded, Roman garden design reached its remotest corners though its eastern provinces were not noticeably influenced by Rome, as the designs of Babylon and Persia had long been established there. But in Europe, the Roman influence in garden design can be seen even today in the topiaries and sculptures of famous gardens all over Europe and England. The British fondness for topiaries in the eighteenth century, when almost every large garden had one, has its beginnings in the Roman occupation of the island, though the trend was established by the Dutch in the seventeenth century. But then, Dutch formality and topiaries too, have their roots in ancient Rome.

After the fall of Rome, gardens disappeared from Europe and re-emerged only in the medieval period when there was a certain amount of political stability. Around the tenth century, gardens began to dot the landscape which had been successfully denuded by the crusaders and marauding Goths and Visigoths.

The Chinese, despite dynastic changes, Mongol invasions and political upheavals, continued to create breathtakingly beautiful gardens right up to the twentieth century when a large number of old gardens were destroyed by the People's Army. Even the nomadic

Mongols, who were considered totally uncivilized by the Sung Chinese, did not do as much damage to this ancient and great civilization as did Mao's little men, who in their ignorance considered beauty elitist and the destruction of it their bounden duty. With the ravaging of the gardens they ravaged their own civilization. But fortunately, detailed descriptions and paintings survive which bear testimony to the sound gardening knowledge of the people. The features of classical Chinese gardens were carried forward right up to the twentieth century—man-made bridges, cascades, lakes, carefully chosen rocks, an abundance of flowers, meandering streams and walkways were all part of the grand design.

Chinese garden design first unfolded in Europe in the fourteenth century, in the writings of Marco Polo, who described the gardens of the Sung emperor. That account did somewhat influence European gardens of the time but it was not really felt until centuries later in the 1800s when European and British gardens, taking a leaf from the Chinese manual, shed their stifling formality. In south-east Asia, Chinese garden design had a lasting impact, which even today, is based on principles laid out more than 3000 years ago. But it is the Eastern spread of the Chinese garden design into Japan that has produced the most unique style. The purpose of these gardens was not simply to provide the viewer with pleasure; it was far more esoteric—appealing to the soul as much as the eye. Hitherto gardens the world over were designed to provide food and pleasure in that order but the Japanese infused into them a mysticism and spirituality which turned these gardens into spiritual havens, especially after the advent of Zen Buddhism.

The Japanese imported a fully mature culture from China around the fifth century—writing, silk-weaving, painting, Buddhism, poetry, ceramics and garden design. The first

The early European garden

landscape garden with a lake, as recorded, was laid out around the imperial palace at Nara in AD 607. Some of the main features, such as the bridge and lake, were constructed by a Korean craftsman who was called the Ugly Artisan because he had white spots on his skin, probably leucoderma. A bridge spanned the lake in contemporary Chinese fashion along with other typical features, and for the next few centuries, the Japanese faithfully copied Chinese gardens. An eighth century screen from the imperial treasure house, Shosoin, depicts a lady seated on a pitted rock by a lake; nearby is a tree with a twisted trunk. Rock, lake, tree—all elements of a Chinese garden. Early in the Heian period (794-1185), an imperial park was laid out, and the dominant feature was a lake dotted with rocky islands. The Chinese believed that the Immortals lived on islands in the ocean called Peng-lai, and replicas were a permanent feature in the imperial gardens of China. The Japanese had no such belief, but they faithfully followed Chinese garden designs right up to the eleventh century. A rare survivor of early Heian gardens is the Saga-no-in, where the Emperor Saga had retired in 823 AD. His lake, bordered by cherries and maples, once had islands linked by rocky outcrops, and the 'cascade' in the north bank is probably the earliest 'dry cascade', which was later to become a part of Japanese gardening tradition. The emperor was passionately Chinese in all things, so it is quite safe to assume that this putative Japanese feature is in actuality a Chinese prototype, though the Chinese usually shunned such abstract symbols. They preferred their reality with its magnificent beauty, and

The Japanese garden

being essentially a pragmatic people, the abstract was confined to the world of ideas. The Heian Japanese, like the Chinese, adored brightly coloured flowers which were grown in great profusion, quite unlike the gardens after the twelfth century which owed their austerity to Zen Buddhism. These gardens were spare, colour was kept to the bare minimum and there were never more than a couple of dominant features. Zen influenced all aspects of Japanese life—poetry, painting, fabric design, pottery and garden design. Zen is austere and metaphysical, and the gardens are a reflection of these Zen ideals. Moss gardens bereft of bright flowers, vistas of swept sand seas, bamboos lit by a single stone lantern—the gardens were designed to evoke quiet contemplation rather than boisterous exuberance. Almost every feature was a metaphoric representation of an abstract idea. The opulent and lush Chinese garden with its grand design and myriad facets, gave way to smaller gardens, pared down to the bare minimum. Zen eschews 'too much'. This is best expressed by Yoshida Kenko (1283-1350), the reclusive Buddhist monk who wrote, 'I should call it a mark of vulgarity to have all manner of gadgets within easy reach . . . a forest of br ushes . . . profusion of stones and plants in your garden.' Cleanliness, personal as well as in the surroundings, is a Zen precept, and the garden is never slovenly or loud. Every scattered petal or leaf is there because it is meant to be. The typical Zen garden is a small walled enclosure usually just beyond the abbot's living quarters. These gardens are for viewing rather than participating in, unlike the earlier Chinese-style 'stroll gardens' where people walked on gently curving paths or boated on the lakes to see the changing vistas. These single-positioned gardens began early in the Heian period but were perfected after the induction of Zen Buddhism in Japan. The acme of Japanese gardens, however, is the tea garden of the sixteenth and seventeenth centuries which is firmly rooted in Zen Buddhism. The 'Way of Tea' as other 'ways' is Taoist in origin and was absorbed by Ch'an Buddhism which became Zen. By following the 'way' one attained self-containment and oneness with the cosmic energy flow. In the tea gardens, creativity replaced imitation and the metaphoric Japanese garden burst out of the cocoon of Chinese traditions.

In Japan, Zen permeated into all the art forms and whether it was a haiku, a sumi-e or a garden, the artwork had to evoke *sabi* (isolation), *wabi* (austerity, moderation), *aware* (impermanence) and *yugen* (elusiveness, mystery), if it was to meet the high standards set by the masters. As with the seventeen-syllable haiku or the few brush-strokes of the sumi-e, the garden too, must be profound yet simple and austere. Artifice was used to create naturalness, and the whole inspired meditative contemplation.

Of all the Japanese gardens, the most esoteric and metaphysical by far are the 'dry gardens'; the most famous being the Ryoanji Temple garden. Five groups of rocks are arranged in a sea of raked white sand. There are no flowers, no shrubs, and the only bits of greenery to be seen are the strips of moss between the rocks. This stark, arid garden nevertheless affects even those unacquainted with Zen, and the deep, profound philosophy behind it is palpable. There is nothing superfluous, nothing in excess. Zen influence can still be seen in the small modern gardens which are carefully planned to evoke the gentle calm and solitude of a distant landscape. Even the most casual and unambitious garden will have a quiet dignity and harmony. Flowers are not grown in profusion, there is no riot of colour—just a touch provided by a camellia or azalea. The emphasis is on subtlety and texture—hard/soft, smooth/rough, dull/glossy. Many dispense with colour altogether. Mosses, grass, bamboo, low pruned bushes, a pine or two, a small path, a lantern, a few rocks, all symbolic, form the basis of these gardens. The elaborate was replaced by long austerity.

As Japanese gardens were maturing, Europe sank into the Dark Ages and gardens disappeared from the scene. But the relatively stable political climate in the Eastern empire (Greece, Asia Minor) saw gardening rise to new heights. Hellenistic traditions remained but in many cases, the gimmickry of wondrous gadgets superseded aesthetics. The feature most often seen was a tree of gold or silver on which artificial birds perched, flapped their wings and warbled. When shaken the branches sprayed perfume or wine! These gardens were Persian in character except for the gadgetry which owed its existence to the advancement of mechanical sciences in Greece.

The Persians had perfected their garden design centuries before the birth of Mohammed, but for practical purposes, all Persian-style gardens built after the seventh century are called Islamic, for it is the aggressive spread of Islam that carried the design far and wide, from Spain in the west to India in the east. Only in Turkey did the rigid, geometric Persian design meet its Waterloo. The Turkish people have long been influenced by the cultures of both East and West—Greece, Rome, Babylon and Persia, thus making them far more cosmopolitan than the Persians. The Persian garden design altered radically when it went to Turkey. Extreme formality gave way to a charming lack of order, hard lines softened and blurred, strong axial points were discarded, and waterways did not run at right angles to each other. Flowers, shrubs and trees were grown wherever possible; the formal, enclosed flower beds were dispensed with. Gardens spilled over where they willed in a more haphazard fashion than anything seen in Spain, Persia or Mughal India. Though there were no water channels, water did play a major part in the garden design. Pools and fountains were an important theme; in fact, the Turkish people were so partial to fountains that they were seen not only in gardens but also in city squares and village streets, wherever they could be installed. Evliya Celebi, in his book *Narrative of Travels*, written in the seventeenth century, remarks that if he were to describe all the gardens and walks in Istanbul, it would be an exceedingly long work.

Coastal Turkey is blessed with a more salubrious climate than either Iran or India and the weather gods show great clemency there. The Sea of Marmara and the Bosphorous make Istanbul pleasant even in the worst summer months making protective features redundant. The gardens of this ancient city have a sense of open-ness, though enclosed in high walls, and the architecture and design reflect the various cultures that have influenced the city. Turkey has been exposed to Greek culture from the days when Troy was flourishing, Roman culture, after the first century, and to neighbouring Persia. The Greek influence was well-entrenched. There is a legend that the Megarians went to the Oracle of Delphi and were told to build a city on the Sarayuburnu. They went to Asia Minor and built their city, which they called Byzantium after their leader, Byzas. One hundred and fifty years later the Persians conquered it, but a century later the Greeks took it back. The Romans deposed the Greeks and made it their eastern capital, and in the fourth century they renamed it Constantinopolis, after Emperor Constantine who converted to Christianity. For centuries the city was a haven for men of science and learning, but in 1453, Mohammed II conquered Constantinople, renamed it Istanbul and altered the culture forever.

Mohammed II was an astonishing man who not only delighted in planning the gardens of his palaces and mosques, but actually worked in them whenever he could spare the time. The enormous gardens at Topkapi, which were far more extensive in the fifteenth century, were greatly influenced by Islamic design features and from this time on the Islamic style became dominant.

Many beautiful flowers and shrubs are native to Turkey—tulips, roses, narcissus, the cypress and Judas trees to name just a few. The sultans, nobles and wealthy citizens built summer palaces and dwellings (*yalis*) along the coast and gardens were laid out behind the houses. These terraced gardens tumbled and ran down to a natural belt of trees and shrubs where walkways curved among the pines and other indigenous trees. Early Turkish gardens reflect the Greek influence with the colonnaded courtyard and pool to provide cool and shade. The later, Islamic influence introduced fountains, a profusion of flowers and pavilions connected by paths, but without the overall geometric pattern and structural rigidity.

In the mid-nineteenth century, Charles White, who wrote *Three Years in Constantinople*, describes the gardens near the Bosphorous. In the flowering borders, vegetables were grown; vines, roses and other climbers were trained on walls, fences and trellises. Parterres, edged by clipped box-hedges, were filled with orange and lemon trees, bay and lilac bushes. The gardens were filled with flowers —lilies, tulips, sunflowers, larkspur, mignonette, lupins, sweet peas and convolvulus were planted around groups of shrubs and small trees such as the pomegranate. They grew geraniums, carnations, stocks and fuchsias in flower pots which stood on terrace steps and walls. The walks were shaded by vine-trellises and each parterre had a central pool or fountain. Secluded areas on the hillsides were planted with fig, walnut, pine, cedar and chestnut. Most private gardens had at least one kiosk, either in a tiled courtyard or at the water's edge. Persian design influenced the kiosks and pavilions built by Mohammed II, and these Ottoman-designed pavilions became a garden feature in Egypt during the Ottoman rule. The delightful gardens of Turkey are the result of 2500 years of intermingling of peoples of diverse cultures, who brought with them not only their traditions but also plants from their native lands.

With Islam, the Persian/Byzantine garden design spread eastward into Central Asia, Afghanistan and India, along the whole of the North African coast and throughout the Mediterranean, especially Spain. During the Moorish caliphate, there were more than 50,000 villas built in the Valley of Guadalquiver in Spain, all of which had gardens much like the jewel-like one at Al-Hambra which was built between 1248 and 1354. Unfortunately, the zealous Crusaders destroyed most of the buildings and surrounding gardens at the end of the fifteenth century but thankfully it was restored in the nineteenth century. The Al-Hambra had colonnaded courtyards with pools and fountains, insulating it from the world without by containing it within walls.

The finest Islamic gardens in Iran and Afghanistan were created between the thirteenth and fourteenth centuries. Marco Polo, who spent nine months in Tabriz in north-east Iran, describes fabulous gardens with *chaarbaghs*, water courses, shrubs and trees. Timurlang, more renowned for his wanton cruelty, laid out some of the most exquisite gardens of the time. In Samarkand, he planned gardens filled with flowers, groves of flowering and fruiting trees, and vineyards. In one, water was diverted from the central stream to run among the trees to create a natural waterway. Dilkhush (Heart's Delight), Chinar Bagh, the New Garden and the Garden of Paradise were all laid out by him and are vividly described by Clavijo, the Spanish envoy who went to Samarkand in 1404. As a young man, Babur saw these gardens, and his passion for gardens may well have begun in the gardens laid out by his ancestor.

Babur laid out the first of the great Mughal gardens in India. These were pleasances of water, meadows, trees and flowers but unlike Al-Hambra, architecture was not the main feature. Babur had the soul of a nomad. In India, after the classical period, there are few records of gardens. But gardens there were, as is testified by the *Upavana Vinoda*, a treatise on plants and plant life written sometime between the 12th and 13th century. There were elaborate gardens in Nalanda and Sarnath, but with the disappearance of Buddhism in the seventh century, they fell into disuse and decay. In the south, gardens remained intact for much longer, unaffected by the political upheavals of the north. After the tenth century, garden style and architecture was influenced by Islam, and by the time Babur conquered Delhi in the sixteenth century, the Indo-

Islamic architecture and garden design was well entrenched. The Mughals brought it to the state of the art and their gardens had few rivals in the Islamic world.

Babur, despite his ancestry (he could trace it to both Timurlang and Ghengis Khan), was an extremely cultured man, and his love for flowers and gardens ran deep. He created gardens wherever he went. When he took over the city of Kabul he laid out ten gardens in the city, the remains of some of which can be seen even today. The one in Istalif, close to the Paghman mountains, had chinars, oaks and Judas trees growing near a natural spring. On the hillside was a round seat and a stream was diverted to flow past it. Along the banks he planted sycamore and chinar saplings. He also planned and laid out the garden around what was later to be his tomb. When he conquered India he did no less, but he had to face obstacles that would have daunted a lesser visionary. The flat northern plain of India had no rising ground for terraces, no natural springs and streams; most were monsoon fed, and the climate totally unsuitable for the flowers of his homeland. Only in the brief winter months could he grow his beloved irises, hyacinths and tulips. Unlike Timur whose bloody raids and sack of Delhi were unparalleled in their carnage, Babur was no predatory raider. What he did inherit from his nomadic ancestors was a need for wide open spaces. That coupled with a lifetime spent as a soldier swept away any hankering he might have had for the security of walls. He chose to live in his *chaarbaghs* rather than the confines of the palace. As in Kabul, his gardens in India were terraced, with strong axial points and water courses, and since the winters were not as harsh as those of Farghana and Kabul, he was able to expand the utilitarian aspects of his gardens. His extensive terraced gardens were essentially open-air palaces in which he lived all the year round. The Kabul winters used to force him indoors; he could move to the great encampments in the meadows and gardens outside the city only in spring. But in India he was bound by no such constraints. Each terrace in his garden was designed for a specific purpose—reception areas, baths, mosque, living quarters and a pavilion for public audiences. Babur's genius as a landscape artist is seen in his choice of sites, his flair in the use of local flora, his ability to turn a disadvantage into an advantage and his sense and employment of space. His gardens were designed for living in, not merely for viewing.

His descendants, especially Jehangir and Shah Jahan, inherited his love for gardens, and of the two, Jehangir was the more ardent lover of nature. Kashmir was the area he loved most. 'The flowers of Kashmir are beyond counting and calculating', he wrote and commissioned his court artist, Mansur, to paint over a hundred of them. When he went to Kabul, he visited Babur's gardens, 'seven in one day'. The gardens of Vernag, Nishat and Shalimar were all created by him. Jehangir's ideal garden was the one laid out in Sihrind. As he describes it, 'on entering the garden

I found myself immediately in a covered avenue, planted on each with scarlet roses and beyond them, arose groves of cypress, fir, plane and evergreens . . . Passing through these, we entered what was in reality the garden, which now exhibited a variegated parterre ornamented with flowers of the utmost of brilliancy of colours and of the choicest kind.' There was a pond in the centre of a green parterre and an octagonal colonnaded pavilion which could seat 200 or more quite comfortably.

Shah Jahan's talent lay in architecture, and in his gardens, though he did plant flowers and trees, the buildings dominated the landscape. His genius is seen in the Red Fort of Delhi and his beloved Taj Mahal in Agra. The gardens around the Taj Mahal are ambitious and the waterways are almost wide enough to be termed canals. The walks are tree-lined and the enclosed squares planted with trees and shrubs—all the basic traditions of the Islamic garden—but it is the white marble edifice that draws and holds the eye, making the gardens paltry. Not so in Nishat or Shalimar, built by Jehangir. The gardens hold pride of place.

After Shah Jahan, garden style in India became static, without a touch of individuality. Most of the gardens built by these phenomenal Mughal gardeners—Babur, Jehangir and Shah Jahan—were neglected, and little remains of their former beauty. But in the bare bones—water courses, paths, central pools (most now dry)—one can see how lovely they once must have been. The Mughals built three types of gardens—courtyard gardens, tomb gardens and the Paradise gardens, the last much like the gardens of the ancient Babylonians and Persians.

Not long after Babur built his gardens in Kabul and India, Shah Abbas I of Iran conquered the region of Mazandaran (1596-97) near the Caspian Sea, and he experienced the same delight as Jehangir did when he first entered the Valley of Kashmir. He built a number of palaces and dwellings along the caravan routes, and each was surrounded by a garden. In doing so he was merely doing what Persians had done for more than 2000 years. Over the centuries, wherever the centre of power was located in Iran—whether Tabriz, Shiraz, Isfahan or Herat—palaces and houses were built and gardens surrounded the homes of nobles, court officials, governors and the like. Timur's son Shahrukh built some exquisite pavilions and gardens in Herat and he also renovated the existing ones which were falling into ruin. The gardens of Shah Abbas I rivalled those of Shiraz, a city as famous for its gardens as it was for the production of books. A miniature illustrating a collection of poems dating back to 1396, contemporary with Timur's reign, depicts a small garden surrounding a palace. A stream has been diverted to flow within the garden, water lilies grow in the pool, and willows with violets at the base line the banks of the stream. Shah Abbas I's gardens, 200 years later, were very similar; the ancient Persian design had scarcely altered over time. Thomas Herbert, who wrote *Travels in Persia* (1627-29) describes a garden situated in the desert outside Isfahan which was much like what Abbas I built in the north. The garden was filled with fruit trees; peaches, pomegranate, pears, plums, cherries and apricots. It had streams and artificial grottoes, stone pools lined with marble and an airy mansion which had twelve rooms with covered balconies for viewing. Shah Abbas I died in 1629, when Herbert was in Isfahan. 'Gardens here for grandeur and fragrance are such as no city in Asia outcries.' Shah Abbas I was the greatest creator of gardens in Iran, the equal of the Mughal emperors in India.

Shah Abbas I was succeeded by Shah Safi, whose successor, Shah Abbas II, passionately loved flowers and gardens. He built the famous *Chihil Sutun* (Forty Pillars), a fabulous garden pavilion surrounded by trees under-planted with rose bushes to line paths, flower beds and shrubs which were divided by water channels. Twenty wooden pillars surrounding a large rectangular pool support the roof; the reflection of the pillars in the water is said to have inspired the name 'Forty Pillars'. Another gem of a garden laid out in the seventeenth century was the Sa'atabad (the Abode of Felicity), and so much did Shah Abbas II hold it in esteem that he commissioned Mirza Hadi (Ramzi) to write a poem in its praise. The manuscript, copied and illustrated for the British Library in the nineteenth century, contains twenty-nine paintings of the flowers described by Hadi. These include larkspur, irises, hyacinths, violets, willows, narcissus, tuberoses, tulips, poppies, blossoms of fruit trees such as apple, peach and cherry, lilies, white jasmine and several varieties of roses.

Modern Iranians still have their gardens, as any visitor can tell you. Walk through a door in a wall on a dusty road and you will enter a world of peace and tranquillity which even the smallest of gardens seem to provide. Though the grand gardens of the Sassanian kings no longer exist, Iranians still delight in gardens and whether grand or simple, the layout with its central pool or fountain, water channels running at right angles to enclose flowerbeds and shrubs, has not changed since Cyrus the Great laid out his garden in the sixth century BC.

European gardens disappeared with the Roman civilization. The cities were ravaged by barbarian hordes, but the physical remains of this past were to shape the gardens of the future. Gardens first reappeared in the relative calm and peace of the Christian monasteries, in the tenth century. The plants in these gardens owed their existence to their usefulness rather than their beauty. The cloister garden usually had a herb garden, a well, a shaded path leading from the garden to the building and pot plants. For a long time these were the only gardens in Europe, until the Gothic gardens appeared towards the end of the Crusades. These gardens, influenced by the Islamic design, were usually rectangular and divided into the traditional four or eight sections, but paths and not waterways divided them; and instead of a central pool, there was a well which later became the vertical feature in the garden.

In thirteenth century Italy, the Islamic influence was even more pronounced. Emperor Frederick II had spent much of his youth in Sicily, and as a result, had developed a great admiration for the architectural and garden traditions of the Saracen emirs. Giovanni Boccaccio, author of the *Decameron*, described the royal gardens in Naples. The main feature was a vast lawn lined with statues, interspersed with seats. Many flowers were grown in summer but evergreen shrubs and trees formed the permanent features. In the *Decameron*, Boccaccio also describes small walled gardens which lay beyond private chambers or lawns with seats and a central tree, often a peach or orange. One of the most renowned gardens of fourteenth century Europe was Hesdin in Picardy. This garden was designed like the gardens of West Asia, with an array of automata and elaborate use of water. Hesdin was laid out by a Crusader who returned to France in 1270. The design was based on gardens he had seen in Syria and Palermo and for several centuries, this garden had no rival in Europe.

With the gradual return of political and economic stability, people now had the calm to enjoy the good life. A sign of the times was the passion for rediscovering the splendours of classical antiquity, but it was only in the fifteenth century, during the Renaissance that gardens made a real comeback. Tapestries and paintings of the time depict a number of flowers popular then. The gardens were still enclosed within walls to keep out the troubled world but, by the end of the fifteenth century, they had begun to open up. It all began in Florence where the walls of the medieval enclosures, having served their purpose, were torn down to expand the gardens. By the sixteenth century, disassociated parterres began to appear, one behind the other, to lengthen the axis, and sites of new villas were chosen more for scenic beauty than defence. In the typical Renaissance garden, the various parts were united by walks or steps to form a composite whole, emphasizing the unity of home and garden. Stone, statuary and fountains were lavishly used, and grottoes, small pavilions and urns formed part of the garden plan. Gardens such as these did not exist in classical times but the various elements certainly did. The flowers most often grown, as seen in the famous Unicorn tapestries commissioned by the Duke of Burgundy in 1449, are sour cherry which is depicted in all four tapestries, sweet violets, periwinkle, the English daisy, wild strawberries, calendula, wall flowers and pansies. Forget-me-nots, wild orchids, irises and carnations were prized for their clove-like scent; lilies and stocks were also very popular. During this period, container gardening became a rage. A Florentine architect, Leon Battista Alberti, designed a garden in which myrtle, ivy, juniper, vines and lemon trees were grown in wide terracotta pots with brightly coloured flowers around the base.

The age of exploration at the end of the fifteenth century saw the arrival of many unknown species of plants in Europe. The first influx came from Persia, and later, the Moors brought a host of new plants. The second came with the Spanish explorers. They brought back the Love Apple (tomato), which until the nineteenth century, was used purely as a decorative plant for the berries were thought to be poisonous. The earliest New World plants to be introduced, along with potatoes, capsicum and tomatoes, were French and African marigolds, the Marvel of Peru, nasturtium, tuberoses, passion flowers and canna.

By the sixteenth century, gardens were flourishing everywhere in Europe and the British Isles. Some were ostentatious, others had a quieter beauty, but all had exotic plants from the Americas. Parterres became de rigueur as did a dramatic use of water. Flowers were used more than ever before, but since their season was short, they were not among the permanent features in the garden.

The French invaded Italy in the late sixteenth century and Italian style gardens became a common sight in France. The first to acquire a semblance of sophistication was the Chateau of Anet, though it still remained inward looking. Essentially, it was still a medieval garden, although it had incorporated the idioms of the sixteenth century Italian garden.

In England, floriculture became widespread only at the end of the sixteenth century. A large number of plants were imported from Spain although the relationship between the two countries during Elizabeth I's reign was strained. Prior to this, English gardeners did not have much to work with and the gardens served a different purpose. Plants grown were either used in medicine or as food. The early Tudor knot gardens had intricate geometric designs, usually edged with either dwarf box or marjoram, unlike their French counterparts which had bright flowers. It was only in the sixteenth century that the word 'border' first made its appearance, meaning a bed bordering a wall or the pattern in a knot garden. The seventeenth century saw the import of many plants from the Americas. The fact that there were nursery men to buy them and there were published works which contained information on many foreign plants does suggest that gardening was becoming an increasingly popular pastime. The list in John Parkinson's *Paradises* contains plants from North and South America, Turkey,

The arbour

Persia and other parts of Asia, and even one from South Africa, which Parkinson calls the 'marine hyacinth', today called the water hyacinth. But the great gardens of England were not even a mote in the eye.

In seventeenth century France, gardens opened up; the central axis was extended to beyond the garden proper and moats were converted into an ornamental body of water on one side and a decorative canal on the other. When Louis XIV ascended the throne, he took over the entire team of artists employed by his predecessor, including the landscape designer Andre Le Notre, and laid the foundations of the magnificent gardens of Versailles. Though the French gardens in the north retained their Italian flavour, the general taste now ran to the baroque. This required variety, and an unlimited vista. The Italian *giardine segreti* which till then was a place of seclusion, hidden from the general view, was now used to provide a setting for theatrical entr'actes, and the compartmentalized Italian garden was unified to form a whole. The Persians wove their flower gardens into their carpets and took them indoors, the French laid out their flower carpets in their grounds and went out to view them. Flowers were planted in intricately designed beds and borders which covered huge areas. With the French dominance in eighteenth century Europe, French garden styles became almost universal and Versailles the model for all palace gardens. In Italy, Russia, Germany and Holland, French designs were faithfully copied; where they differed, it was because of climatic and geographical constraints and not due to innovation. In Holland, gardens flanked the canals and as water was not deemed a luxury, there was an absence of pools and fountains. Another feature typical of the Dutch garden was the topiary which was well suited to the intensively cultivated land. The Dutch were also partial to geometric design in the overall pattern. It was these garden plans that William and Mary took to England in the late seventeenth century.

In Spain, the Italian patio gardens gained popularity and were designed much like the traditional Greek gardens with colonnaded open-air pavilions and pools to provide the much needed shade and cool during the summer months. Though the French style was seen in La Granja

The French garden

and a few other places, the extended French garden remained alien to the Iberian Peninsula. The English, though thoroughly committed to the French design with its geometric patterns, included lawns and gravel walks in their gardens thus altering the character of the garden. The French vista lay on the main axis; in English gardens vistas radiated like rays from a semi-circle. With the accession of Williams of Orange and Mary, the Dutch influence became widespread and Dutch topiaries, though they had doubtless existed before, became the fashion. The gardens of Wichendon House, which were celebrated as the cynosure of Dutch aesthetics, were laid out by the fifth baron in the last quarter of the seventeenth century; the whole garden was an elaborate and complicated topiary! But by the eighteenth century, the English love affair with the formal Dutch style was on the wane. Also, people were becoming increasingly aware of the natural world, particularly flowers. The strait-laced formality gradually gave way to a charming disorder. The rigid lines and geometric form had lost their allure. Poets like Alexander Pope and Joseph Addison saw no beauty in topiaries and questioned the custom of cutting and shaping trees and shrubs into forms more suited to sculpture. They advocated the restoration of free-form and encouraged a revolt against artificial symmetry. The Chinese influence, first felt in the seventeenth century, also helped in promoting the naturalistic style. Trees were allowed to assume their natural shapes, large expanses of water were redesigned into natural-looking ponds and lakes, streams meandered instead of running straight; paths became irregular and parks and inner gardens were connected. Lancelot 'Capability' Brown completed this merging of parkland and garden. Called Capability because he always spoke of a place as having 'capabilities of improvement', Capability Brown made a fashion of smooth, rolling lawns and rotund clumps of trees. Gardens no longer hugged the house.

But it must be mentioned that long before Capability Brown rid the gardens of geometric designs, Bacon, it appears, did not find the rigid knot gardens of his time with their definite lines attractive. ('As for making knots or figures with divers coloured earths . . . you may see as good sights many times in tarts.') Another difference lay in the purpose of flowers. In Tudor England, unlike the later gardens, scent took precedence over all else, but naturalists like Capability Brown discarded scent and the flowers such as 'gilly flowers of all varieties and musk roses', and replaced them with water, trees and grass.

Most garden planners were in accord with the naturalists in their abhorrence of geometric design and extreme formality. They preferred what Bacon envisioned for his heath. 'I wish it to be framed as much as may be to a natural wilderness.' Then there were others who advocated the dramatic and the bizarre. These savants were inspired by the remote past and exotic lands described by travellers and explorers. Yet another school favoured a garden of poetic sundries with features that evoked surprise, astonishment and wonderment. Wandering around these gardens one came across follies, pagodas, bridges, ruins covered with ivy and the like. But this fashion too soon lost its popularity in England though it caught the fancy of Europeans and was as widely emulated as Versailles had been a century earlier. In Italy people went so far as to destroy Renaissance gardens to make place for the new *anglo-chinois jardin*, as the French called it. Its influence was seen as far as Portugal, where *le jardin anglais* was created in Queluz.

In the late eighteenth century and early nineteenth century, Europe was flooded with exotic plants thanks to increasing trade and travel. Flowers became an integral part of the garden but the flower garden as we know it was limited to cottages in the country and small towns. In the cities, the flowers were relegated to enclosures within large gardens. Soon botanical specimen gardens were in vogue but these gardens sacrificed aesthetics for exotica and their popularity did not last long. Terraces with masses of flowers overlooking the parkland became a prominent feature but the undiscerning use of plants that imports and plant breeding made available resulted in a tasteless mess. By the end of the nineteenth century, efforts were made to create aesthetically pleasing gardens and a balance between beauty and rarity was achieved. J.C. Loudon urged people to take the gardens out of the hands of architects, planners, painters and the cultivated dilettante and leave them to professional plantsmen. William Robinson, who had much to do with the revival of old-fashioned flowers, attacked both the ceremonial and collectors' gardens, arguing that botany was a science but gardening an art. The Rev. Samuel Gilbert, in his book, *The Florist's Vade-Mecum* (1683), mentions violets, daffodils, snowdrops, hyacinths, roses, honeysuckle, carnations, polyanthus and other flowers that were hardly seen in the gardens of nineteenth century England. These had been replaced by exotica and hybrids. Robinson demonstrated in his own gardens that plants look best where they grow best, but the true revolution was brought about by the horticulturalist Gertrude Jekyll and poet/novelist Vita Sackville-West. They, influenced by Robinson, advocated free-form and brought cottage garden flowers back into fashion. They adopted the informality and rich palette of cottage gardens, laying it over a substructure of concealed regularity, to bring the art of the flower garden to its zenith. If the eighteenth was devoted to great landscapes, to the exclusion of flower gardens, the nineteenth century saw overly-intricate bedding schemes and fussy detail. With Jekyll and Sackville-West, the twentieth century saw the amalgamation of the best of the two forms. The craft rather than the art was on the rise in the nineteenth century, but the craft was widespread and numerous, and smaller, private gardens began to appear. The rich were no longer the sole proprietors of gardens; people of all walks of society found time to cultivate plants.

In the twentieth century, there was a marked enthusiasm for horticultural pursuits everywhere. The rise of gardening and horticultural societies brought an interest in the individual plant resulting in the cultivation of outstanding specimens for competitions. In the 1920's there was a great upsurge of plant breeding, and introduction of new plants which continued well into the second half of the twentieth century took gardening into a new arena. Horticulture, both as a profession and a hobby became more widespread than ever before. But in garden style and design the past still played a prominent role.

Now one can see a desire to maintain and reproduce old gardens (sadly lacking in India) in Europe, England and America. Another trend is the revival of scent in the garden, a fact that would have pleased Francis Bacon and the people of his time, when scent took precedence over everything else, and purely ornamental flowers were relegated to some corner. In France, the sixteenth century garden at Villandry has been restored; and in the USA, the colonial garden in Williamsburg—a typical Anglo-Dutch garden—has been refurbished. In Kyoto many of the old gardens which have not been swallowed up by modern city blocks have been replanted and restored to their former beauty. But a distinctive modern idiom is missing from most newly laid gardens.

In India, the great gardens of the Mughals and the gardens created by the English lie neglected. Weeds grow where flowers should, and trees are planted in existing gardens with a total disregard for style, aesthetics or design. This sorry state of affairs is seen in almost all public gardens. There is no effort being made to recreate old gardens. Not so with the Americans. At the Cloisters Museum in New York, a garden has been created using the flowers, most of which have been identified, depicted in the Unicorn tapestries more than 500 years ago.

All modern gardens are based on designs and styles established over the last 1000 years, the truly modern note is patently absent. In the US, gardens frequently reflect the Japanese style but though exotic and fresh in America, the style itself belongs to a time long gone. Until fairly recently, gardens were built exclusively for personal use by kings, nobles and wealthy citizens. Modern gardens, the large ones, are largely created for the use of the general public, but landscape architects and planners are more concerned with the functional aspect and space utility than with beauty. The chief goal is to provide for the activities of the urban dweller rather than refresh his spirit, which is a pity, for now, more than ever before, there is a need for calm and tranquillity. The English and Japanese are passionate gardeners but the high cost of labour and space constraints have made it impossible to lay out gardens in the grand style of the eighteenth century. All the great gardens of today were made when there was time to create them and leisure to enjoy them.

Gardeners' Jargon

If you've just joined the club and are stumped by words such as 'blanching' or 'bolting', don't panic—or bolt. Take comfort in the fact that every gardener once felt as you do. This compendium will allow you to hold your own with the best of them.

Aerial (of roots)—These form above the ground either as support or to absorb nutrients from the air.

Alpines—These are not simply plants that grow in the Alps. These are all the small, delicate plants that grow in high-altitude regions. Usually grown in rockeries or cool-houses.

Annuals—Any fast-growing plant which completes its cycle—from seed back to seed—in a year or less.

Axis—The main stem, root or branch in relation to its own branches.

Biennial—A plant, which when grown from seed, has a life cycle of two years. Usually flowers in the second year.

Blanching—Very simply, whitening a plant by excluding sunlight. Done to vegetables like celery.

Bolting—When a plant prematurely starts to produce seed. Usually happens in hot, dry weather.

Bract—A modified leaf immediately below the flower; some are more colourful than the flower.

Bud—A condensed, undeveloped shoot or flower.

Budding—Method of propagation in which a bud growth is inserted in a slit in the bark of another plant so that the tissues unite.

Bulb—A modified stem surrounded by fleshy scale leaves which contain stored food.

Catch crop—To grow fast-growing crops like lettuce or radish in a vegetable patch lying empty between crops.

Compost—Rich, organic manure made of decomposed vegetable and animal matter.

Conifer—Any tree or shrub that produces its seeds in cones. Yew is an exception—though a conifer, it has berry-like fruits. Almost all conifers are evergreens.

Crop-rotation—Changing the vegetables in a patch from year to year.

Crossed—Cross-pollinated.

Crown—Top of a tree, and the top of certain rhizomes from which shoots appear.

Cultivar—A plant that has been cultivated and refined. In short, a civilized plant.

Dead-heading—Cutting off dead flowers to encourage more flowers.

Deciduous—Plants that shed their leaves at the end of the growing season.

Delicate—Plants that need cosseting when taken out of their natural habitat. Hardy plants don't need special care.

Disbudding—Removing superfluous buds to direct all the plant's energy into producing a few superb blooms. Plants for flower shows are usually disbudded.

Dormant—The resting period of a plant.

Drill—A straight, narrow hole in the ground or in large containers, to plant a seed. A drill is usually made with a stick.

Dwarf-stock—Thanks to the wizards of horticulture, a great many shrubs and trees are grafted on to a stock so that they remain small.

Earthing up—Making a mini pyramid around the base of a plant, either to blanch it or support it. Done to leeks and celery to prevent them from turning green. It is also done to potatoes to encourage tubers to grow higher on the stems.

Evergreen—Any tree or shrub that does not shed all its foliage at one time. It sheds and replaces foliage almost continuously, but not so that you notice. Firs, pines, oaks, camellias and junipers are some.

Eye—An embryo bud on a tuber or stem. Looks like a dried up pimple.

Fertilizer—Anything which improves soil conditions by adding vital nutrients. Broadly divided into organic (natural) and inorganic (chemical) compounds. Organic: manure, compost etc. Inorganic: chemicals that perform the same function but over the years will kill the soil.

Frost—The outside limit for the coldest part of the year.

Fungicide—A chemical to fight fungal diseases such as black spot or mildew.

Genus—A super-family comprising several species which together are distinct from any other group.

Hardening off—Gradually getting a plant accustomed to a different climate.

Hardy—Any plant that can live through harsh conditions such as arid heat or severe cold.

Heading in—Temporarily putting a plant in the ground before installing it in its final place. This usually happens if you haven't prepared the bed or pot. The root ball is put in a shallow trench and covered with earth.

Herbaceous—Any plant which has soft stems rather than woody ones. Some herbaceous plants are annuals, others perennials.

Hoe—A tool used to keep the ground free from weeds. It cuts the plants off in their prime, just below the soil.

Humus—This is supplied to the soil by decomposing animal or vegetable matter—this organic material makes the soil rich and dark. Most plants like humus-rich soil except cacti and some succulents.

Hybrid—Plants that have been especially bred by cross-fertilization of different species or varieties, usually for colour and size of the flower or for hardier and tastier (moot point) vegetables and fruit. Seeds from hybirds never run true to form.

Hydroponics—A term introduced by Dr W.F. Gericke for growing plants in water, without the use of soil.

Insecticide—Anything organic or inorganic that kills insects.

Inter-crop—A fast-growing crop sown between slower maturing plants.

Lateral shoot—A shoot growing sidewards from the leader.

Leader—The growing shoot by which a main stem advances; usually a creeper.

Leaf mould—Decayed dead leaves which improve soil condition and soil fertility.

Loam—Good, fertile soil rich in minerals. Not wet and sticky or sandy and dry.

Mulch—A ground-cover made of any kind of organic, biodegradable material such as leaves, straw, wood-shavings, shredded paper etc. Spread around the plant, it helps retain moisture in the soil and enriches the soil as it decomposes.

Naturalize—To make deliberately planted bulbs and other plants appear as though they have grown wild. They are left to multiply wherever they are planted.

New wood—A stem or branch from the current year's growth.

Node—The joint on a stem from which leaves or a stem may grow. Bamboos have very distinctive nodes.

Peat—Partially decomposed organic matter of mosses and sedges from boggy areas.

Perennial—Any plant that can go on, more or less, for decades or centuries.

Pinching out—To remove tender tips of shoots with your fingers. This, when done to trees or shrubs, will induce branching. It also helps produce more flowers in annuals and fruits in fruit trees.

Plant—Anything smaller than a tree or shrub.

Planting out—Moving a young plant from a sheltered spot to an open, sunny site.

Pleach—To intertwine branches such as in a hedge plant or a shrubby tree.

Pricking out—Moving a seedling from a smaller box to a larger one so that it has more space to grow in.

Propagation—Increasing plant stocks either by seed, cutting, layering or grafting.

Pruning—Cutting back a shrub or tree to encourage it to produce more flowers and fruit. Also used to shape a hedge, bush or tree.

Scandent—A plant with a climbing habit.

Semi-hardy—Plants that cannot take extreme climatic conditions.

Shrub—Basically a bush with hard, woody stems and branches. Unlike a tree, it doesn't have a central trunk. However, many can be trained to look like small trees.

Slurry—A liquid manure, usually made of cow or horse dung.

Snag—Superfluous stems which are the result of bad pruning.

Soil pans—A layer of pebbles or clay-like strata which lies a few inches below cultivation level. This must be broken up when digging and forking.

Spadix—A spike of small flowers closely arranged around a fleshy axis and typically enclosed in a spathe.

Sphagnum—A bog moss which decomposes to form a type of peat.

Stock—A plant which receives the graft called the *scion* / a plant that roots itself.

Strike—When a cutting roots.

Succulent—A plant with thick fleshy stems and leaves which usually grows in arid regions.

Sucker—A shoot growing below the grafted joint, from the root-stock. If the plant is not grafted, it grows from the main stem below the ground.

Tilth—Cultivation. When the soil is dug up and turned over, the resulting soil condition is called tilth. The deeper you dig, the better the tilth.

Timezone—Climate varies from area to area. Gardeners consider the right season rather than the right months.

Topsoil—The soil on the top of the ground which in nature, is very rich in humus. Sub-soil, which is infertile, lacks bacteria.

Transplanting—Removing a plant from one spot or container and planting it in another.

Tuber—Swollen underground root or stem that acts as a storage organ.

Variegated—Any plant that has more than one colour in leaf or flower. To retain the effect, the plant usually needs a sunny position.

Variety—A plant which varies from others of the same family in some aspect like petal formation, colour etc. and retains that difference in the succeeding cycles.

Weed—Basically any plant that you have no use for. But for the gardener, weeds are those plants which will deprive his (don't fly into the boughs!) plants of nutrition by growing around or near them.

Whorl—An arrangement of leaves and flowers around a stem, all emerging from one point like the spokes of a wheel.

Amateur Gardeners' Common Mistakes

Nobody's perfect, and all gardeners make terrible mistakes at some time or the other—even the best of them, which is heartening. But the beginners tend to make some glaring (and very often expensive) mistakes in the most rudimentary areas.

The Fifth Law of Gardening

It always rains after you've watered the lawn.

—The Devil's Bedside Book

a)   Neophytes tend to water too frequently or too sparingly. When water is only sprinkled, only the soil on top gets wet. In the case of potted plants, the bottom and sides remain dry. In hot areas, plants need a thorough soaking. They should be watered lightly only during the rainy season.

b)   They use pesticides and fertilizers indiscriminately, especially when planting young shrubs, saplings or annual seedlings. Pesticides should be applied only when seedlings mature into young plants, otherwise they'll die along with the pests.

c)   Amateurs tend to plant saplings of large trees too close to the house or compound wall. They don't bother to check the height of telephone or electrical lines, and as a result, when the tree matures, the crown has to be sheared off and the tree is mutilated. Choose a smaller tree if you don't have the space.

Planting too close to the house will disturb the foundation. Keep a distance of at least 40 ft between large trees and buildings. The roots of large trees are very strong borers.

d)   Beginners pay little or no attention to the soil. They buy expensive plants, put them into poor soil and expect them to thrive. In a garden, soil is of the utmost importance.

e)   Fledgling gardeners rely too much on *maalis* who know next to nothing about plants and their requirements. They would do better to consult a few books on the subject.

f)   Few beginners actually *do* any gardening. *Maalis* do what has to be done—digging, manuring, planting etc. Nor do they bother to supervise since they know even less than the *maalis*. The *maali* may use poor compost or the wrong feed and the beginner won't know a thing. Beginners usually don't know the difference between good and bad manure. There are very few good *maalis* available, and like rare birds, are sighted once in half a dozen years. Do not rely on your local *maali* to give you a beautiful, thriving garden.

g)   Pesticides are often used too late, when the damage is already done.

h)   Seeds are sown too early or too late in the season. Bulbs are planted out of season and are expected to flower. Most bulbs are plants that belong to cool climates and flower between twelve to sixteen weeks after planting.

i)   They tend to overwater bulbs which rot as a result. Bulbs should be watered sparingly until the shoots appear, and heavily afterwards.

j)   They tend to use manure that is not well-rotted. Fresh manure destroys the roots.

k)   They do not read the fine print when applying chemical pesticides and fertilizers. These must always be used with care or you could end up with more dead plants than living ones.

Cultivation and Watering

Odours that rise
When the spade wounds the roots of a tree,
Rose, currant, raspberry, or goutweed,
Rhubarb or celery, . . .
It is enough
To smell to crumble the dark earth

'Digging'—Edward Thomas

For a garden to be truly successful, the most important thing after weather and climate is the condition of your soil. You can't do much about weather and climate but you can do plenty for the soil. Most garden plants thrive only in soil that is loose, open, not too wet, not too dry. To achieve this, you must dig, and dig deep, turning over the soil. Good soil is friable, open, and easily crumbled, allowing roots to explore without hindrance. In some gardens soil may be too heavy, in others, too light. To correct this, you must dig, turn over the soil and add bulk manure such as cattle manure and leaf mould. And this organic matter needs to be frequently renewed.

The First Law of Gardening

The Rake you step on is always teeth up, so that it not only injures your foot, but smacks you on the mouth with its handle.

—The Devil's Bedside Book

The next factor is water. 'Water is beneficient to all things but does not contend. It stays in places which others despise, therefore it is Tao,' says the Tao Te Ching. Water is vital not only for us but for all plants. Water them as much as they need and no more and for this, you must know your plants. Plants that are native to desert areas need less water than plants which grow in marsh lands. When watering, always water from above to simulate a shower of rain. Leaves as well as soil should be watered.

In order to get the best out of your plants you must know their water requirements. This is being repeated because it is absolutely essential for a healthy garden.

For if you will have a tree bear more fruit than it hath used to do, it is not anything you can do the boughs, but it is a stirring of the earth and putting new mould about the roots that must work it.

—Francis Bacon

Never water plants during the middle of the day, when the sun is blazing. The droplets on the leaves can act as burning glass and scorch the leaves. If you have watered the garden well in the morning, the soil beneath the surface will remain moist even if the topsoil is dry. If you have potted plants out in the sun and you see them drooping, lift the foliage and water the soil only. If they are not drooping, don't water even if the soil is dry. You can water them in the evening.

Young trees when newly transplanted into the ground, or a newly potted plant, should be watered carefully. Do not flood the pot or the ground until the plants are well established. They will die if you do so. In winter when the plants are resting, and during the monsoon, trees need little watering. When plants are dormant, water only if the weather is very dry.

All roots are avid water-hunters and go deep into the soil, so surface dryness does not matter when plants are in the ground. But it does matter to potted plants. Light watering is bad for plants in the ground or in pots. The water does not penetrate deep into the soil, and the roots remain close to the surface causing shallow root growth.

- Superficial watering is as bad as not watering at all.
- In India, it is foolish to water during the monsoon months. Only potted plants that do not get the rain will need some watering. Those standing out in the rain better have good drainage holes and well-drained soil or you could end up with a whole load of dead plants due to water logging.
- In dry weather, it is better to water thoroughly every alternate day rather than to sprinkle lightly every day.
- Small seedlings, unlike established plants, need small doses of water every day as do plants in small pots.
- In very dry areas where there's hardly any rainfall and your daily water-supply is inadequate, it is necessary to flood the garden every three or four days. Water till the ground is saturated and let the water soak deep into the earth. This method however, has some disadvantages. It can change the character of the soil, forming a hard cake on the surface. To prevent this, fork the soil the morning after.
- Lawns must be watered thoroughly and evenly.

SOIL

Soil is to the plant what the mother is to a child in the womb. Undernourished, poor soil will produce weak, unhealthy plants. Most novices don't pay any attention to the soil and then wonder why their plants are dying or looking straggly.

The first thing when planning a garden is to attend to the soil. I cannot over-emphasize this point. Débutant gardeners will spend money on exotic plants, gardening implements, fancy containers and garden features but tend to completely ignore the soil. If you truly want a lovely garden, put your money into the soil. A beautiful plant does not need any embellishment; don't gild the lily. Work instead, on improving the soil so that the plants can achieve their true potential.

Pool soil is soil that is lacking in bacteria and other living micro-organisms which live in humus-enriched soil. Sir E. John Russel, author of *Soil Conditions and Plant Growth*, found that one tiny gram of good, rich soil, which contains both vegetable and animal manure, has 29 million living bacteria, all necessary for plants. Chemical fertilizers over a period of time kill these bacteria, thus killing the soil. Sparingly used they can be beneficial,

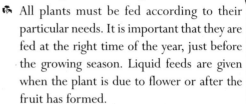

Dos and Don'ts of Feeding and Watering

- All plants must be fed according to their particular needs. It is important that they are fed at the right time of the year, just before the growing season. Liquid feeds are given when the plant is due to flower or after the fruit has formed.

- *Do not* feed seedlings until the roots are fully developed.

- *Do not* feed plants when they are in full bloom; they have already absorbed all they need for flowering.

- *Do not* feed a plant if the leaves are yellowing when they shouldn't be—that is, when it is not time for the plant to shed its leaves.

- *Do* feed a plant a before it is about to flower, but take care not to overfeed.

- *Do* feed the plant when you see new growth, such as new shoots and leaves.

◆

- Overwatering kills more plants than underwatering.

- Plants in ceramic containers should not be heavily watered as the soil retains moisture. Check the soil before watering.

- Plants in clay pots need regular watering as the soil dries out quickly.

- In damp weather, water plants only when they require it.

but organic fertilizers are by far the best. In your hurry to have luxuriant plants, don't emulate the American farmers who a few decades ago, in their frenzied efforts to take advantage of high prices, used so much chemical (read inorganic) fertilizers that they virtually killed the soil. Enrich your soil with organic fertilizers; there are plenty to choose from.

Good loamy soil is a mixture of sand and clay with large quantities of rotting vegetable and animal matter, which when broken down, forms humus. Soils are predominantly sandy, clayey, chalky or peaty. Good soil usually has to be made. Acid soil has too much humus, alkaline soil has too much chalk.

Different plants like different soil conditions, but all plants need soil that contains potash, nitrogen and phosphorus in varying quantities. Potassium encourages flowers and growth, phosphorus develops strong stems and good roots, and nitrogen gives leaves their rich green colour (chlorophyll) which the plant needs to manufacture its food. When starting a garden you can do one of two things: either you can get plants that grow in poor soil—and there are quite a few that do—or you can enrich and cultivate the soil in order to grow what you want. For the lazy beginner I would strongly advise the former.

(Nature herself tells you whether your soil is alkaline or acidic.)

Leaf Indicators
a) Poor growth, yellow colour—lack of nitrogen.
b) Greyish-coloured growth—lack of phosphates or potash.
c) Tall spindly plants—not enough light, or too tightly packed.
d) Rich green leaves, thick stems—plentiful nitrogen.
e) Blanched leaves—too much lime, organic manure needed.
f) Patchy leaves—insufficient potash.
g) Dark-coloured leaves which crinkle—acid soil, lime needed.

When starting a garden, you must find out if your soil is *acidic* or *alkaline*. Soil-testing kits are not available in India, but good chemists stock a pH-testing solution which is basically the same thing, except cruder. If the soil test shows less than pH 7, it is acidic; high readings mean that the soil is alkaline. Most plants like a balance of the two. If your soil is too acidic or alkaline and it is too much of a bother and expense to alter the composition, you will have to restrict yourself to plants that tolerate those conditions. For instance, azalias, camellias and rhododendrons love acidic soil; they die if the soil is chalky.

Don't expect nature to do it all for you. She needs help too. Like all living things, plants need air, water, sunshine and food. In a garden, the food and water have to be supplied by you, otherwise the plants will starve, wilt and die.

Root and Fruit Indicators of Soil Conditions
a) Too bright red (as in apples)—either lacks nitrogen or there is too much grass around the tree.
b) Blotchy tomatoes—lack of potash.
c) Blanched fruit—lack of nitrogen.
d) Slow in ripening—excess water or nitrogen or a lack of phosphates.
e) Failure to ripen—lack of potash.
f) Stunted roots—acidity, poor drainage, hard-packed soil or a lack of lime and phosphates.
g) Good root development—well cultivated, slightly acid soil.

Stiff clayey soil soil can be lightened by using lime about 5 grams to a square metre, but bulk manuring is by far the best. For a flower and vegetable garden, you will need 8-10 kg of manure per square metre. Resist the temptation to add sand to lighten it. This is a fatal mistake made by many gardeners. Sand forms a macadam-like skin on the surface of the soil, suffocating it. Soil needs to breathe too.

In the plains of India, the soil is often dry and sandy or silty. This poor soil cannot nourish your plants. Bulk manure with lime will rejuvenate the soil and build it up.

MANURE AND MULCHING

And to you Corpse, I think you are good manure,
But that does not offend me.
I smell the white roses sweet scented and growing.
—Walt Whitman

A plant needs about fifteen elements to make its food. Some are drawn from the soil and some from the air. In its natural habitat, a plant gets all it needs but when taken out, the plant's needs have to be supplied—nitrogen, phosphorus, potassium and, on occasion, lime. There's plenty of nitrogen in the air, but plants, except those of the bean family, cannot tap it; they depend upon the nitrogen in the soil. You can supply the deficient elements by using suitable manures. Cattle and horse-dung manure are rich in nitrogen, with smaller quantities of phosphates and potash. Bone-meal contains plenty of phosphates and wood-ash is a good source of potash.

Behold this compost! Behold it well!
Perhaps every mite has once formed
part of a sick person—yet behold!
The grass of spring covers the prairies,
The bean sprouts noiselessly
through the mould in the garden,
The delicate spear of the onion
pierces upward,
The apple-buds cluster together
on the apple branches . . .
—Walt Whitman

Compost

This is well-rotted vegetable, leaf and animal manure, and is very necessary for the healthy growth of plants. It is the best of all manures and is rich in nitrogen, phosphates and potash. Do not give plants manure that has not broken down.

To make compost: If you have enough space in your garden, you can make your own compost. It will be superlative if you do it right. Nature makes compost slowly, but you can hasten the process by adding 'starters' to your heap. The compost will be ready to use in six to eight months, but like wine, the older it is, the better it gets. A gardener's compost is usually made up of the green stuff he can come by—leaves, cut grass, soft weeds and kitchen waste.

The pit: Choose a spot 6 ft by 6 ft by 10 ft in some unused corner of the garden. If it is smaller, make it deeper. Set the dug earth aside in a heap. Fill the bottom with a 6-inch layer of leaves, over this put a 6-inch layer of grass cuttings, and then a layer of straw. Top it off with kitchen waste, like vegetable peels, leaves, seeds, waste bits of meat and fat, and fruit peels. Drench the layers with water and then spread a thin layer of fresh cow-dung and a little powdered lime. Use wood-ash if you can get it; dust it on the top of the dung and lime. When this lot settles, keep building up the layers in the same order. It will take three to four months to fill the pit. Make sure the leaves and grass are sun-dried before adding to the pit. Air is essential for decomposition, so when the pit begins to fill, turn the contents over to aerate them. Compost takes longer to decompose in colder regions.

Always sun-dry the greens you have collected for the pit. If sun-dried, they pack lightly, allowing air and water to circulate. This is essential for the process of decomposition.

Don't use woody-stemmed branches and twigs; just the soft greens. Don't add thick leathery leaves. Kitchen waste like egg-shells and bits of fish, meat or chicken can be added.

Lime and wood-ash are used to prevent the compost from becoming too acidic.

Finally, cover the pit with a wire mesh.

Liquid Manure (Slurry)

The acacia tree smells of acacia,
In the garden there is a smell of
roses and manure.
—Melih Cevdet

This is given to plants when they are about to flower or when the fruit has formed. You can make slurry by mixing fresh cow-dung with water in the ratio of 1:4. Add two cupfuls of wood-ash if available. Let the mixture stand for a week to ten days, stirring daily. When it is ready, mix water and slurry in the ratio of 4:1 and apply to plants. Those in the ground will need more than those in pots.

Green Manure for the Vegetable Garden

Everyone, unless they are exceedingly dim-witted, would prefer vegetables that are not saturated with pesticides and ripening agents. Growing even a few vegetables can add greatly to the quality of the food on your table. If you don't have a kitchen garden, you can grow vegetables in pots and tubs. If you do have a vegetable garden, you are one of the fortunate ones. But to get a good crop of vegetables, your soil will require heavy feeding, for vegetables are greedy plants, and most being annuals, grow rapidly. Cattle manure mixed with well, rotted leaf manure is best for the plants. When the plot is lying fallow in the hot months, or between the cold season and the hot season vegetables, it is time to feed the exhausted soil with green manure, that is, green crop legumes. Use quick-growing annuals. Cut the plants just before they flower and bury the leaves and tender stalks in the ground. Dig up the roots and turn the soil over before you bury the greens. This will provide the soil with much-needed organic matter and humus.

Good garden soil is made up of two parts soil, one part leaf mould and one part farmyard manure. Sheep-dung manure is available at most good garden centres.

Lime

Lime is essential to all plants, some need more, others very little, but all need it. Lime sweetens sour earth and greatly increases the fertility of water-logged soil which has been drained. Lime is available as quicklime, slaked lime and limestone. Quicklime when moistened gets hot and froths, forming slaked lime. Slaked lime, when left in the open, forms limestone. In general, limestone is the best for a garden. Lime should not be given to plants along with the manure. It should be added to the soil a month before planting.

Mulching

Mulch is a covering on the soil which prevents loss of moisture from below. Mulching is done in hot, dry and cold weathers to conserve the moisture in the soil. For the mulch to be effective, the space around the plant should be free of weeds. The best materials for mulch are dry mosses, hay, straw, grass clippings, sawdust and compost. Mulch can also be made of finely forked soil which in dry weather becomes powdery and stops undue evaporation of water from the soil below. But it is not really recommended as a brief shower can solidify this layers which will form a cake around the plant and sub-soil moisture will be lost Organic mulch is by far the best.

If you live in an area which has spells of hot, dry weather and extremes of sunshine and rain, mulching with leaf mould is the best. This helps keep the soil cool. If you are fortunate, you will be able to procure peat manure. A good mulch is about 3 inches thick.

How Much Bulk Manure?

This depends entirely upon how good or bad your soil is. Poor, light, sandy soil in hot, dry areas needs large quantities of bulk manure; rich, loamy soil needs far less. Average soil needs about 6 kg per square metre. The first lot should be added in February/March, the second in September/October, making it 12 kg per square metre per year. For poor soil, increase the amount but don't overdo it—the soil could become acidic. In flower beds, very heavy manuring will produce more leaves than flowers. Spread the manure evenly and dig into the soil. Organic matter when dug deep improves the tilth.

PROPAGATION

Seeds

If you plant in good soil and at the right time, your plant is sure to grow. Seeds of flowering plants, especially annuals, are usually sown in seed-boxes and kept sheltered from the vagaries of the weather. Seedboxes can be shallow pots or any containers which have holes in the bottom. Good drainage is as important for seeds as for plants.

> *When beams of wisdom strike*
> *on soil and clay*
> *Receptive to the seed, Earth*
> *keeps her trust*
> *In springtime all deposits she repays,*
> *Taught by eternal Justice to be just.*
> —Rumi

Preparing the seedbox: Place a layer of crocks on the bottom of the container, with the concave side facing down. Fill with seedling compost and moisten it. Spread the seeds thinly and cover with a layer of compost.

Compost for seedboxes: One part soil, two parts leaf mould and a sprinkling of fine, clean sand. Mix and air the compost. Make sure there are no grubs or eggs of insects, or your seeds are doomed. To ensure there are none, many gardeners pour boiling water over the compost and dry it out before using.

Planting: If planting directly in the ground, be more generous with your seeds. There's an old English adage that goes 'One for the rook, one for the crow, one to die and one to grow.' This is especially true of seedbeds. Pigeons and sparrows are sure to make a meal of at least half your seeds. The soil in seedbeds should be light and rich in compost.

Seeds: There are plenty of both foreign and local seeds available in garden centres and nurseries. Some will germinate well, with others you will get just a few seedlings. Local seeds from a reliable nursery or garden centre will give you almost 100 per cent germination. Some foreign seeds will not germinate at all. This is the seed's way of objecting to the climatic conditions they are not to its liking.

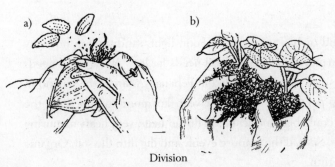

a)   b)

Division

Division

This is the only form of division that would stump a mathematician—the number increases instead of decreasing! Many plants are best propagated by division rather than by cuttings or layering. Ferns, violets,

kunia

nsy

Double Poppy

Anemone

primulas and bulb plants are some. The process is really quite simple—lift the plant out of the soil and split it into several portions, each of which can be replanted to give you a new plant. If the roots are tough and thick, some leverage must be applied to lift the plant but try not to damage any of the roots. In the case of bulbs, remove the bulblets and replant so that they grow into full-sized bulbs.

- When sowing in seedboxes, the boxes should be shaded before germination, but once the first pair of leaves appear they must be exposed to more light. If the plants are over-crowded, thin them out or else the seedlings will get sickly and die. Transplant the ones you remove to a previously prepared seedbox. Once they have four to six pairs of leaves, you can move them into the bed or large pots which have been prepared to receive them.
- Germination of seeds can be very erratic—some germinate in days, others can take weeks or even months. Then again, seeds of a particular plant may not do what you expect them to do. Some seeds, unless given all the right conditions, may not germinate at all.
- Young seedlings should be watered every evening except during the rains when they should be watered only if necessary. Don't wait until the topsoil is dry and cracking.

Cuttings

It's quicker to reproduce shrubs, trees and other plants by cuttings than by any other method. The cutting will yield a plant truer to the parent plant than a seed will; it will practically be a clone. With seeds there's a chance of a throwback—the plant could end up looking like its great-grandmother. But this can never be the case with a cutting.

Cuttings should be made from young wood; the upper shoots of the plant are best for producing flowers and fruit. They will flower much quicker than plants grown from seeds, usually by the second season. Low-side shoots make healthy plants, but these are slower to bloom and are usually shy of fruiting. Old wood is never good for cuttings; the shoot must be energetic. Some plants do take from hard wood, but in general, the half-mature wood of a year's growth is the best. Cuttings can vary in thickness. They can be pencil-slim or as thick as a man's thumb, depending upon the plant.

Making a cutting: Cut the stem just below a leaf bud or node. The cutting should not be more than 6-8 inches long. Strip away all the leaves except the pair on the tip. Use a sharp knife and cut at an angle. Some plants need cuttings with a 'heel'. To make one, tear off a small branch with a 'heel' of the parent—that is, a piece of bark and stem attached to the branch—and plant.

Planting: When planting, one-third of the cutting should be in the soil and planted slightly aslant. Do not crowd the cuttings. Press the soil firmly around them.

Cuttings should be cut and planted at the end of the mother plant's dormant period, just before active growth takes place. In the case of plants which are at their best in winter, cuttings should be made just before the cold weather sets in. But for most tropical trees and shrubs, the best time is just before the monsoon rains. They should be watered lightly till the rains arrive. Some cuttings will root within six to eight weeks, others are quicker. Cuttings from fast growing plants strike more quickly than those from woody, slow-growing ones. Sometimes lateral shoots appear; this is an indication that the cutting is using its reserves, not that the roots have formed. Don't transplant until the roots are well developed.

Transplanting

Most plants do not mind being moved, provided you do it at the right time of the year—when they are dormant. Seedlings of annuals and cuttings, however, are transplanted when they are growing. Your beds or containers should be prepared before you transplant. Cloudy days, preferably those with a light drizzle are best for transplanting, but they are not always available, especially for those in the northern plains. For most of us, the best time to transplant is in the evening. Make a small hole in the soil, put the

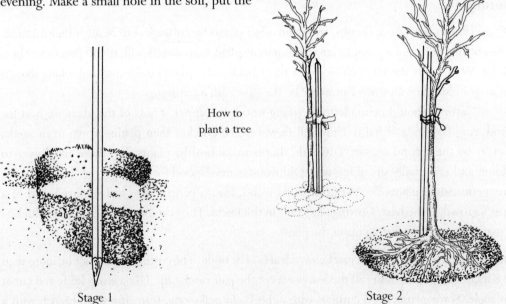

How to plant a tree

Stage 1

Stage 2

plant in and firm the soil around it. Do not crush or injure the roots and never force the root-ball into a drill that is too small for it, enlarge it first. Don't plant the cutting too deep. The top roots should lie just below the surface of the soil. After planting, press the soil lightly but firmly around the plant. Transplanting more than once checks the growth of the plant and is necessary to keep plants dwarfed. This is important for plants growing in containers. The size of the container should increase gradually, till the plant is finally in its permanent pot.

Ancient civilizations the world over observed that planting and transplanting with the waxing moon was beneficial to plants. This sounds like a lot of hogwash but science has now found that this belief was based on sound knowledge. Lunar rhythms affect the earth's magnetic field, which in turn affects the growth of all living things. The gardeners of yore discovered this from experience, and by trial and error, not from laboratory tests. I would strongly advise you to follow this. You will have very few casualties in the garden.

Grafting

Grafting is the technique of binding two plants so that they fuse into a unit which continues to live, the two parts retaining their own characteristics. The 'stock' has the roots and lower trunk, and receives the 'scion' which will form the upper part of trunk and branches. The stock and scion are generally of the same species, except when grafting cacti.

Grafting has many uses. It is used to cultivate the tree and improve it. A damaged tree can be saved by grafting it onto another. Flowering trees will produce flowers of different hues, as will grafted bulb plants. Some trees are the better for grafting. White pines, which are not easily propagated from seed, grow faster and more vigorously when grafted on to the hardier black pine. Grafting will also give you many varieties of a plant. The grafted plant will look like the scion, similar colour and form but the seeds from the grafted plant will produce a great many varieties. However there are some disadvantages to this method of propagation. First, a certain amount of skill and proficiency is required; second, the graft may not heal properly, and may look unattractive. Unsightly shoots may start growing from the stock, and if not removed, the scion will die. Have no qualms about removing these. This sophisticated field is not for amateurs. Don't graft if you don't have the experience—you'll only suffer disappointment when the graft doesn't take.

Plants most suited for grafting: All types of fruit trees, pines, woody flowering shrubs and creepers are excellent grafting material. Fruit trees are particularly suitable for grafting. They start fruiting earlier than trees grown from seeds, and if the rootstock is properly selected, they often bear heavier crops. Roses, when grafted, will give you far more beautiful blooms, and if you collect the seeds, you can get yourself some new varieties. And grafted roses flower earlier.

When grafting, make sure that the 'combium' (the growing layer of the two parts) is not exposed to the air. Grafting wax, which is made of beeswax, tallow and resin, should be used before binding. You may not find grafting wax in local garden centres, but you can easily make some yourself.

Making grafting wax:

<u>Ingredients</u>
Six parts crushed resin
Six parts beeswax
One part tallow

Melt the tallow in a heavy pan and add the beeswax. When the mixture starts to boil, add the resin, little at a time, stirring continuously till it has melted. Boil for five minutes and remove from the fire. Strain through fabric such as cheesecloth, and cool. Once cool, you must knead it until it is firm and doughy. Roll into small balls and store.

Some gardeners use melted paraffin wax, but the above mixture is far superior.

If you don't wish to make grafting wax, use any lip balm made of beeswax. Make sure it does not contain menthol.

Grafting Methods

In the tropics, tongue grafting (in which the stalk and the scion are cut to make the ends tongue-shaped) is more common than straightforward grafting which is popular in temperate regions. The reason for this is not known.

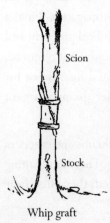

Scion

Stock

Whip graft

Lateral grafting: The graft point should be made as low as possible on the stock, preferably hidden in the soil. The scion should be cut into a wedge, 2 inches long, and the incision in the stock should be of the same depth. Insert the scion into the stock and bind with any natural fibre and apply grafting wax. New growth on the scion will tell you that the graft has taken. At this point the stock should be cut off at an angle above the grafting point. Cut cleanly and neatly without leaving any unsightly bit sticking out.

Whip grafting is the simplest and most common method. The stock and scion must be of equal thickness and age. The stock, one to three years old, should be cut 4-6 inches from the ground and the cut end should slope neatly to the top, the point and hip being flat. The lower end of the

Scion

Stock

Saddle graft

scion is cut similarly and should sit squarely on the stock. Place the two together and bind tightly with tape and cover with grafting wax.

The *saddle graft* is much the same as the whip, except that the end of the stock is wedge-shaped and it fits into a notch on the scion. Both stock and scion should be of the same thickness. This method is often used to graft shrubs and small trees.

Cleft grafting is done when the stock is older or thicker than the scion. The stock is sawn off 6-10 inches above the ground. Using a sharp knife, cut a wedge-shaped cleft in the trunk and slip the scion into the opening. The scion should fit snugly. Place the scion on the near side—the inner bank of both stock and scion should meet. Sometimes, two scions are used, one on each side of the cleft. Take special care when binding this graft.

Crown grafting is usually done to spruce up an old tree. The best time for this is during the plant's growing season when the bark peels

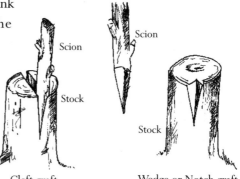

Scion

Stock

Cleft graft

Scion

Stock

Wedge or Notch graft

away easily from the wood. The stock is sawed 8-12 inches above the ground. Slit the bark, open it up gently and fold the flaps back. Now insert the scion and bind carefully. More than one scion can be inserted. When worked with a number of scions around the edge, a crown effect is created, from which this method gets its name.

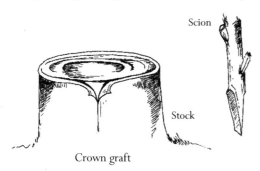

Scion

Stock

Crown graft

Inarch or Upright grafting is generally used on fruit trees. Take a rooted cutting of a two-year-old plant and pot it. This will form the stock. When established, slice 2 inches of bark with a thin layer of wood still attached to it. This is done on one side of the stem. Do the same to the scion which you have been growing in another pot, or in the ground. Place the stock near the scion, bind the two sliced areas of the stock and the scion together and cover the binding with grafting wax.

Scion—
a branch of
a growing
plant in the
garden

Stock—
a rooted
cutting in a pot

Bud grafting is used on roses and fruit trees. The 'eye' of one plant, together with a piece of surrounding tissue, is inserted into a slit in the stem of another plant. Most nursery gardeners use this method and it is best for the dry regions in India. The stock must be hardy and easy to propagate by cuttings. The bark should peel away easily. The bud should always be from the current year's growth. Choose a cool rainy day to graft. This will prevent the bud from shrivelling up. Make a T-shaped incision on the stock and slide the scion in. Secure in place and bind with tape. Bud grafting is done in the case of apricots, cherries and peaches. Oddly enough, these fruits belong to the family of roses, Rosaceae.

Layering

Layers take longer to root than cuttings, but where cuttings refuse to root, layers often succeed. In this process, a branch from the parent is induced to root and then separated from the parent.

When layering, choose a healthy, pliable branch and bend it down to the ground. At a point where there is a leaf bud, on the underside of the branch, directly beneath it, make a cut, and slice the bark upwards for an inch or so, to form a tongue. Keep the tongue away from the branch by inserting a couple of matchsticks or a pebble. Insert the cut area into the soil, a couple of inches deep, and peg it down. If the branch is thick, use two pegs, one on either side of the tongue. Loosen the earth before pegging the layer. Keep the pegged branch shaded and don't let the soil dry out. The layer will root within four to six weeks. When the layer has rooted, cut it away from the parent in easy stages. Make a small notch and keep deepening it gradually until it separates.

Air-layering: This is a very popular method in India and China, especially in the case of fruiting and flowering trees and shrubs. As in layering, choose a healthy young branch and make a tongue below a leaf bud. You can also cut a ring around the bark, an inch wide. Surround the area with leaf mould or dry moss in a 2-inch thick layer, and wrap the ball in jute or coir matting. Tie on

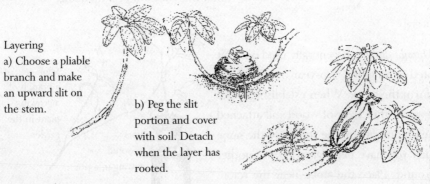

Layering
a) Choose a pliable branch and make an upward slit on the stem.

b) Peg the slit portion and cover with soil. Detach when the layer has rooted.

Air Layering
c) Make a cut on the stem and hold the slit open. Wrap in moss and cover with jute or plastic film. Remove when stem has rooted.

either side, leaving the mouth open for watering in very dry weather. In moister areas, strap around, and keep the mouth closed.

> *Cut off a foe like an old gardener cuts off the protruding branches of a creeper.*
> —Rig Veda

The moss or compost should remain moist at all times but should not be soaking wet. Many people use plastic to wrap the ball. This is fine in cold regions where warmth is required to facilitate rooting, but I would not advise you to use it. Too much warmth and moisture will rot the layer. If you have no option but to use plastic, keep the mouth open. Branches that have been air-layered will take between two and four months to root well.

PRUNING

Pruning is something most amateur gardeners regard with apprehension. If you are a newcomer to this exalted field, you are right to fear it. Pruning requires great expertise and skill. Not all plants are pruned in the same way or at the same time. Some don't like heavy pruning and others don't like pruning at all. If you have no experience, the rule is: 'Too little is safer than too much.' The best way to learn pruning is to watch an expert at work. If you can't, there are some basic guidelines you can follow.

There are three main reasons for pruning—to shape a plant, to encourage new growth, and to get rid of weak or dead wood.

The best time to prune *evergreens*, which grow and flower in the summer months, is in the cold season. January is a good month. This will give the plant time to get over the shock of being pruned, and by spring, it will have recovered to produce healthy vigorous new shoots. If pruned later, spring growth is lost and new growth is slow to appear.

For the majority of deciduous shrubs and trees, pruning should be done a month after leaf-fall. *Winter flowering* plants should be pruned after flowering.

Spring and summer flowering plants should be pruned after flowering or fruiting, to encourage new shoots which mature in the following year.

General cleaning and trimming can be done during the monsoon, as this is the growth time for most plants in the tropics.

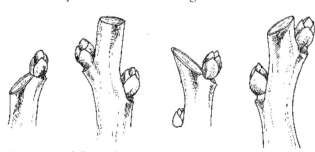

Pruning cuts, left to right: too close to the bud; too far away from the bud; sloping the wrong way; correct

Don't prune in autumn when the plant grows vigorously, just before the onset of winter.

Don't prune when the weather is very hot and dry, and if there are hot winds blowing.

Don't prune plants which have been newly transplanted.

How to Prune

Use a sharp knife or secateurs, and cut cleanly at a slant, about half an inch above a leaf bud. Cut up and out so that the top of the slant faces out. Remove dead wood and superfluous shoots which have already carried fruit or flowers and are not needed as a frame to bear new shoots.

When pencil-slim wood is cut, it will throw out closer to the cut, but when thick branches are cut, some may die back. The dead snags should be cut off in the next pruning season.

When pruning, you must know if your plant produces flowers on one-year-old wood or two-year-old wood. Good judgement is required for pruning. Heavy pruning produces vegetative growth, and if done to fruit trees, for instance, will produce excessive leaf and shoot growth.

Pruning sends a plant into shock—a healthy plant can stand up to pruning but a weak plant may be severely affected and die.

Vigorous climbers and shrubs must be pruned drastically, or else they will grow wild.

Finally, when buying your plant, ask your nursery man what kind of pruning it can take.

Pruning Methods

Thumbnail: This requires pinching out two to three leaves from the tips

Heading back: The upward growth of a plant is cut back to induce spreading branches.

Light pruning involves removing spindly growth and cutting back wood that is pencil-thick.

Heavy pruning involves cutting back thick branches which form the frame of the plant.

Pollarding consists of cutting back a tree to encourage new plume-like growth.

Root Pruning

When a tree is shy of flowering or fruiting, gardeners resort to root pruning. Very heavy root growth produces leaves at the expense of flowers and fruit. A narrow tunnel is dug under the tree and the taproot is severed. The more common method is to dig a circular trench three to four feet deep and a foot and a half wide, about 6-10 ft from the trunk, depending upon the size of the tree. The lateral roots are exposed by the trench and these are cut cleanly and removed. After a couple of weeks, the trench is refilled with the soil you have kept aside. The soil should be mixed with compost before you return it to the trench. This drastic treatment should be reserved for trees and shrubs that refuse to fruit or flower even after proper manuring and feeding.

The tree is traumatized by root pruning. It's wiser to prune in semi-circular halves, every alternate year.

TREE PLANTING

> *I think that I shall never see*
> *A poem lovely as a tree.*
> —Joyce Kilmer

One of the greatest advantages of gardening in India is the infinite choice of fast-growing trees. They attain stature and a well-defined character in five to eight years. Many trees, if grown from cuttings or air-layers, will produce flowers and fruit in just a couple of years. If you have a large garden, you can plan to have a tree in flower all through the year.

> *Ease your weary limbs,*
> *stranger, under this—*
> *Truly the soft breeze speaks*
> *through the green leaves.*
> *This is indeed a place to*
> *take your ease,*
> *And dear to wayfarers in the*
> *intense heat.*
> —Theokritos

When planting a tree, one is tempted to buy the largest specimen available and transplant it into the garden. Do that only if you have the expertise, and know your trees. For a beginner it is best to begin with young saplings. It may take a little longer to get results, but it will survive the transplanting. The older the tree, the less it likes to be moved.

When planting trees, it is essential to prepare your pit well in advance. The soil should be dug deep, turned over and enriched with manure and compost. If you are adding lime, prepare the pit six to seven months in advance.

Planting

When planting, dig a hole $3^1/_2$ ft deep and 3 ft in diameter. If the soil is poor, dig to a depth of $4^1/_2$ ft and 4 ft across. Keep the soil aside. Now refill the pit—for every five parts of soil, add one part of well-rotted cattle manure mixed with 1:5-part leaf mould. Make sure the manure is old and free of pests. Fill the pit to a few inches above ground level and water thoroughly. The soil will sink and the loose earth will settle. Then let the

> *Who does his duty is a question*
> *Too complex to be solved by me*
> *But he, I venture the suggestion*
> *Does part of his that plants a tree*
> —J.R. Lowell

soil dry. Once dry, make a hole large enough to take the root ball of the sapling, and plant your tree. If you have moved the tree from your surroundings, make sure there is a large clod of earth when lifting. Make certain the taproot is straight when planting. If the sapling is removed from a pot, gently loosen the roots that have been compressed, and spread them out. The collar of the sapling should be level with the top of the pit. Fill the hole and press the earth firmly around the collar. The best time for planting is with the arrival of the rains. Some trees can be planted in February/March. If you plant before the monsoon season, the young plant should be protected till the rains come.

Know your trees before you plant them and visualize the space they will occupy when full-grown. With a bare patch of land there is a tendency to plant too many trees. A large tree needs 30 sq. ft of area around it to grow healthily. One medium-sized tree is quite sufficient for a small garden. Don't plant large trees in a small garden; big trees have roots that go deep and spread wide in their search for nutrition, and the other plants in the garden are no match for them. Only if you have a huge garden can you indulge in a copse of large flowering trees, or create a little glade or a leafy arbour.

Care

If you want a straight trunk, you must stake the sapling. This also prevents it from being battered by the wind. Use some padding between the trunk and the stake to prevent the bark from being bruised.

Newly planted trees need watering from time to time in the hot dry months, but too much watering will prove disastrous. Make a deep drill in the soil and water only if the soil below is dry. When watering, water deeply. Young trees can be shaped by lopping off the lower branches which later will be too close to the ground. As a rule, garden trees are chosen for their naturally graceful form and it is not necessary to prune them. Choose trees suitable for the climate and the size of the garden.

Do not allow grass to grow around the tree until it is at least four to five years old. Occasionally, fork the bare earth.

- Pits should be prepared at least six months before planting a tree.
- When planting grafted trees, the graft should be just below soil level. If the point of union is higher, there is not much you can do.
- Never remove the ball of earth around the roots.
- Fruit trees are generally pruned and cleaned towards the end of their dormant period. January is the right time in most cases.

Soil Mixture for Fruit Trees
Six parts soil
Three parts well-rotted manure and leaf mould
One part wood-ash
One part bone-meal

Compost for Fruit Trees
One part cattle manure or compost
Half part wood-ash
Half part bone-meal

Fertilizers

Trees will not produce fruits and flowers if one simply plants them.
There is much you have to do if you want quality as well as quantity.
—Lore from the Upavana Vinoda

You may think that this chapter is out of a witch's almanac, and rubbish it as a lot of superstitious, mumbo-jumbo . But if you are clued up you'll know organic gardening is one of the 'in things', part of the ecology and environment drive. This 'in thing' was commonplace not so long ago, when plants were fed what nature supplied us with. Chemcial fertilizers are the new kids on the block whose influence hasn't been very salutary. Their benefits are short-term ones. In the long run, these chemicals destroy the soil which they are meant to nourish. Chemicals should be used sparingly or in dire conditions. The only people who advocate the regular use of chemicals are the manufacturers themselves.

A plant basically requires three things: nitrogen, potash and phosphates, with small quantities of other trace elements. All these can be supplied organically. Besides compost and manure, your kitchen can supply you with some excellent fertilizers that will be greatly appreciated by your plants. Since that's not sufficient—it never is—garden centres are stocked with various types of organic feeds and fertilizers. The difference between the two is the former is used to feed the plant, the latter, to feed the soil.

The Big Four

- If your soil lacks nitrogen, dig in well-rotted dung of animal manure which also contains some amount of phosphates.
- Wood-ash (and no other), is rich in potash.
- Bone-meal is an excellent phosphate.
- Powdered lime is the best remedy for acidic soil.

FROM THE WITCH'S ALMANAC

- 🌿 Weak or wilting plants need a booster; some sort of tonic. Give them sugar dissolved in water. Just as it is for us, it's a good source of energy for them.
- 🌿 *Daal* washings (skinless varieties of *masoor*, *moong* etc) are a mild *liquid feed*. Give it to them regularly.
- 🌿 A more potent feed is the bloody water which meat or fish has been washed in. It is criminal to throw away such an excellent feed. Give it to your plants.
- 🌿 Fruits, flowers and vegetables thrive on liquefied blood. Get half a kilo of blood from a butcher (it can get coagulated) and mix it in a bucket of water. Give a cupful of this mixture to your plants at regular intervals when fruiting and flowering; they'll thank you for it.
- 🌿 For the slow growers, or if you want some plants to grow exceptionally tall, give them a little diluted beer—yes, beer—regularly during their growing period and watch them grow. A beer drinker somewhere in England (where almost everyone is a gardener) used to chuck his leftover beer out of his window, into a bed of hollyhocks. The hollyhocks in the other beds did reasonably well but those growing beneath the window shot up to a height of 18 and a half feet! The yeast in the beer helps plants grow tall.
- 🌿 All leguminous plants help fix nitrogen in the soil. There are some very pretty wild ones which also make excellent ground covers.

Compost pit

🌿 Nettles in the garden receive ruthless treatment. They are hacked down, dug up and thrown out. But nettles benefit all plants growing near them. They stimulate the plants, and if added to a compost heap, hasten the decomposing process and enrich the manure. Grown in controlled clumps,

Good manure can be made by turning vegetable waste into compost. Every 6 inches of vegetable waste should be covered with a fine layer of compost to hasten the rotting process. The heap should be turned over every three weeks and watered if the weather is dry. A wire cage makes a good container for compost.

they only do good. The soil in which nettles have been grown is very rich in plant nutrients—nitrogen, silica, proteins, phosphates and formic acid among others.

- 🌿 Don't throw away kitchen waste—just add it to the compost heap if you have one. If not, boil the waste in water and give that soup to the plants when cool. A very good *liquid feed*.
- 🌿 Azaleas, and especially camellias, enjoy a diet of tea leaves. Small wonder, since the two are first cousins. Don't throw away tea leaves if you don't have camellias. They make a very good mulch for any plant.
- 🌿 Ferns also enjoy a drink of weak tea.
- 🌿 Banana skins are rich in plant nutrients. Lay them below the soil. They decompose very quickly, providing the plants with magnesium, calcium and phosphates.
- 🌿 Rinse out milk packets or bottles into a plant. The milky solution makes a mild feed.
- 🌿 If your milk has gone bad, give it to plants that like calcium.
- 🌿 If you want your soil to be rich in humus, put in plenty of leaf compost mixed with animal manure.

SYMBIOSIS

This is the process when two organisms live together for mutual benefit, like the Yucca and the Yucca moth. Some plants when grown together, have a symbiotic relationship. Old gardeners knew about this long before the scientific term was coined. They discovered this by observation and found that some plants were soil brothers. The old timers were blissfully unaware of root excretions or organic activity; they just knew the plants grew well together.

In a flower garden, appearances matter, but in a vegetable garden, plants can be grown symbiotically without having to worry about aesthetics.

Marigolds

Plant them among your vegetables and flowers. The root excretions from this plant kill whiteflies and nematodes in the soil. This can create mayhem in your flower beds but with some planning and discretion, they can be used quite effectively. The best for the purpose is the small variety, *Tagetes minuta*, with maroon and yellow flowers. They are very good for tomatoes and potatoes and a little less so for everything else.

Nettles

A walk in the hills or in the countryside will show you that anything growing near nettles is lush and healthy. Nobody wants nettles in the garden, least of all the gardener. But they appear to stimulate the plants near them. Fruits, vegetables and flowers, all benefit from them. The worst thing about them is not their drabness, it's their sting! It's advisable to wear thick gloves when working with them. Fruit trees are seen to produce more fruit when they have nettles growing near them.

Parsley

Roses like parsely growing near them. So do flowers in the flower garden, and we're lucky it's such a pretty plant. It's attractive *and* you can eat it! In the vegetable garden, it's good for tomatoes. In the flower beds, it can be grown as an edging or between other low-edging plants.

Tulsi

If grown near fruiting or flowering plants, tulsi keeps them free of pests.

Vegetable garden plants

Coriander and *anise* discourage insects. Coriander can be used effectively even in a flower garden as it is a pretty, delicate plant. If allowed to flower it has spikes of tiny mauve-white flowers.

Onions and *garlic* are not only good for roses but in the vegetable garden are good brothers to carrots.

Peas, beans and *turnips* are all good for each other.

Carrots are good for beans, lettuce, onions, garlic, mint and turnips.

Peas are good for beans, cabbages and leeks.

Potatoes like soil in which peas have been grown.

Radishes are good for most vegetables.

Dandelions are bad for most vegetables and flowers.

CHART

Plant	Likes	Dislikes
Beans	Carrots, radishes	Lyssop
Beetroot	Onions, kohlrabi	—
Broad beans	Carrots, cauliflower	Onions, garlic, shallots
Broccoli	Dill, French marigold, and soil in which potatoes had been grown	Strawberries

Brussels sprout	Dill, carrots, French marigold and soil in which tomatoes or potatoes were grown	Strawberries
Cabbage	Early potatoes, dill, camomile, sage, rosemary, mint	Onions, garlic, leeks
Carrots	Beans, lettuce, garlic, mint	Strawberries
Cauliflower	Dill, mint	Chives, onions, garlic, leeks
Celery	Cabbage, leeks, tomatoes	—
Cucumbers	Lettuce, radish, beans, sunflowers	—
French beans	Carrots, beets, cucumber, maize	Onions, garlic
Leeks	Celery	—
Lettuce	Radish, carrots, strawberries	—
Peas	Radish, carrots, cucumber, beans	Sunflowers, tomatoes
Potatoes	Beans, maize, cabbage, peas	—
Radish	Lettuce, chervil, nasturtium	Onions, dill
Runner beans	Maize, beets, cabbage, cucumber	Mustard
Spinach	Strawberries	—
Strawberries	Radish, lettuce, carrots	—
Tomatoes	Asparagus, parsley, French marigold	—
Turnips	Peas	—

FERTILIZERS FROM VEDIC INDIA

Ancient Sanskrit texts on agriculture and gardening have devoted many pages to feeding plants. You'll either be astonished and pleased, or revolted, depending upon whether you're squeamish or a fanatic vegetarian. But illuminating it will be. What the ancient sages recommend will come as no surprise, however, to the cognoscenti.

Good, rich soil is one that contains plenty of decomposing vegetable *and animal* matter. The forest floor where all plants grow is not only nourished by rotting plants and leaves but also by the bodies of creatures great and small who live in the forest and die there. Their bodies return to the soil and enrich it. Our ancestors were well aware of this fact. They fed their plants with ghee, milk, the meat of pig, deer, jackal and rhino (we'll have to pass that) among other animal flesh. They also had a pretty fair knowledge of climatology, plant physiology, fertilizers and manures. The *Atharva Veda* has a verse on plant nourishment in Chapter 281. Later texts on the subject contain detailed instructions on plant care. Even Kautilya, author of the *Arthashastra,* took time off from problems of governance and finance to write about manures. It's impossible, in this day and age, to use all that is recommended in the ancient texts, but there is plenty left over for us to make good use of.

Enriching compost for agricultural use was made of pulses, barley, sesame seeds, goat and sheep dung, fish and cattle flesh and fat.

Sukracharya is very precise: 'If you want healthy plants they should be fed with stools of the goat, sheep, cows, water as well as meat. Growth of trees can be helped by the application of water with which fishes are washed and cleaned.'

Again: 'The powder of the dungs of goat and sheep, the powder of *yava, tila* (pulses) beef as well as water should be kept together (undisturbed) for seven nights. The application of this water leads very much to the growth in flowers and fruit of all trees.'

> *Today's gardening gurus will tell you about the benefits of fish manure, blood-meal, bone-meal, and manure made of bird droppings. Guano, a manure made of the droppings of sea-birds, is greatly prized. Peru is the world's largest exporter of guano.*

Kumpa

This appears to be the grandmother of all manures. When the ancients talk of flesh, fat and marrow, it can be that of any animal. Offal from the butcher will do just as well.

Kumpa was widely used in ancient India. The *Upavana Vinoda* suggests as much:

'One should boil the flesh, fat and marrow of deer, pig, fish, sheep, goat, rhinoceros in water and when it is properly boiled, one should put the mixture in an earthen pot and add into the compound milk, powders of sesamum oilcake, *masa* (lentils) boiled in honey, the decoction of pulses, clarified butter and hot water. There is no fixity as to the amount of any of these elements. When the said pot is put into a warm place for a fortnight, the compound becomes what is called 'kumpa' water which is very healthy (for plants in general).

The Vrksayurveda by Surapala has a simpler recipe: 'Water in which dung, fat, flesh, marrow, brain and blood of a hog have been put together and which is burried underground for a fortnight is called kumpa.'

- For very young trees, a porridge of fish and sesamum seeds is recommended.
- A vine will bend under the weight of flowers and fruit if fed with chicken dropping, manure and a broth of flesh and fish.
- For sweet, juicy pomegranates, copious amounts of sugar water and a soup of flesh should be given to the plants.

🐾 Orange trees benefit from a broth of jaggery, milk and meat.

🐾 Any meat soup is good for date palms, coconuts, bamboo and lotus.

🐾 All flowering plants greatly benefit if fed a broth of flesh and blood.

🐾 Fruiting and flowering trees will be laden if watered with milk, and the fruits have been found to be very sweet.

🐾 Vines benefit from chicken manure, washings of fish and meat. They will bear abundant flowers and fruit.

For the small urban gardens of today, your kitchen will supply you with enough raw material to make excellent manure. 'What you can eat, your plants can' is the general rule of thumb. For obvious reasons, deer, rhino or jackal meat cannot be used, but the butcher has all that is needed, and the better gardening stores stock goat and sheep manure. A soup can be made from all the bits and pieces you remove when cleaning fish, chicken, mutton, pork and beef, and given to the plants. A soup of vegetable and fruit peels will be greatly appreciated by your plants, and your reward will lie in their health and beauty and the quantities of flowers and fruit they produce.

Lore from the Upavana Vinoda

'Mango trees bear very fragrant and sweet fruits at an early date if they are watered with a decoction of milk, together with the fat of deer, jackal, elephant, horse etc.' (In other words, any animal fat will do.)

'If one waters the roots of vines with the compound liquid made up of the stools of fowl, flesh and fish, straw and husks of paddy, they bear fruit and flowers and grow.'

'If a Vilva tree (Bael) is watered with clarified butter, milk and honey, it bears fruits which are sweet to the taste, full of fleshy substance containing a scanty number of seeds.'

'White mustard, plantain leaf, fish, pig, and cat manure mixed with clarified butter to form a thick paste should be smeared on the trunks of fruit- and flower-bearing trees and woody shrubs to keep them free of disease and to ensure they bear fruit in great quantities.'

Pests and Diseases

Worms, insects and other pests, seen and unseen, of many kinds and many
names, male and female, leaders and followers, I destroy you root and branch.
—*Atharva Veda*

Every gardener would like to do precisely that, for the garden is a place where 'fat caterpillars drift around, and paradisial grubs are found'. And the gardener can do without them.

Plants have so many enemies, both great and small, that a major part of gardening is keeping them in check, if not eradicating them altogether. Only a few plants like the sundew can make a meal of pests. Caterpillars are voracious eaters and can decimate the leaves of your plants in days if left unchecked. Aphids suck the sap, eelworms eat up roots, and fungi can make plants terminally ill. These creatures certainly have a right to live, but preferably outside the garden, or if you're nasty, in someone else's garden. Crows, birds, dogs and cats can be a problem but enemy number one is insects. Barring a few—bees, butterflies, ladybirds— the rest are positively unwelcome.

Common garden pests that sometimes appear on house plants are usually carried in on a pot from outside. Remove them by hand.

Unfortunately, these pests cannot be completely eliminated unless the garden is small. In large gardens, they can only be controlled, either directly or indirectly. Those that creep and crawl can be destroyed, and those that fly can be discouraged, but fungi can only be treated; you can't stop the breeze from spreading the spores around. In the case of blight, prevention is better than cure. Keep your plants clean and healthy and you'll rid yourself of a major problem. A healthy plant is usually impervious to fungal attack.

> *What is a weed? A plant whose virtues have not been discovered*
> —R.W. Emerson

The most important factor for healthy plants is soil condition—it must be open, friable and well-drained. If you dig deep and cultivate the soil, many insects that dwell in the earth will be destroyed. Get rid of all the weeds around the plants; clean soil is less likely to harbour pests than weed-covered earth. Weeds by nature are tough, and pests don't bother them. However, all weeds should not be removed; the leguminous kinds increase the nitrogen in the soil and make a pretty ground cover.

There are few animal pests in cities other than pet dogs, cats, sparrows and pigeons, but all these can be dealt with. Unruly pets can be trained and birds can be discouraged by putting up streamers of foil or bits of paper wafting in the breeze. Rats are difficult to discourage if they have found a source of food, and they are very destructive. But they can be trapped and got rid of.

The most formidable enemies are the insects, and all gardeners, amateur or expert, wage a constant battle with them. Get rid of one and a host will errupt like myrmidons. Only in a small garden can the gardener emerge victorious. But it is a brief victory. For a while there is respite and then the war begins again.

Snails, slugs and caterpillars must be hand-collected and destroyed. You cannot afford to be squeamish unless you want your garden ruined. The worst of the bad lot are snails, beetles, butterflies in their larval stage, nematodes and aphids. Turning over the soil destroys the eggs of those insects that lay them in the ground, but many lay their eggs when the plants begin to flower and fruit; their timing is very good! Gardeners must deal with them as they emerge.

There are so many pests to deal with, the list is endless—thrips, grasshoppers, termites, chewing and sucking lice, caterpillars, wireworms, crane flies, eelworms, slugs and snails to name just a few. This short list is enough make an amateur shudder and vow never to have a garden. Sometimes a combination of circumstances allows pests to thrive—climate, soil conditions, and a certain amount of neglect on your part—but with a few drastic measures they *can* be eradicated. The signs to look for are wilting shoots and leaves, seedlings nipped off just above or below the ground, and chewed-up leaves. Your method of attack will depend upon the type of insect you are dealing with. If it is a leaf-biting one, the leaves should be sprayed with an insecticide, if it is a root-nibbler, the soil must be treated. The leaf-eaters are beetles, caterpillars, snails, grasshoppers etc. Aphids, thrips, bugs and scale insects pierce and suck the sap. Crickets feast on the tender shoots of seedlings. Ants run off with seeds, tend and herd the aphids, and some types even attack live wood. Nematodes and eelworms attack the roots and to deal with these horrors, you must bore holes in the soil and pour in liquid pesticide. But you shouldn't have any nematodes in the first place if you have forked and turned the soil over thoroughly or checked it if in pots. To destroy the enemy, you must know it well.

All insects change form during their existence. They start off as eggs, when they can't do any damage, but in the next stage, the larval, they are demonic, wicked and bad. They just feed, and feed, and feed on all the tender leaves and shoots they can get their mandibles into. Then they enter the pupal stage when they, thankfully, go to sleep for a while before emerging as adults. And then again, with many of them, you'll have to begin all over again.

Preventive measures are the most effective. Turn over the soil, sun it and remove all the creepy-crawlies you find. Powdery little mounds of soil will tell you where the crickets are holing up. When there is an out-and-out invasion, you will have to get drastic and use chemical pesticides. For most soil pests, a mild solution of phenyl is quite enough to destroy them. If the plant is in a pot, just repot with fresh, clean soil.

THE ARSENAL

Most remedies mentioned here may appear fatuous at worst and absurd at best, but science has caught up with some old wives' tales and we find that there's more to them than we thought. They are not the product of vague, slightly imbalanced minds. The difference is that the old wives didn't get their knowledge from laboratory experiments but through long years of observation. Plant with the waxing moon and not the waning moon, say the old folk, and now we know that lunar rythms affect the earth's magnetic fields. In ancient India, many plants were worshipped and fed with ghee and honey; now we know that these ingredients are as good for plants as they are for us.

If you have a small garden or a pot garden, you shouldn't have any serious problems and you will not have to resort to drastic means such as chemical pesticides. If, however, you have a large garden, you may need to use them on occasion. In that case, consult your nearest garden centre. There are various pesticides available—some are suitable for sucking insects, others for biting insects and still others which are used for soil pests. Find out what your requirement is.

Insects, all without exception, cordially dislike *turmeric*, and will not attack plants treated with it. For leaf-biters and piercing and sucking insects, a solution of turmeric and soap makes an excellent repellent. Put two teaspoons of turmeric powder into 1 litre of water and add half a teaspoon of soap, *not* detergent. Spray young leaves and shoots. If you need something stronger, say for a colony of aphids, add the tobacco of half a cigarette to the solution and let it stand for twenty-four hours. Then spray the infected plants with this solution. The aphids will die instantly. Repeat the process for two or three days if the aphids stubbornly persist in living.

Turmeric powder can be dusted on the leaves to get rid of the biters. If dusted on *aphids*, they drop off. If the aphids are ensconced in the calyx of flower buds, pour in a little turmeric powder. Soon the aphids will meet their maker, since the ants which nurture them will not go near the turmeric-coated area. Grind turmeric with tulsi leaves and rub the mixture on the stems of plants attacked by scale insects. That will kill the ones on the stems and prevent colonization.

Ants deposit aphids on the tips of the tender shoots and care for them. To prevent the ants from carrying the aphids up, make a thick paste of soap, tobacco and turmeric, and rub this on the base of the trunk. This will stymie the ants.

Camphor is a great repellent. Moths, spiders, caterpillars and other pests cannot abide it. You can protect your garden from several pests by occasionally spraying the plants with camphor solution. When it percolates through the soil, it carries on its good work there.

A decoction made of *neem leaves* is an excellent pest-control agent. Boil neem leaves in water, cool and strain. Spray plants with the solution and use the leaves as a mulch.

Neem cake, when mixed with soil, prevents soil pests from breeding. There are plenty of neem products available in the market.

Neem oil if rubbed on the base of plants, will prevent the creepy-crawlies from climbing up.

If your plants are prone to *leaf-curl*, hang camphor balls on them. Leaf-curl is caused by fungus which does not like camphor.

Aphids are the bane of any garden and pesticide-manufacturers will encourage you to spend a small fortune on their products. Don't waste your money and time. Most gardeners will tell

Of Aphids

These bear young in enormous numbers and the young begin feeding from birth. Numerous generations can be produced in one season . . . Apart however, from the direct damage they do, aphids also transmit many viruses from plant to plant.

—Prof. W.W. Fletcher

Aphids are green, black or red, winged or wingless and are found on the underside of leaves and young shoots. They attract ants. Wash them off with a soapy solution followed by clear water, or use an insecticide.

you that aphids remain unless you use a very strong pesticide. Rubbish. That will destroy the aphids and your plants as well. The good news is that when the good Lord made aphids, he also made *garlic*. Grow garlic around the plants that are prone to aphid attack and you will find plants free from the pest. *Roses* are especially vulnerable to

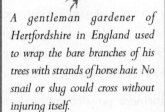

A gentleman gardener of Hertfordshire in England used to wrap the bare branches of his trees with strands of horse hair. No snail or slug could cross without injuring itself.

aphids, greenflies and blackflies. A few cloves of garlic grown around the plants keeps the aphids away. Garlic also seems to prevent leaf-curl and other fungal diseases. Try it—it works like magic! The rose appears to absorb some substance released by the garlic which the aphids have no taste for. Try this on one rose bush, and use chemicals on the others. You'll soon stop wasting your money on chemicals. All members of the *onion family* are excellent insect repellents, but garlic is by far the best.

Ants for some reason do not like *lupins*. Rub the trunks or base of plants with crushed lupin leaves and ants will give them a wide berth.

To get rid of *snails* in the garden, put a little *beer* in a couple of old jam bottles and lay them on the side. Snails like beer; they will crawl in and discover too late, that they're trapped. All you have to do is cap the bottles and throw the snails out of the garden if you cannot bring yourself to kill them.

Nasturtiums are nature's answer to the woolyaphis and white fly, which attack many fruit trees and some flowering shrubs and trees. Grow nasturtiums around the infected trees and train them up the trunks. The trees will soon be pest-free. In the case of healthy trees, they act as a preventive measure.

Marigolds, especially the small yellow and maroon ones (*Tagetes minuta*), are good for everything in the garden. Insects—both the ones above and below the soil—cannot abide them. True, they are not pleasantly scented, but

White flies settle on the underside of leaves making them mottled and sticky with 'honeydew' which attracts ants. They multiply at a great speed. They, along with their eggs and larvae, should be sprayed with insecticide.

then insect repellents are not supposed to be. Both the aroma of the flowers and the excretions from the roots are invaluable for flowers, vegetables and greenhouse plants. The root excretions kill *nematodes* and destroy *white flies*. Plant marigolds wherever you can in the garden—in the rows of vegetables, among the flowers and near creepers—to keep them insect-free.

> *The Marigold was sacred to the Aztec goddess of Agriculture. In ancient Mexico, it used to be planted among the rows of corn and beans.*

Soap-water (not detergent), especially if it contains a little *washing soda*, if thrown into flower and vegetable beds keeps them free from insects. Treat the beds once in ten days or once a fortnight. Frequent treatment with soap water will destroy young plants, so don't overdo it.

All parts of the *thuja* make an excellent *pesticide*. Dry and pound the leaves, and add the powder to the soil mixture when potting or repotting. If the plants are in the ground, loosen the topsoil and mix with powdered thuja.

A good deterrent for leaf cutters and suckers is a decoction made of *tulsi (basil) leaves* to which a little *turmeric* is added. Turmeric/soap-*tulsi* solution will also keep *leaf-miners* (larvae that tunnel through the leaves) at bay. Chrysanthemums and nasturtiums are frequently attacked by leaf-miners.

A very effective *pesticide* for *soil pests* such as *maggots, nematodes* etc. is the *tomato plant*. Dry and powder the plant after it has finished fruiting and add the powder to the soil. I have found that pomegranate peels and bitter gourd scrapings have the same effect.

All fungi, except mushrooms and the bloom on cheese, are lethal to what they grow on. Warmth, damp and shade are necessary for fungal growth. Plants that are out in the full sun, or even partial sun, during the hot summer months will not be attacked by fungi. Some fungi attack leaves while others attack the roots, and it is the latter that one must guard against since the damage is usually detected too late to save the plant. We never see the beginning of the attack, and by the time we realize what's happening, the deed is done. Plants with root diseases usually have to be dug up and destroyed; there is no cure. The best way to avoid *blight* attacking the roots is to treat the soil before planting with *turmeric*, powdered *thuja* or *neem cake* and other *neem pesticides*. If a branch is attacked by fungal rot, it must be cut till the healthy wood and the cut must be sealed. The dead wood should not be left around in the garden; it should be burnt or thrown far away.

Fungi that attack leaves can be easily spotted and dealt with a fungicide spray such as *turmeric* solution or decoction of *neem* or *tulsi* leaves. Lemon juice is also effective, if you have enough lemons to spare. Water in which *tobacco* has been steeped is also an excellent fungicide.

Tobacco is a wonderful pesticide for both soil and leaf pests. A *soap* solution in which *tobacco* has been steeped is a very effective leaf-spray. Get raw tobacco leaves from the market, add them to a solution of soap and water, and boil to make a concentrate.

> 100 gm tobacco
> 5 litres water
> 20 gm soap

This solution should be cooled and then used. For a spray, one part of this solution should be mixed with three parts of water.

Phenyl, which is found in most homes, makes a very good insect repellent. Mix one part of phenyl with twenty parts of water and use for soil or leaf pests.

Soft soap and *kerosene* when mixed with hot water is excellent for leaf pests, especially the piercing and sucking types such as *thrips, aphids, bugs* and *scale insects*. To make the solution, mix one part of soap with ten parts of hot water and two parts of kerosene. If the plants are under severe attack by *aphids* or *scale insects*, use a mixture of *phenyl*, *kerosene* and *soap solution*.

2 parts phenyl: 1 part kerosene: 40 parts soap water. How much you need depends on the size of vessel you use to measure one part.

When sowing seeds, mix them with *turmeric* powder and sow. Ants will not steal them.

Nematodes attack the roots and the plant forms knotty galls around the collar. Once the plant is infested, there is no real remedy; it must be uprooted and destroyed.

The soil should be turned over, sunned, and treated with a pesticide made of *pheynl* and *tobacco* solution. Leave the soil untouched for two to three weeks and then turn it over again. Do not plant anything until the soil is free from *nematodes*.

In a large garden, if only a few plants are infected with fungus, it is not worth buying or making special fungicides. Just sponge the leaves with a solution made of equal parts of *water* and *methylated spirit*.

NUGGETS OF COMMONSENSE

- Prevention is better than cure. Well-treated soil that has been cultivated will not harbour pests.
- Never use fresh manure—it will contain maggots and other pests. It should be well-rotted and dried out if it has been damp for too long. Check for pests before applying.

❧ Never spray plants when the sun is high. They should be sprayed either in the morning or late in the evening.

❧ Do not use chemical pesticides without reading the instructions, including the fine print.

❧ Keep the plants clean and always destroy infected plants that have been uprooted in order to prevent disease from spreading to healthy plants.

Red spider mites appear in hot, dry conditions. Regular misting of leaves is a good preventive. These creatures are almost invisible and suck the sap. The leaves turn yellow and brown, and shrivel up. A soap and tobacco solution will solve that problem.

Red spider mites

Grey mould (botrytis) attacks the leaves and stems of many indoor plants. First, fuzzy grey patches appear, and then rot sets in. Remove and destroy the infected parts before using a fungicide.

Mealy bugs look like specks of cotton and can be easily detected and controlled. Knock them off with an old toothbrush and spary the plant with *neem solution* in which tobacco has been steeped.

Thrips can also be controlled as their presence is easily detected by the silvery sheen and speckled markings they leave on leaves. These small, black, flying insects suck the sap from buds, flowers and leaves. They can be destroyed with a *soap solution* or *insecticide*. Add tobacco if necessary.

Thrips are small, black, flying insects which suck buds, flowers and leaves. Thrips will drop off if you shake the plant.

Garden Design Concepts

The loveliest of gardens, whether Japanese or English (very passionate gardeners, the English), always have a sense of contentment. There are sheltered areas with a hint of mystery, apertures leading excitingly into other areas, containing an element of surprise, and nooks filled with enchantment.

All successful gardens are essentially personal, and this is true of all gardens, whether they are the formal eighteenth century gardens of Europe, the deceptively simple tea-gardens of Japan, the great park gardens of China in the second century BC or the Persian gardens of medieval Shiraz and Isfahan. In all these gardens, there is a quality of selectiveness. It's impossible to incorporate all garden design features in one garden without making it an eyesore, much like a tastelessly overdressed woman. The best way to learn about garden design is to look at the great gardens; if you can't see the real thing, photographs will serve the purpose. Rely on your senses and analytical abilities and discard all that does not appeal to you. Should you like some feature, check if it will fit into your garden design. Gardens are infinitely complex, and without editing, can become a vague collection of effects rather than a set of concepts followed through. Even the most informal garden is the result of great care and thought. The most beautiful gardens are a feast for the eyes (and nose, if scented) rather than a collection of numerous botanical specimens. All serious gardeners, whether beginners or experts, have a bit of the collector in them, but the expert will be concerned with the overall beauty of the garden rather than the rarity of the plants in it. Whether planting a hedge, building a pergola or a doorway, look at other gardens famed for their beauty and incorporate or modify the features and use only what will fit in with your scheme of things.

🐾 The most obvious elements in a garden are the vertical features—trees, tall shrubs, trellises etc.—which rise up from the ground. But the horizontal element is as vital—

it's the vista seen when sitting in the garden or in the house. Too much of any element can become boring, whether mown grass or gravel patches. Too many flagstone paths or brick-paved areas can be dreary and arid. Try for a harmonious blend of material and texture underfoot.

🌿 Even a small change of level can make all the difference in a garden. A flat, unbroken expanse is tedious at best. Some of the best gardens rely on texture for effect—hard flagstones with soft lines of hedges and pergolas. Texture should be designed into the garden plan—it can remain constant, as with stone, or change with the seasons, as a bank of trees. Many great gardens are a blend of large-leafed and small-leafed plants in varying shades of green. Bare branches against a winter sky can be as effective as when crowned with leaves. A variety of textures—stone-grass, gravel-grass, moss- gravel, brick-shrub, stone-low hedge etc.—provide the contrasting effects of hard and soft.

🌿 The day and the year bring changes in shade and light, and these changes add to the drama being enacted in the garden. A serious gardener will plan for them. There are few sights more lovely than sunlight bursting through trees or streaming into a doorway. Trees and doorways can be positioned to capture the slanting rays of the evening sun. Almost all textures are related to the play of light and shade. New leaves glow as light filters through them; others like camellias glisten, and still others like the silver oak and willow shimmer silver and green in the wind. In India, shade is used not merely for effect, it is essential if one is to enjoy the garden. In hot places, contrasting greens and reflections in water are an integral part of a successful garden.

🌿 Colours can make or mar a garden. Getting them right in a garden is akin to a good sense of colour in clothes or interior design. True, in nature, colours never clash, but in a garden, with plants from all over the globe, it will be wise to choose good colour schemes. Yellows, whites, blues, greens; peach, apricot pink and cream; reds, crimson, oranges with cream or white. A mass of blue and mauve can be spectacular. In hot countries, few things are as soothing or pleasing as greens with just a touch of colour here and there. In this case, plants should be chosen for foliage texture rather than their flowers. Add a small, sparkling fountain and it can become a tiny paradise.

🌿 Perspective is as vital as texture and colour. It takes the eye from the foreground to the horizon. In a small garden, it leads the eye from the house to the line of control. Perspective gives a sense of relative space—what's closer appears larger. The finest example of the use of perspective is the garden of Versailles in France. Louis XIV created the masterpiece of formal garden design, but Capability Brown's gardens in England are no less. Too much emphasis on geometry and formality can take away the enchantment and beauty found in less informal gardens. Today there is too little thought spent on garden design and that has resulted in a loss of style and charm. Perspective requires careful handling and a certain degree of understanding. Think of a garden as a painting and find the vanishing point. Halfway down a garden, what lies behind and on either side must look just as good as from the main vantage point. Retain some element of surprise, something not anticipated and seen only when one reaches it.

🌼 The most successful gardens are those which are a joy throughout the year. Plant shrubs and trees which are deciduous along with the evergreens chosen for flowers and foliage. In a large garden, you can have permanents (shrubs and trees) which, if chosen with care, will flower throughout the year. A walk in the city parks will tell you which trees flower when.

🌼 Today there is a great conflict between informal and formal garden designs. Let your garden design be ruled by your preferences, what is available and what grows best in your climatic zone. The loveliest gardens are a judicious mixture of the two—a little formality closer to the house and informal beyond. If you want a wild, informal design, make certain you have the required skill. The wild, untamed look requires much expertise. Don't seek to change land with natural falls, irregularities and curves; incorporate them into the design whether formal or informal.

POINTS FOR GARDEN PLANS

🌼 Know what you want and visualize it.

🌼 Understand line and form.

🌼 If planning from scratch, use graph paper and a soft pencil.

🌼 Check the area and see if you wish to hide an ugly wall or pipe, an unsightly shed or the neighbour's intruding roof.

🌼 Check existing shrubs and trees, and if flowering or fruiting, design around them. Remove if they are diseased or not what you want.

🌼 Decide how much you want to spend in terms of time and money.

🌼 Include quick-flowering plants if you don't have any.

🌼 Check climate and local weather patterns. Is the garden open or sheltered?

🌼 Find out which part of the garden gets the full sun and which lies in the shade, and plant accordingly.

🌼 Check your soil—sandy or clayey, rich or poor.

🌾 If necessary, put a layer of new topsoil.

🌾 Prepare ground for planting. This means digging, hoeing and cultivating it. Feed the soil and remove all weeds.

🌾 Don't worry if you are a beginner—nature and thousands of nursery men are on your side. There are innumerable plants to choose from—just know what you want before you buy, but find out if what you want is what you can have. Don't be carried away by exotica—expensive plants you don't know how to look after. It is a very discouraging experience when they die on you. Choose hardy, reliable species native to the area. Buy healthy plants if you don't have the know-how to nurse the sickly ones.

🌾 Don't expect some kindly old gardener to help you decide and choose your plants for you.

🌾 Go to good nurseries and garden centres.

🌾 Don't take the advice of friends who know as little as you do.

🌾 If you are planning a big garden with a pool, arbour, pergola etc., get a landscape architect to advise you and to work out the cost.

🌾 Don't go to *maalis* for advice.

🌾 The cognoscenti have definite views about their gardens. They know what they can have and what styles they can incorporate. If you don't have the know-how, read some books on garden design and they will give you an idea of what you can do with your garden.

🌾 Garden design and ornamentation depend solely upon the space you have. Don't crowd it. Remember: too little is far better than too much. It is more difficult to remove a permanent feature than to add one.

🌾 Some have a preference for formal gardens, others for informal ones. The former needs space. You can't have a formal garden in 30 sq yd.

🌾 The garden should have a certain flair and style. Style never goes out of fashion, as in clothes, but fashion quickly goes out of style. Don't follow trends blindly. Use your sense of aesthetics when planning your garden and forget about being trendy. Consider your soil, situation, house and boundary walls. They may not accommodate the plan you visualize.

🌾 Look at great gardens but don't imitate slavishly. Sure, the best ideas come from them, but don't set out to create a replica if you can't replicate everything.

🌾 Have the courage to implement your own designs. Remember, rules can be broken. Experiment in order to achieve what you desire.

🌾 Remember, an informal garden requires more design input than a formal one does.

❧ If you are starting a garden late in life, you cannot have plants which mature late. Nor do you have the energy and time to spend on maintaining it. Get trouble-free, quick-resulting plants.

❧ When planning your garden, visualize what it will look like when it is mature. For example, trees, as they mature, will dominate the garden; so plan for that. Leave space for them. Similarly with lush creepers and dense shrubs.

❧ Formal gardens should contain one special feature around which the whole design evolves. It could be a seat under an arch, a paved pool, a bird-bath or a sundial. It could be a combination of a seat and pool with a sundial, a fountain, or a statue under an arch. If the site is long and narrow, the main feature should be at the far end, as a climax to the arrangement. A central position will create an effect of extreme formality. Walks, shrubberies or an avenue leading to an informal garden counter this in very large gardens. Only if the garden is enormous can you have extreme formality. And even then it should be broken up by using water with overhanging trees and meandering paths. There must be harmony, however large and formal the garden. A slope in the garden is ideal for a flight of ornamental steps. If there is a gentle slope, a little levelling will give you a few shallow steps, but the steps should fit naturally into the design. Steps can be used to break the monotony of a path or lead to some garden feature such as a seat or a sunken pool. A secluded terrace is always welcome.

❧ Brick and stone are always more pleasing than concrete.

Some Features for a Large Garden

A well-designed large garden can have quite a number of garden features without appearing tastelessly ornate and overdone—just as long you don't include every concept. It can incorporate various styles which, if properly visualized and executed, will blend to form a composite whole. Needless to say that to achieve it, your sense of aesthetics must be well honed. A large garden can happily accommodate many garden ornaments which give it a certain emphasis and accent. Unlike the garden which is constantly evolving, these are solid and static. Urns, seats, sundials, statues and columns serve as a foil to the living plants around them. Just don't clutter them up like goods in a second-hand shop; their placement should have a definite purpose in the scheme of things. Remember: too few is far better than too many, particularly when there is uncertainty. Arches, doorways, paths and steps can lead you from one portion of the garden into the next,

The Third Law of Gardening
Gimmicky devices don't work.
—The Devil's Bedside Book

each with its own ambience and style, but the change should be gradual and should be sensed before it is seen. For instance, a path leading from a sunny flower garden to a secluded one with a fountain should reflect the change in mood.

GARDEN PATHS

Paved paths are decorative but should lead somewhere—to a seat, pool or glade. They may be narrow or wide, winding or straight, depending upon the garden style. Paths may be made of brick or stone, rough or dressed, gravel or mossy. In places where the ground is hard, paths can be laid on ordinary soil with a dressing of gravel. Then water and roll the path. In places where the earth is soft and silty, the foundation is important, as especially in India, where it has to withstand the monsoon rains. Paths should be slightly higher in the centre to ensure good drainage. A word of caution: if the incline is too steep, the surface dressing will be washed away. The ideal slope always has a gradual incline. A turf path is more attractive between a bank of shrubs and flowers. Get hardy grass—the springier, Mexican or Nigerian turf will get worn away by constant trodding.

To lay a foundation: Dig up the path to a depth of 4-6 inches and ram down the bottom till it is absolutely firm. Spread 3 inches of clay mixed with plenty of broken brick rubble. Roll till firm. Paving, whether brick or stone, should be laid on this surface. If you intend to use grass, put a layer of topsoil (6 inches) on the foundation.

HEDGES

If the hedge is being used to protect the property, it is best to plant thick, thorny shrubs or rampant, thorny creepers. But if the hedge is being used as a screen, a dividing line, or to flank a path, choose one that which will be most suitable, especially in terms of height. Decide beforehand if the hedge should be flowering or evergreen (and that again will depend upon your garden style). The most attractive thing about a hedge or fence is its continuity and ability to contain. Successful gardens have a long view with small contained areas usually defined by a fence draped with creepers or a well-clipped hedge.

LAWNS

The effect of the lawn should be such that it lets the eye behold a vast expanse of green unbroken by flower beds, unnecessary paths or dotted by too many shrubs (for details on cultivating a lawn *see* 'Bamboos, Grasses and Reeds').

BIRD-BATHS

A fairly large bird-bath on a pedestal is eminently suitable for a formal or semi-formal garden. The material used should ideally be

Bird-bath

marble or stone and the design classic. The bird-bath for a wild or natural garden should not be stylized, though the materials used can be marble or stone. Many people prefer a concrete bird-bath faced with bricks or tiles, made either of ceramic or clay. The best position is usually the centre of a lawn or in a formal flower garden. In the hills, a bird bath can be placed in a formal herb garden.

SUNDIALS

Sundials look divine in a garden with a Mediterranean feel or in a courtyard garden, or an enclosed herb garden. It can resemble a bird-bath, except that on top, instead of a basin, there is a dial and a gnomon. For best results, materials used should be stone or marble. A sundial belongs to another age, and if done right, can bring the past into the present.

FLOWER BEDS AND BORDERS

Flower beds and borders are easier to manage if they are not scattered all over the place. Group them together, unless you are aiming for a wild, informal look (and that takes a lot of doing). The beds can be close to the house or in a contained formal or semi-formal area of the garden. The beds will require an open sunny position, away from shading trees, excepting those flowers that prefer shade or semi-sun. Shade from the house in the late afternoon does no harm.

ARBOURS

One of the most enchanting garden features is an arbour set into a recess among trees, overlooking a large expanse of the garden. Some of the loveliest arbours were designed by the 'Wizard of Durham', Thomas Wright. He was something of a polymath—astronomer, architect and garden

An arbour

designer—and lived in eighteenth century England which had some of the most delightful gardens of the time.

An arbour can be built of wood or cane, or brick if you desire a more permanent building. All surfaces should be covered with creepers. A high pitched roof can be very attractive. An alternative is the traditional Japanese or Chinese roof, especially if the arbour is rectangular. The arbour may be round, hexagonal or octagonal with as many entrances as you please. In India, you can have a thatched roof made of rushes, or clay tiles for a slightly formal look.

ESPALIERS

For those living in the hills, an espalier on the south side can make an interesting garden feature. The tree is grown against a brick wall with horizontal 'shelters' or tiles set into the wall. Trees used for espaliers are usually fruit-bearing and of medium height, such as peach,

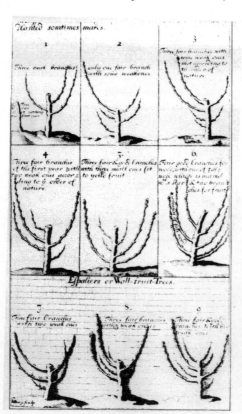

plum, apple and apricot. They are trained on the trellises or framed in such a way as to make hedges. In eighteenth century England, a common sight was fruit trees trained onto kitchen or garden walls. The problem with all espalier work is forcing the branches to spread horizontally. Espalier trees are suitable for walks or avenues but they can also be used as wind-breakers to protect greens and other plants.

Training: Plant a young tree in early spring or at the onset of the monsoon, up against a wall. Cut back the growing shoot to a pair of healthy branches. Strip the leaves, leaving the leaf-buds intact, and spread the branches horizontally. Every year, as new branches appear from the first two or four pairs, they too have to be trained to grow horizontally. The main branches should not exceed

An engraving of a fruit tree growing against a brick wall with horizontal 'shelters' or tiles inset in the wall.

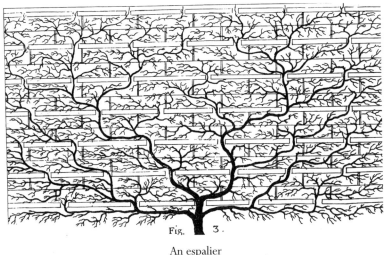

Fig. 3.

An espalier

four pairs. All other branches will grow from these. Cut off all unhealthy branches. The same treatment is used if the tree is to be trained on a frame. Initially, the branches may need to be tied to the frame.

In India, in the plains, custard apple, dwarf sapota, hybrid guavas and hybrid mango trees can also be used.

PERGOLAS

Pergolas are the loveliest way to display profusely flowering creepers such as roses, petrea, convolvulus, bignonia, etc. Pergolas can be made from stone, well-seasoned hardwood, or brick. If you prefer, you can use concrete slabs that imitate stone. But somehow, in a garden, natural materials are more satisfying and aesthetically far superior to concrete.

Pergolas may be single or double. The double pergola should be connected at the top, both across and along the sides to form a walk underneath. If using wood, tar the portions that have to be imbedded into the ground and treat the rest with a preservative. The wood must be well-seasoned, otherwise it will either warp or rot over the years. A single pergola has one line of pillars, each joined to the next by a wooden bar. It can be used to outline a lawn or provide a colourful backdrop. A pergola breaks the flat, tedious planes in a garden by introducing height. In a new garden it adds maturity by taking away the raw appearance before the trees have grown large enough to make their presence felt. A good height for pergolas is 6-8 ft from ground level. A double pergola should be a little higher for the walkway to be comfortable. The thicker the pillars, the higher the pergola. You can reduce the height only if using slender pillars—about half a foot lower. In a small garden, a down-sized pergola, with three to four pillars about 4 ft high, can make a very interesting garden feature, especially if used as a backdrop for a bench or a tiny, sparkling fountain.

If you are going to use heavy creepers, the pillars must be sturdier, having a thickness of 14-16 inches. But if the creepers are light, the pillars can be 12 inches thick or even more slender, especially if the climbers are allowed to ramble along a looping chain or a bar. If using brick, especially in a windy area, the pillars should have an iron core (such as a rod) to give them strength. If the pergola is wooden, the bars on the top must be made of well-seasoned wood, with a thickness of at least 6 inches. As a rule, the connecting bars rest on their narrow sides and those across a double pergola, on their broader sides. With a double pergola, the pillars should be settled in first, before installing the two length-wise bars. The ends of the bars, when left jutting out and cut at a slope or rounded, add a flair to the feature.

Some Creepers for Pergolas and Arches

Jasminum rex—This creeper has milk-white flowers and small, dark green leaves. The flower, though not scented, appear in profusion during the hot months. It is easily propagated by cuttings.

Lonicera odoratissima—(*see* 'The Perfumed Garden')

Creeping Tuberose (Stephanotis floribunda)—(*see* 'The Perfumed Garden')

Thunbergia—*Thunbergia mysorensis* has yellow-red flowers that hang in long, loose sprays. *T. grandiflora* has pale blue flowers, large and wide open. This creeper is more robust. Both are natives of India, where they are often seen running over hedges. There is a white variety which is often seen in the foothills of Sikkim. *T. Fragrans* has creamy-white scented flowers.

Golden Trumpet (Allamanda cathartica 'Hendersonii')—This vigorous climber has bright, orange-yellow flowers which bloom profusely. *A. aublettii* has golden-yellow flowers.

Nepal Trumpet Creeper (Banisteria laurifolia)—This vigorous climber has bright yellow flowers and rigid dark green leaves. It blooms in summer.

Bougainvillea—There are eighteen species of this South American genus and are named after Louis de Bougainville, the first Frenchman to cross the Pacific. They are sturdy, robust and very showy. The colour lies in the brightly-hued bracts; the real flowers are insignificant. Some varieties flower intermittently while others flower almost throughout the year. *B. glabra* has magenta-purple bracts. There are some very splendid crosses that bloom throughout the year.

Such as *B. Spectabilis* (lilac-rose). There are many hybrids available, in almost every colour double and single—orange-pink, pink, pink-white, white, mustard yellow, magenta-white and deep purple.

Rangoon Jasmine (Quisqualis indica)—(*see* 'The Perfumed Garden')

Echites caryophyllata—It is very useful for growing up columns and pergolas. It has clove-scented white flowers which appear from June to September. It is propagated by layers or seeds.

Petrea volubilis—This is among the world's loveliest creepers. Called the Purple Wreath or Queen's Wreath in its native Caribbean islands, it has long sprays of mauve-purple flowers which bloom profusely. The sepals are lighter than the corolla and outlast them. In the northern plains, the flowering period is brief—barely a month and a half. It does best in a mild climate.

Winter-flowering Creepers

Congea tomentosa—It has lovely mauve bracts that look like petals, and puts on a display from December to February. There is a white variety, *C. alba*.

Holmskioldia sanguinea—This is a woody climber and has rust-red small candlestick-like flowers which bloom from October to December. It must be cut back after flowering. Needs a sunny position.

Porana—(*see* 'The Perfumed Garden')

ARCHES

Small pergolas, gazebos or covered arches should be an integral part of gardens in the plains, unless they are minuscule. To sit out in the garden on a hot, blistering day is no joy, but to sit under a heavily canopied pergola or arch is sheer delight even in mid-summer. Rustic wooden arches are ideal for semi-formal or informal gardens. Wrought iron is an alternative. A highly formal garden (always providing it has the space) can accommodate a stone or even a marble arch into the design. The other ornaments such as a bench or pool near a marble or stone arch should counterbalance its 'hardness', and the creepers used should not be too delicate. Large-flowered creepers such as a *Thunbergia* are ideal. An arch plonked in the middle of a lawn, in the centre of a flower bed, or just anywhere, simply looks silly. The arch must have a purpose—it should either span a path, or serve as a gateway in a hedge leading into another section of the garden, stand at the end of a lawn, serve as a covering for a seat, or stand at the head of a flight of stairs. An arch without an agenda is ridiculous to say the least.

Do not use wooden arches if there is a danger of white ants in the area or if the soil is very acidic. In these circumstances, metal is preferable. A curved arch can be made of light iron rods bent to form double posts. The rods should be 4-5 ft apart and the gap filled with a wire netting. The span of the arch will depend upon the width of the steps, path or seat. Very low arches are not attractive and serve no purpose whatsoever. The arch, at its centre, should be at least 8 ft high. Make sure the posts are well embedded in the ground. A packing of brick, rubble, both around and beneath the underground portions helps keep them in place.

GARDEN POOLS

Of all the elements in gardening, the most significant is probably water, especially in a hot country like India. Babur, Akbar, Jehangir and Shah Jahan created immense gardens with water as the central theme. Water adds magic, mystery and romance to any garden, whether it is a tiny pool or a huge artificial lake. Water provides movement in an otherwise static environment.

Comforting that crisp, gentle sound of water, even so comforting to sit on a stone, very still and wait for something to happen.
—John Galsworthy

In India, the main problem with a garden pool is mosquitoes. The menace is very real, which is why many people do not want a pool and it is certainly not prudent to have one if you live in a malarious district. But there's no real risk in other places, provided the pool is not situated close to the living area and it is kept scrupulously clean. Mosquitoes avoid areas where tulsi grows, but you can't have a ring of tulsi around your pool—it's neither aesthetically pleasing nor will tulsi grow too close to water. It does not like sodden soil.

One option is to spray the pool with insecticides during the mosquitoes' larval stage, but by far the best option would be to stock the pool with fish like *Aplochilus* and *Panchax* which eat the larva. There are several indigenous varieties of fish which will serve the purpose. They need minimum care and attention, which is not the case with the imported varieties. Visit your local aquarium and find out what is available.

Barring mosquitoes, a garden pool is a thing of beauty. During the hot summer days, it lends a cool serenity, and at night it can be pure magic especially if you plant the right flowers around it. White arum lilies, scented iris, a small arbour or arch with trailing jasmine and scented water lilies along with clumps of bulrushes can make the pool idyllic.

The ideal form for water in a garden is a small winding stream falling in a series of cascades, forming little pools. A close second is a pond in a natural hollow, but in the dry northern plains you will be lucky if you can have a small tank.

The simplest way to make a pool is to sink a barrel or a moulded plastic tank into the ground. You can also excavate the earth with the soil heaped on the side, and with a little imagination, this can be turned into a delightful garden feature.

Small Pools

These look better on a raised section or a semi-paved area. They can be made by sinking half a barrel or an industrial tank into the ground. You can even make one by sinking a section of a sewer pipe with a concrete floor sealed with bitumen. The pool should be lined with PVC or rubber sheeting which will be able to withstand the pressure of the water. It is easier to move should you need to shift the pool. Miniscule pools can be made by sinking an old basin or plastic tub into the ground. Don't even consider the readymade plastic or fibreglass pools. Their installation is simple but they'll never cease to look artificial. The pool should be positioned in an open space as water plants require a lot of sunshine. If it's under a tree, leaves will fall in, rot and stink, and kill the fish you stock. Always keep the pool clean—you may need to clean it every year.

Plan the pool on a graph paper, and having planned it, peg it out on the chosen site. Decide what you're going to do with the excavated soil. Remove all stones and line the bottom with sand 2 inches deep. Then position the liner so that it overlaps equally all around, and weigh it down with bricks. The liner will be pulled to the centre as you fill it with water. Cut off the excess material, leaving a 10 inch overlap which should be placed flat on the earth and paved over.

Natural Pools

This is an ambitious project which will need far more effort, time and patience. First, you must know what a natural pool looks like in the first place. The hard lines of the tank must be broken and softened, and the plants should be spaced out to create a landscape effect. Plant a couple of creepers on a far bank and encourage some sprays to hang out and reflect in the water. Others should be allowed to ramble at will. A clump of dwarf bamboo, a quick-growing flowering tree and a few flowering shrubs will provide the high points you need. Lilies, ferns, creeping herbaceous plants and rushes will add to the visual impact. Grow the ferns in the shade of overhanging vegetation. To make sure that the water is visible from a distance, the near bank should be gently sloped. Plant with rushes and grass. Zephyr lilies naturalized in the grass will add a lovely touch to the overall effect. You can group a few large boulders in the water to form an island. Plant suitable grasses and small shrubs in the crevices.

Planting in a Pool

The best containers for pool planting are plastic baskets with holes in the sides or plastic-coated wire baskets. Line the basket with old jute sacking and fill with a layer of rich topsoil and compost. Put the plant in and cover with a layer of pebbles to prevent the soil from being washed away. Lower the basket gently into the pool. Plastic containers are far more practical than clay pots as they are easy to remove when you wish to thin or divide the plants. Water lilies, however, are best planted in wide-mouthed clay pots. The compost should be a mixture of four parts garden soil, two parts well-rotted animal manure and a couple of spoonfuls of any phosphate-enriched organic plant feed. Consult your nearest garden centre for the best one. Plug the sides of the pot with a lump of cement, and stand the pot on bricks. The young plant should be at least 3 inches below the surface of the water. When it grows, the leaves will reach the surface. If you see the leaves are growing above the surface, remove the bricks. Later the pots can be broken up and the lilies planted in the bottom, together with the earth around the root ball. The tank or pool should only have a few inches of water when planting. Once you have put in all the plants, fill up slowly.

A paved pool is a visual delight but it will require an expert to construct and it does not come cheap. If you are still determined to have one, make sure the shape is simple and that it has a prominent place in the scheme of things. Gaps in the paving or scattered paving will allow you to grow plants informally around the pool. If it is to look its best, the rim should be at least 2 ft wide; if the garden is small, the rim can be smaller and plants like narcissus, with their heads hanging down, can be planted at the edge with marvellous effect.

Checklist

- Consider the amount of water needed for fish *and* plants when calculating the depth. Remember, the water level will rise during the monsoon, so allow for a margin of 6 inches. Lilies, depending upon the variety, need, 1.5-3 ft of water.
- Fill the pool with water and leave for a couple of weeks. Empty and scrub the tank with clean water and refill. Repeat this process twice before putting in the soil and plants.
- Allow the earth to settle before stocking with fish and plants.
- Grow water plants that clean and aerate the water.
- Don't overstock with fish.
- Keep the pool free of rotting vegetation, dead frogs and the like.

🐟 When draining the pool, leave at least 6 inches of water for the fish. A little bit of old water will do no harm. Put in fresh water immediately, gently and slowly.

🐟 If the pool is small, don't grow too many water lilies.

🐟 Lotuses do well only in fairly large pools or tanks.

Some Plants for Pool Gardens:

Trees—willow, weeping willow, bottlebrush, wattle.

Bulbs—spider lilies, arum lilies, zephyr lilies, amaryllis, iris.

Bamboos and grasses—Pampas grass, fox-tail grass, bulrushes, golden bamboo, dwarf bamboo.

FOUNTAINS

A fountain is an extremely romantic and enchanting garden feature. Even a small one can create a magical effect at any given time, whether in bright sunshine, a misty morning, or in the moonlight. The fountain may be in a small pool, in a Persian courtyard garden or in a Mediterranean patio garden. But it requires engineering expertise to install one—pipes have to be laid and the mechanism installed. However, the effort and expense are well worth it. On a small patio, the site for the fountain should be carefully considered. The cascade should rise no higher than the radius between the fountain and the edge of the basin. If the pump is too powerful, water will shoot over a wide area. Fish will appreciate the extra oxygen the fountain produces, but water lilies and other aquatic plants dislike a heavy, constant spray.

A fountain

Small-space Gardening

This was one of my prayers: for a parcel of land not so very large, which should have a garden and a spring of everflowing water near the house.

—Horace

The saddest thing about our cities today are the gardens which are shrinking at an alarming rate. For most folk the garden is just a strip of a balcony or a tiny terrace. But don't let that bother you. You can do plenty with that little space, whether it's a rooftop, terrace, patio or balcony. With some imagination and ingenuity, you can have an enchanting little garden right out of a fairy tale. If you have some land to work with, so much the better.

The tiniest garden is often the loveliest.
Look at our cottage gardens, if you need to be convinced.
—Vita Sackville-West

Small gardens have some definite advantages over large gardens. The best is that there is scarcely any wretched weeding to do. Also there aren't too many creepy-crawlies, and the ones that are there can be dealt with single-handedly. In extremes of climate, you can grow plants in the balcony which would perish outdoors. But to create a little gem of a garden, you'll have to design, plan and style it just as you would a large one.

The Plus Points of a Small Garden

No digging. No hoeing. No tilling the earth. No soil cultivation. Few pests.

DESIGN

In India, 99 per cent people think garden design is a load of rubbish. Plant some trees, flowers and shrubs, throw in a few garden ornaments, and bingo, you have a garden. But tell them to choose a three-piece suit or a saree with a total disregard for design, and they'll be horrified.

Design is vital to a small garden because your space is limited. The planning and selection of plants have to be almost flawless if the garden is to be successful.

> **3 Rules for Small Spaces:**
> - Optimize use of space.
> - Do not select plants that are too big.
> - Plan for the whole year.

- The garden must be attractive all year round because you can see the whole in one glance. Don't waste space on plants that have a brief season and spend the rest of the time looking drab and shabby. Choose plants which look attractive even after flowering and fruiting. The lush green foliage can be used as a backdrop for other plants.
- A small garden is an extention of the house and should give you extra living space. It can make a very attractive addition if properly designed.
- Keep the design simple and charming; you don't have the space to be grand and it's never good to be pretentious. Don't clutter up the garden with too many ornaments. Always design around one focal point.

POTS IN A SMALL GARDEN

Place the pots in strategic spots: tall plants should be placed at the back, smaller ones in front. To create perspective, place the plants with darker foliage at the back and the lighter greens in front. This is a must for all small gardens.

The pot garden can be made more interesting if you have containers in different sizes and shapes. Exotic-looking plants, unusual in shape or foliage, with a very modern approach to line and form, look better in angular pots. Fussy, pretty ones suit pots with a curvature. Break the levels when placing pots. Don't tuck pots away in a dark corner—they get neglected.

You can do wonders for your small patio or terrace if it can accommodate a tub. You can create a mini-landscape in it, complete with a small tree, rocks, flowers etc. Tubs can be used to grow a mass of annuals or you can use them as the foreground in some part of your garden. Cover the sides with a pretty creeper which has a habit of trailing, or one that can be trained to grow downwards (and nobody will know you have a tub). The tub can also be used to grow herbs and vegetables, some of which can be very attractive.

To get a sense of height you can use pots vertically. Place them at different heights against a wall and the wall will soon be in bloom. Vertical gardening allows you to maximize the number of pots you can accommodate. You can also obtain stature by stacking together three to five terracotta pots in gradually diminishing sizes against a wall or in a corner.

GARDEN IN A YARD OR TERRACE

If you have a small outdoor yard or a fair-sized terrace, you can create a magical effect by using a few tricks. And these simply don't work in a large garden; they'd look plain stupid. You can create space and depth by placing mirrors in strategic places such as under an arch which is against a wall. To complete the effect, have a creeper growing over the arch, and voila! you have a window looking out into another space. You can put a door into a wall or into a hedge, giving an impression of something beyond the door. With a few props—a stone lantern, rocks, the correct plants—you can have a little Japanese garden filled with serenity and tranquillity.

You can have a little Mediterranean garden with a small trellis, a few large urns with tumbling flowers and bits of wrought-iron furniture.

A Persian garden can be made in a courtyard or a walled-in terrace. A few pomegranate trees, a small tinkling fountain or a little pool in the centre, a mandarin orange or two and some bulb plants, and you have an utterly enchanting little garden.

If you have a rectangular bit of land behind the house you can do quite a few things with it; with the right features you can have two or more gardens with different moods in that one space. Pave the bit of land just beyond the door and have a path leading from it to some part of the garden where something is happening—a fountain with a bench, a sundial, a covered arch with a bench etc. Grow a small hedge or make a low fence with a door, about a third of the distance from the paved area, and beyond that create a space with a different ambience. If the door of the house opens onto the narrow side of the plot, you can have a hedge with an interesting aperture to give you three areas to work with. You can divide the sections with a simple pergola or a trellis draped with flowering creepers, if that's where your preference lies. If you like the dramatic, have a really large ornament at the far end of the garden. An arbour or arch over a couple of shallow steps can make a very interesting feature in a rectangular plot.

Fernery

If you have a preference for green coolness rather than flowers, your shady balcony or terrace can be converted into a cool, fresh green haven. Use plenty of ferns, a few dwarf palms and other foliage plants to get the effect you want. Put in a cane chair or two and you could be in a tropical paradise. To complete the picture, throw some birdseed on a ledge and you'll have the birds as well. The long summer days will be more endurable if you have a cool space to escape into.

There are so many plants to choose from that you'll have difficulty making the right choices. If you want a touch of colour, grow a few zephyr lilies or saintpaulias along with your Brussels-lace ferns, philodendrons, monsteras and areca palms. Most modern gardens, small or large, do not include a fernery; lawns are more fashionable now, but a lawn cannot give you that feeling of being in the coolness of a forest that a fernery can. The walls of the balcony can be covered by training creepers up the surface. Corners can be used very effectively for a palm, filling in the rest of the space with gradually smaller foliage plants. Ferneries are especially suited to a small space; you need so few plants to create that feeling of another time and place.

A fernery or green garden is just the thing for people who want a garden but don't wish to devote too much time to it. Ferns, once established, need little care, as do many foliage plants. Potted shrubs and bulbs need far more attention. Once the plants are established, there's not much for the gardener to do. If you are a beginner, don't try growing mountain ferns in the plains; you'll be disappointed. But there are plenty of others to choose from.

SOME POINTERS

- Bare corners in balconies can be instantly softened with a few well-chosen foliage or flowering plants.
- Hanging baskets can be used to break the levels and you can have some even if you live several stories high.
- Tubs and containers can be spectacular when filled with masses of flowers or one to three flowering shrubs strategically placed with the tall ones at the back.
- A garden with one level is flat and uninteresting. Place pots on metal frames, bricks, stones, or anything to break the levels. Breaking the level will also let you have more plants.
- Have window-boxes if you want to optimize on space. The boxes can be attached to a wall, leaving the ground free for other things.
- On a balcony or terrace, use potted creepers to cover a blank wall. As the creepers are potted, there's no fear of them growing rampant. There will be scarcely any need for pruning.
- When selecting plants, select for sun, shade and partial shade. See how much area gets sunlight and how much lies in the shade; design the garden around that. Unfortunately, your plan will be restricted by this.

SOME GARDEN STYLES

The Japanese Tea Garden

Rikyu, the sixteenth century Zen monk and the first master of Chanoyu or the tea ceremony, built a garden in Sakai. The garden lay on a hillside above the dark blue sea. When all was done, he invited his guests. The first thing the astonished guests noted was that the master had almost blocked out the view of the sea with shrubs and trees. But when they stooped to take water from the stone basin, they glimpsed the sparkling sea through

The art of 'leaving something to be discovered' was called the 'artist's flower' and it was a guest's duty to discover this folower. This became a part of the gardener's art and it was achieved by understating rather than emphasizing.

the gaps between the shrubs. They then understood the master's intention—he wanted them to feel the bond between the drops of water in the basin and the infinite ocean. The means used were refined and subtle, and an open vista of the ocean was too obvious. He had followed the cardinal rule—never too much of anything, not even the ocean.

For the Japanese, the highest beauty lies in nature, and this philosophy has permeated into every aspect of their daily lives. Though garden designs were imported from China, they were very quickly Japanized, and by the time Rikyu built his garden, little of the Chinese influence remained. The tea garden, a haven of peace and serenity, is a concept all their own.

The tea ceremony was imported from China sometime during the twelfth or thirteenth century and was a pastime of the nobility, held in palaces and palace gardens. The nobles were given ten types of tea to taste and had to name the tea and the place where it grew. In time, the tea ceremony became popular with all classes, but it was Zen Buddhism which forever changed the nature of the ceremony—from one of pomp and opulence to one of refinement and austerity. Chanoyu became the means by which inner harmony was restored. The soul's equilibrium, disrupted by the problems of daily life, could be restored by spending time in an atmosphere of calm and beauty, simplicity and serenity.

The masters drew their inspiration from the simple cottages of peasants and fishermen, and the gardens were built to bring home the sense of *wabi*, one of the chief principles of Japanese art. *Wabi* can be best explained as a sense of moderation, simplicity and the sadness that arises from the inexorable pattern of life.

One does not have to be a philosopher or a monk to enjoy the calm beauty of a tea garden. For one, it is designed for a small space, and the style is practical though the purpose is philosophical, but the philosophy need not concern you. The small size allows the designer to concentrate on every aspect, right down to the smallest detail; and the result is very satisfying. In today's polluted, stress-filled, tense world, the secluded calm of these gardens is needed more than it ever was in sixteenth-century Japan. A half hour spent in such environs is far better than an hour on the shrink's couch—and cheaper!

The garden ought to suggest a forest retreat deep in the mountains. For this you need some evergreens and there are plenty to chose from—juniper, thuja etc.—which can withstand some heat. Then you will require a lantern, water basin and an informal path, all preferably of stone. Make sure the stones have a weather-beaten look to capture a sense of time.

Subtlety is the hallmark of a Japanese tea garden. The gardener should conceal his art rather than make an exhibition of it. Nothing is blatant—the play of light and shade, the lantern, the position of the rocks and shrubs, the basin or the wickergate. Avoid the ostentatious or flamboyant.

The central feature is the stone path. Only a lover of the arts will be able to appreciate the careful deliberation in the selection and placement of the stones. The shape and the distance between the stones determines the pace and rhythm of the visitor's progress. Traditionally, the path wound gently like a mountain path but there were some masters who preferred straight clean lines. One was Kabari, the seventeenth-century master. 'The path', he said, 'should be six parts useful and four parts beautiful.' Another master, Oribe, inverted the ratio. You are the best judge in deciding which ratio will apply to your path.

The tea garden is very careful of the guests'needs. *Tobiishi*, literally 'flying stones', were added to the beaten path to ensure the comfort of the guests. The stones, set raised above ground level, ensure the visitor's feet don't get wet from dew or raindrops. The distance between the stones is decided by the average length of a man's step. The visitor should not have to trot or leap from stone to stone. The aim is a sedate walk which will give him time to view and appreciate his surroundings, and take him to the tea house.

Tobiishi (The Stones): The size of stones must be proportionate to the width of the path and its length. You can't have huge stones on a small path. You may as well pave it and adopt some other style. The stones should be at least a foot in diameter and, though irregular, there should be some uniformity in shape. There should be no hollows or crevices which could cause the visitor to trip or stumble. For those who prefer geometric forms, the stones can be rectangular or square.

The tea garden, though small, usually comprises two sections. There is an outer garden which leads into the inner one, divided by a rustic gate. The gate can be made of bamboo,

A baron once asked Sen no Rikyu to lay the stones of the path. Rikyu was a long time in thinking and placing down the stones. The baron thought that an affectation. After the master left, he moved one stone, just a fraction of an inch, certain it would go undetected. But the next day when the master arrived, he took one glance at the path and moved the stone back to its former position, much to the embarrassment of the baron.

rough beams or rushes. The *tobiishi* form a part of the outer garden. In the inner garden, there should be a water basin with a long-handled water scoop.

The Basin: Tomes have been written about the shape of the basin and its placing. The basin, like the tea bowl, is an object of beauty as well as utility. Its main function is to make the guest comfortable when washing his hands. It must not be placed too high so as to make the visitor stretch, or too low so that he has to stoop. The visitor should be able to take water without any discomfort.

The basin varies in size, depending upon the owner's taste, but there are some definite rules. It must be harmonious with the rest of the garden and it must be unobtrusive. The weather-worn stone must evoke a sense of time long gone.

The water for the basin is usually carried by a bamboo pipe, but if you use a metal one, disguise it. The pipe must be kept scrupulously clean on the inside. The basin may be small or large, but not too much of either. It can be square, oval or round. The ideal basin is a weathered stone hollowed by water. Most masters preferred weathered stone but there were some who used dressed stone. The most famous of these is the Enshu basin which is hard and square and uncompromising.

Some masters think the basin should be placed low, among grasses and ferns so that the visitor, when he kneels, will smell the fresh scents of earth and grass.

The stones that lie under and beside the basin have definite uses. The one under is large enough to accommodate the basin with enough space left over for a lantern or candle on a dark evening. The other is used to place a vessel containing warm water for the visitor's hands on a chilly evening.

The basin must always be kept clean and covered when not in use.

The Stone Lantern: This feature, imported from China in the sixteenth century, is placed not too far from the basin. Initially, lanterns were used to light the garden for the night-time tea ceremonies which usually lasted until dawn. Later, under Zen influence, they were used to guide the visitor through a dark garden into the lit tea house, symbolizing the light of knowledge which dispels the darkness of ignorance. But symbolic or not, the lanterns were there for a practical purpose—to light the path. Old texts state that the light should not be too dim or too bright. There should be enough light on a dark night to prevent the guest from stumbling but never so bright as to weaken and dim the moonlight. On full-moon nights, unless absolutely vital, it should not be used at all. The light is not there to dispel the darkness; rather, it is meant to enhance its charms.

The lanterns have either three or five parts. The three parts symbolize heaven, earth and

belia

e flower'

Alyssum

Daisy

man, and the five parts the elements—earth, air, fire, water and the quintessence. They come in many shapes and sizes; you can decide what is best for your garden. In Japan, lantern-making is still a living art and stone lanterns can be seen in most gardens, big or small.

Moss: This is another essential feature of the tea garden, taking us immediately into a distant mountain forest. Most gardens in the plains cannot have moss, but short, thick turf, unevenly laid, will give you the desired effect.

Other essentials are a small tree with thick branches hanging down, a low winding hedge and a few evergreens. Only one or two small flowering trees are permitted. Traditionally it is the plum, but that's impossible to grow in the plains. Peach trees are hardier and can be grown in the plains, but only with difficulty. A good substitute is the Indian Coral (Parijata) or golden laburnum. The tree should stand discretely by the gate or near the entrance of the house.

As with everything else, colour too must be subdued. There should be no glitter or flamboyance; nothing should dispel the harmony and calm of the atmosphere. Few flowers are used, mainly to offset the greens. But as a result of this restraint, the beauty of a single flower becomes dazzling, something that cannot happen in a flower bed.

You don't have to be a Zen monk or own a tea house to have a tea house garden; you can create one on a rooftop or in a small yard. For most of us in the plains, azaleas, cedars, camellias and pines will have to be substituted by other evergreens and flowering shrubs with a neat habit. This style is particularly suitable for small gardens which can incorporate only one or two garden features. It's also ideal for those who don't want to be burdened with the problems of a flower garden. The style being austere and spare, the owner has little to do once the garden is established.

> *Hideyoshi, the great military ruler of sixteenth-century Japan, wanted to see a convolvulus growing in Rikyu's garden. The master had grown it from an imported seed. The general was invited to morning tea, when the flowers unfurl and crowd the stem. When the general entered, he saw the vine without a blossom or bud. But when he stepped into the dark tea house, he was dazzled by a brilliant whiteness. In a bronze vessel stood a single morning glory still glistening with dew.*

> *Heath grass—*
> *sandals*
> *still fragrant.*
> —Shiki

Cleanliness is a vital part of the tea garden, but that does not imply doing away with nature's delicate touches. Nothing in excess, is the creed, not even hygiene. Moreover, fallen leaves and blossoms add to the beauty, not mar it. Rikyu once asked his son to sweep the garden. When the boy was done, he went to inspect it and professed dissatisfaction. So his son was set to work again but the master was still not pleased. 'What must I do?' the boy asked. 'I've swept the path, raked the leaves, the moss is bright; there's not a speck of dirt anywhere.'

'You still don't understand, my son,' the master said. Silently he went over to a maple tree and shook it. There was a flutter of crimson and gold as leaves drifted down and lay on the grass beneath.

The Persian Garden

If you have a small walled-in yard, a large balcony terrace, or a courtyard inside the house, and are willing to spend some time and money, you can have an exquisite little Persian garden complete with fountain and a pomegranate tree. The only thing it will lack will be a nightingale, but in the northern plains, bulbuls will sing for you just as sweetly. This style is highly possible in the north which has cold winters and a brief but definite spring.

The Persian garden is much older than the Persian empire formed by Cyrus the Great, but it was after he built his gardens that it developed into a highly sophisticated garden design. The Persian plateau is a harsh land with bitter winds and burning summers, and the gardens were designed to shut out the terrain rather than merge with it. These gardens were places of fantasy and enchantment, of sparkling waters, scented flowers and fragrant fruit.

Cyrus the Great built a fabulous garden in 546 BC and called it the *pairidaeza*—a combination of *pairi* (around) and *daeza* (wall). The design of Persian gardens has altered very little since his time. The design was geometric and formal, spaces were cleanly defined and their uses were definite. Flowers, trees and shrubs were planted in an orderly fashion in symmetrical areas. Water, one of the highlights of the garden, was generally brought in. The waterways were arrow-straight and the pools into which the water fell were either square or octagonal. These essential design elements are seen in all Persian gardens, including the great Mughal gardens of India.

Persian garden design was adapted from the ancient gardens of Mesopotamia. There too, water was the main feature of the garden; the larger the garden, the more elaborate the

Morning glory,
so pure
the drew's unseen.
—Kakei

Cherries, cuckoo
Moon, snow-soon
The year's vanished.
—Sampu

Down fall the tears from skies
enwrapt in gloom,
Without this drink the flowers
could never bloom!
As now these flowerlets yield
delight to me,
So shall my dust yield flowers—
God knows for whom.
—Rubaiyat of Omar Khayyam

The Persian garden, a prayer rug,
A fountain filled with burning wine.
Green sky, gold earth and coral
branch,
Its birds in reminiscence lost.
Within this fading shadowy world
The joy of memory's uppermost.
—Nermin Menemencioglu

waterways and pools. Water was not used simply for effect—it was necessary to cool the arid, hot surroundings.

Persian gardens were designed as much for viewing as for walking in. Permament garden pavilions were constructed in various styles, from the simplest, a roof on columns, to the elaborate, a small palace with inner rooms. The pavilions were open on three sides to allow proper air circulation. The larger buildings were two storied, with balconies and airy inner rooms which had sweeping views of the garden.

The Persians favoured flowers that were either brilliantly coloured or perfumed, and trees with blossoms and fruit. They grew pomegranates, peaches, apricots, roses, violets, peonies, narcissus, hyacinth, irises, hollyhocks, lilies and willows. Chinars and poplars were grown to provide shade. And all this among waterways with lilies in pools and the sparkle and tinkle of fountains. It is small wonder that the word 'paradise' comes from the Persian word for garden.

Unlike the Chinese and Japanese, the Persians needed to employ artifice to create the garden of their dreams—lushness amidst aridity, the coolness of water to dispel the heat. They did not imitate nature; they created dreams, for all desert people dream of cool greens, the scent of a myriad blooms and crystalline waters, a reaction in direct proportion to their harsh environs. There's a miniature dating from Timur's reign, of an exquisite Persian garden. It shows a little palace set in a walled garden; the stream outside the wall has been diverted to flow in. The banks are lined with willows with violets growing under them; water lilies crowd the pools and there are day lilies growing in beds. Calvijo, the Spanish envoy of Henry III of Castile, who went to Persia in 1404, describes such a garden in his book, *Embassy is Tamerlane*.

The Persian garden, whether on a grand scale or a simple courtyard garden, most often consists of a central pool, four channels which enclose flower beds, trees and shrubs, paths along the waterways and enclosures. This is known as the *chaarbagh* (four gardens), and these fundamentals are seen in all Persian-style gardens, whether in India, Iran, Afghanistan or Iraq. In the Indian gardens, after Babur's reign, even more emphasis was laid on water to beat the summer in the plains, with pools, series of glittering fountains and long water courses. These gardens plunged even deeper into the realms of magic and fantasy and further away from the surrounding world. Persian poetry is replete with garden imagery, but it was not only the poets who were enchanted. Timurlang, known more for his savagery than for his artistic abilities, created some of the most beautiful gardens of his times. Babur visited them as a young man and was so struck by their beauty, they marked him for all time. All his years in India, he longed for the gardens of Kabul and Herat. There are several descriptions of gardens in his autobiography. 'In 914 AH (1508-9 AD), I laid out the four gardens known as the *Bagh-i-Wafa* (Garden of Fidelity), on a rising ground facing south . . . there, oranges, citron and pomegranates grow in abundance.' The remains of Timur's gardens could still be seen in Kabul until the Soviet invasion of Afghanistan, in 1979. What little remained of the great gardens of Afghanistan was successfully obliterated by the civil war and the American bombs.

If you have a small garden or courtyard and no shortage of water, you can have a miniature Persian garden all your own. You don't have to emulate the strict geometric design if you dislike symmetry. A central fountain surrounded by small plots of flowers, some low flowering shrubs, a small fruiting tree with tidy habits like the Mandarin orange which also has scented flowers, and you have a Persian-style garden. The garden, if square or rectangular, can be divided into two rather than four parts since there isn't enough space. If you have the space, create a *chaarbagh*. The pool need be no bigger than the size of a large basin, which should be at least 1.5 ft deep so that you can grow some water lilies. A scented rose, flowering bush or creeper, will add the final touch. Grow a few evergreens to provide a backdrop for the flowering shrubs. The choice of plants and how many you use will give you the ambience you want—light, airy or a secluded retreat.

- The Persian style is formal. You can get semi-formal but never casual—the central pool and straight lines demand formality. Don't allow the design to get fussy.
- Take advantage of the flowering shrubs, annuals and trees to invite birds and butterflies into the garden. If the space you have gets bright sunshine for most part of the year, with a bit of forethought, you can have flowers all the time.
- One of the best things about Persian-style gardens is that they reduce smog, pollution and the strident sound of horns as they are usually enclosed. An open balcony can be enclosed and a small Persian garden can be very successfully made even in that limited space.
- Many of the plants traditionally grown in Persian gardens will not grow in the plains of India, though they do well in the hills. But roses, which are the delight of every Persian gardener, do grow well even in the plains. So will lemons and some varieties of oranges. Bulb plants can all be grown during the right season, which in the plains is the cool months between October and March. Instead of peach or apricot, you can have a small custard apple or a guava tree. Sweet-scented jasmines can replace the briar roses; jasmines are quite at home in a Persian garden.

You have plenty of plants to choose from, so be judicious, especially if space is limited. A Persian garden is neat; never clutter it up.

English Cottage Gardens

If you have a small plot of land and want a garden that is useful as well as pretty, style it like the old English cottage garden where vegetables and flowers grow together in happy confusion. Cottage gardens date from the Middle Ages when housewives started growing flowers for their beauty rather than their usefulness. Earlier, except in the castles and manors, flowers were grown in the gardens solely for their utility value,

Sir Thomas Herbert, the English traveller, went to Iran in 1627 and described the gardens in his book Travels in Persia. *'The gardens are many and both large and beautiful. Most are enclosed in walls fourteen feet high. They are spacious with plenty of trees, abound in cypresses, chenars, elm, ash, pine and oak' and 'flowers rare to the eye, sweet to the smell and useful in physic.'*

On one side is a gloomy garden . . . Oh, so different from the long irregular slips of the cottage gardens, with their gay bunches of polyantheses and crocuses, their wallflowers sending sweet odours, through the narrow casement . . .
—Mary Russel Mitford

used either as food, in medicine, or to provide bees with pollen and nectar for honey. Pot marigold (calendula) got its name because it was grown in pots, and the petals were used in stews and salads.

The earliest garden flowers were probably brought in from

English cottage garden

the wild—violets, dog roses, primroses and honeysuckle. Later, flowers from the castles and manors drifted down to the cottages, some very exotic. By the sixteenth century, jasmines from Persia and tulips from Turkey were already being grown in England, and by the seventeenth century, cottagers were growing flowers for themselves. Manor gardens changed with the fashion, and many old-world flowers disappeared from those august surroundings and were seen only in the cottage gardens in the country, until they became fashionable once again.

Today's small plots can happily accommodate the informality of a cottage garden—flowers brushing shoulders with vegetables, herbs edging flower beds, all thickly clustered together. You can get as haphazard as you like without worrying if the final outcome will be an eyesore.

Everything that likes the sun—fruit or vegetable or flower—should be grown in the sunny area and all the shade-loving plants in the shade. To complete the effect, grow some flowers whose names you don't know; it will be quite in keeping with the tradition.

Little strips in front of roadside cottages have a simple and tender charm that one may look for in vain in gardens of greater pretension. And the old garden flowers seem to know that there they are seen at their best.
—Gertrude Jekyll

Make Your Own Cottage Garden

- ❧ Grow the old-fashioned varieties of flowers—they are usually scented unlike their hybrid counterparts.
- ❧ Fill the window overlooking the garden with window boxes. That will bring the garden into the room. Plant sweetly-scented flowers or herbs or a mixture of the two. There is nothing like scent brought in by the breeze.
- ❧ Let roses clamber onto your walls. Jasmine and other scented flowers like the Rangoon creeper grow well in the plains.

Today I think
Only with scents—scents dead
leaves yield,
And bracken and wild carrot's seed,
And the square mustard field . . .
—Edward Thomas

- ❧ Grow evergreens behind the flower beds to bring the flowers into relief.
- ❧ Use a corner to grow a clump of tall, flowering plants.
- ❧ Grow things wherever it is convenient for you and suitable for them. You'll see an order in the chaos; let the flowers grow in charming disarray.
- ❧ If you have a tiny kitchen garden, fringe the beds with flowers. In the summer, you can grow portulacas and other summer flowers.
- ❧ Collect wild flowers that grow in the region and add them to your garden. You'll be surprised how pretty some are.

Annuals

He who holds that nothingness
Is formless, flowers are visions
Let him enter boldly.

—Gido

This inscription above the great Zen master's door is echoed by many a poet and seer. Few people are untouched by the beauty of a flower; they are nature's loveliest handiwork and people have risked limb and life to bring them closer to home, into the garden. And of all the flowers in the garden, the annuals are prized and precious, because in their brief span, their excessive beauty brings so much delight.

One thing is certain, and the rest is lies, the flower that once hath blown, foreever dies.
—Rubaiyat of Omar Khayyam

Gardeners are justifiably proud of their annual flowers. Seeds may be eaten up or may not germinate at all. Then the seedlings have a host of enemies—crickets, beetles, snails etc.—from whom they must be protected. The gardener also has to spend many weeks shielding them from the vagaries of the weather. To crown it all, seedlings have different temperaments, and the gardener has to meet their various needs until the flowers unfurl. But no gardener thinks his annuals a waste of time because their lives are so short; in fact, it is this very brevity that makes them so precious. They do not bloom year after year; they have to be grown each time from seed, but those fleeting paradisal months are well worth the labour and the time.

In the hills, annuals flower in summer; in the northern plains, they are grown in the cool season.

For those of us who live in the plains, a garden such as the one described by Batsford and Fry will remain a dream, but for those fortunate enough to live in cooler climes, this garden can be a reality. However, the plains-dwellers need not despair; most annuals will grow and flower during the cool months, from January to March. And though the annual garden has such a short life, it is worth every bit of effort you put in.

Small urban gardens are especially suited to the informality of an annual garden. The charm of old-fashioned flowers, most of which are scented, can be best appreciated in a small garden since the blooms are not oversized. Moreover, a small garden contains the scents.

Most annual flowers are not native to India; for that we have to thank the Mughals, the British, the French and the Dutch who, missing the sights and smells of home, brought these temperate flowers into their tropical gardens. But the Himalayas, from Kashmir to the north-east states, are home to violets, primulas, pinks, irises, lupins, poppies and other annuals, but the gardeners of India never brought them into the plains simply because the plains had so many tropical flowers anyway.

In the plains, a truly herbaceous annual flower garden is possible only if some perennials are treated as annuals. Verbena, carnations, impatiens and others which are perennial in the hills are grown as annuals in the plains. But that can't be helped; one must make the best of the situation.

To achieve a colourful display you need a certain amount of gardening skill and a healthy knowledge of plants and their habits. The plants should come into bloom all together, and that takes some doing. Some bloom in eight weeks, some in twelve, and others in sixteen weeks. Plant at the proper time and you will have a spectacular display. Except in a large, formal garden, annuals are not meant to be grown in regimental order; square, round or rectangular patches of one variety look simply awful. *Mixed planting and irregular lines*

are the best for annuals. Annuals have a free spirit and wild beauty that is killed by straight lines. Arrange small groups so that they merge together, blurring the lines. Do not plant seedlings in regular lines. Keep the tall, straight flowers at the back but grow a few forward to break the monotony. The same should be done with flowers of medium height. The low ones should be allowed to spread and fall spontaneously onto the ground.

A wild, mixed border of flowers looks best against a wall or a dark hedge. Don't grow the flowers too close to the hedge. Leave some space or else there will be severe competition between their roots, and the better-established hedge will steal the nutrients that are meant for the annuals.

All annuals need lots of *sunshine,* so don't attempt to grow annual flowers if your garden lies in the *shade.* Only a few like salvia and cineraria thrive in the shade.

Many annuals are scented so plant for scent as well as form and colour.

In a garden, *contrast* is essential but *harmony* is vital. Few flowers clash out-of-doors, but brilliant colours, if wrongly placed, are apt to kill the more tender shades near them. Mix the pastels and progress to the more brilliant colours, climaxing with the strong, rich hues. Yellow, white and cream are very kind to the pinks and blues. There are many flowers that come in several colours and shades and these are ideal for mass planting in beds. Phlox, snapdragons, cineraria and lineria are some. Some find a mass of blue and mauve-blue flowers dull, but they, I'm sure, have not seen a sea of swan river daisies. And when other flowers in your garden turn to gray as darkness falls, your blue flowers will still glow. The blues are the last to turn grey so it will be wise to grow them near the living area or sitting area.

Avoid complicated designs for the beds unless you have a team of *maalis* who are experienced and skilful, and a huge garden. Keep the outlines simple, which does not mean straight. Intricate designs are not at all restful to the eye or soothing to the spirit.

Beds should not be too small as they could end up looking straggly and messy.

Soil in beds should be well prepared. It should be dug 18 inches deep and a layer of well-rotted manure should be dug in. Break up all clots of earth before adding manure. Water lightly for three to four weeks and remove all weeds as they emerge. Plant seedlings after you have weeded the beds. Every third year a sprinkling of lime should be forked into the soil, a month before you add compost. Never add the lime and manure together. When it's time to plant, dig the beds up again and crumble the topsoil finely.

Many annuals will grow quite happily in *pots*. You can have an annual garden even if all you have is a pot-garden, as long as the area lies in the sun.

SOME ANNUALS

Sweet Alison (*Lobularia, Sweet Alyssum*)

This is a tidy plant which grows 6-12 inches high and is tailor-made for edging. The masses of tiny flowers are usually white, but there is a mauve/lilac variety available. The flowers, as their name suggests, are sweetly scented. The dwarf varieties are only 5-6 inches high. A hardy annual, it can be grown quite easily in pots. Keep pinching back if you want to make it bushy. This is a generous, good-natured plant, the earliest to bloom, and it will still have flowers when most of the others have withered. Annual flowers attract bees and there is a constant hum in the garden when the sun is shining.

Snapdragons (*Antirrhinum*)

Snapdragons come in many colours and shades—orange, yellow, pink, red and white, and all their shades. Pinch back to get a bushy plant.

Swan River Daisy (*Brahycome*)

A very pretty plant with single, daisy-like flowers which are bluish mauve. Other varieties are pink and white. It can grow 12-14 inches high. Pinch back to make the plants bushy.

Candytuft (*Iberis*)

These may be annuals or perennials, but in India, the annuals are favoured by gardeners. The flowers may be white, pink or mauve and the flower heads are flattish. Don't let the plant grow more than 12 inches high. Pinch back.

Cornflower (*Centaurea cyanus*)

These tall annuals are natives of the British Isles. The flowers are usually an intense blue, but there are pink, white and wine-coloured varieties as well. They can grow up to 4 ft in height. Pinch back to make the plant shrubbier.

Sweet-Sultanas (*Centaurea*)

These sweetly scented flowers are natives of Persia. The flowers may be yellow, white, pink or mauve. They grow to a height of 20-24 inches.

Clarkia Elegans

This is a tall annual, and the flowers come in long sprays. They can be white, crimson, scarlet-salmon and shades of pink. The plants can be up to 3 ft tall and need to be staked. The soil should be well drained, light and friable.

Carnations and Pinks (*Dianthus*)

There are about 300 species of dianthus and all are natives of the limestone regions of southern Europe. Sweet williams, border carnations, modern carnations and the single-petalled pinks all owe their existence to the parent of modern carnations, *D. Caryophyllus*, which was taken to England probably after the Norman conquest. These clove-scented carnations were widely grown for their heady perfume. The people of Tudor England used them to spice their wine and called them 'sops-in-wine'. All the old cultivars are perfumed unlike the modern hybrids which are almost perfect in form and colour but have no scent. The old cultivars are usually a deep blood red, crimson, red with white edges or white streaked with crimson. The ones with the strongest scent are the deep crimson and cherry-red varieties.

Clarkia unguiculata 'Elegans'

Theophrastus gave these flowers the name—dias meaning Zeus and anthus meaning flower—literally 'flower of the gods'.

Carnations are usually grown in pots, the pinks are used in borders. Carnations are treated as annuals in the plains but can be perennials with some care. Shade the plants in summer and keep them out of the rain during the monsoon months. They cannot abide excessive dampness. Carnations can be grown from seed but are best propagated by layering or making cuttings of the basal shoots. Cuttings can also be made from the top leaf shoots. The cuttings should be 6 inches long and planted in light compost.

Dianthus

Sunflower (*Helianthus*)

Sunflowers come from the Americas. The annual, *H. Annuus*, is a native of South America. In Peru it was the symbol of the sun god of the Incas. The gardeners of the time vied with each

Helianthus
'Monarch'

other to produce enormous blooms, some with heads as large as dinner plates.

There are many species of sunflowers; some are annuals, others perennials. The colours range from deep gold to light yellow. Heleniums, which belong to the same family *Compositae*, are perennials which carry a number of daisy-like flowers. The tall varieties of sunflowers may grow up to a height of 8 ft, but that is nowhere near the height of sunflowers grown by Crispin de Pass in the Royal garden in Madrid—'. . . they grew to a height of 24 ft; but in Padua in Italy, it is written they attained to the height of 40 ft.'

The sunflower blushed to own the nameless flower as her kin.
The sun rose and smiled on it saying, 'Are you well my darling'.
—R. Tagore

The seeds or plant seedlings should be sown at least 2 ft apart if the variety is large, 12 inches apart if smaller. They can be very effective when grown in informal groups or at the back of a wide, mixed border. Though grown as winter annuals in the northern plains, they can also be grown in the hot months and during the rains. There are many dwarf varieties available.

Sweet Peas (*Lathyrus odoratus*)

This is the old-fashioned sweet pea and most gardeners' first choice for an annual garden, particularly if the garden is small and they cannot accommodate a large variety of flowers. Sweet peas are easy to grow, come in a wide range of colours and have a delicious fragrance

Here are sweet peas on tip toe for a flight,
With wings of gentle flush o'er delicate white,
And taper fingers catching at all things
To bind them all about with tiny rings.
—John Keats

with which they are very generous. They can be trained on to frames or allowed to clamber over a shrub that has shed its leaves or even on to an evergreen one. The maroons and purples have the heaviest perfume but all the old-fashioned varieties—blush pink, mauve and white—have a honey-like fragrance. The frilled varieties, developed in the twentieth century, are very pretty, but not all are fragrant. It would be a shame to plant sweet peas that are scentless, but don't let that dissuade you from planting those varieties. Sweet peas like well-drained, rich soil and a position in the sun.

Wallflowers (*Cheiranthus cheiri*)

Indigenous species of wallflowers are found from the Canary
Islands to the Himalayas. Stocks (*Matthiola*), which belong
to the same family (*Cruciferae*), are from southern Europe.
In England, the summer stocks are called the ten week
flower, because more often than not, the plants flower
ten to twelve weeks after the seeds are planted. The old
wallflowers were a deep yellow, but today there are many garden
varieties which come in shades of yellow, purple, pink, bronze
and white. The winter stocks are the biennials which are sown
in one year and flower in the next.

Stocks have a sturdy habit and are delightfully fragrant. A
double white variety smells like cinnamon-honey.

Cheiranthus cheiri

*Up she got upon a wall
'Tempting down to slide with all
But the silken twist untied
So she fell and bruised and died.*

*Love, in pity of the dead,
And her loving luckless speed
Turned her to this plant we call
Now the flower of the wall.*
—Robert Herrick

For growing wallflowers, the soil should be well
cultivated but not too rich. If you don't want to begin from
seed, plant seedlings which are available in many nurseries.
Double flowers, if grown from the seed of the previous year,
often revert to single flowers.

'Ice flower' (*Drosanthemums*)

'Ice flower' is the name Indian gardens have given these flowers.
They are better known as 'dew flowers' because of the dewy
dots on the leaves which look like tiny sugar crystals. These
low-spreading plants form a dense mat, the leaves are succulent
and the stems tender. The flowers come in phosphorent pinks,
oranges, cream, apricot, white and salmon pink. The plants
thrive in hot, dry regions as they have adapted to growing in extremely dry conditions. These
sun-loving plants will not grow in the shade; the flowers close as soon as the sun moves away
from them. They are grown easily from seed but nowadays, seedlings are available. When
planting seedlings, plant with care as they bruise easily. When grown on a bank, they are truly
a wonderful sight.

Lampranthus are perennials which belong to the same family (*Aizoaceae*). They may be
low-growing spreaders or small, round bushes, 18 inches tall and upto a feet across. There are
many species and most are ideal for rockeries and can be used to drape a wall.

My candied sensations are all glossy, spruce, voluptuous, and fine: they wear a candied coat and are in holiday trim. I seed the bed of larkspurs with purple eyes, tall holly-oaks, red and yellow; the broad sunflowers caked in gold, with bees buzzing around them; wildernesses of pinks, and hot glowing pionies; poppies run to seed; the sugared lily, and faint mignonette, all ranged in order, and as thick as they can grow.
—William Hazlitt

The plants will thrive in sandy, well-drained soil that is not too rich in organic compost. But they are not fussy; any soil will do as long as it is not water-logged or clayey.

Larkspur *(Delphinium)*

These annuals are ideally suited for massing against walls or in informal beds. The perennial varieties do well only in the hills. The annuals grow well in the cool months, in the plains. Larkspurs may be single or double; the long spikes are densely covered with flowers—deep purple, blue-purple, mauve, pink and white. The plant grows 2-4 ft in height.

Hollyhocks *(Alcea [Althaea] Rosea)*

Hollyhocks are very old garden flowers and have been cultivated for hundreds of years. At first, it was thought that the flower originated in China but now the opinion is that their home lies somewhere in eastern Europe.

Hollyhocks can thrive in soil that is neither rich nor very fertile. They are very useful in mixed borders of tall flowers and also as groups in key positions. The large flowers are borne on long stems, some of which can be upto 7 ft tall. They come in every conceivable colour except blue—white, cream, yellows, shades of pink, reds and purples, to one that is almost black. Though perennials, they are treated as annuals or biennials by gardeners. Single and double varieties are available.

Poppy *(Papaveraceae)*

Most poppies are natives of Asia, North Africa and Europe. There are 200 species in this family and many were known to man from ancient times with many species still found in the wild. The opium poppy was cultivated by the ancient Egyptians as is evident from murals and records of the time and has been cultivated for so long in the civilized world that its origins are unknown.

Though Philistines may jostle, you will need rank as an apostle in the highest aesthetic band,
If you walk down Piccadilly with a poppy or a lily in your medieval hand.
—W.S. Gilbert

In India, the most popular poppy is the Oriental poppy (*P. orientale*) which has large red flowers with black blotches at the base of the petals. But the common corn poppy (*P. rhoeas*) and shirley poppies are lovelier and even more fragile in appearance. Corn poppies are a pure, clear red. Shirley poppies, which were developed as late as in 1880, always have a white base with yellow or white stamens. There is not the smallest particle of black, and the flowers are single. All poppies have delicate, short-lived flowers, so fragile that if you 'seize the flower, its bloom is shed'.

Poppies are easily grown from seed. Oriental poppies need deep, well-drained soil and a position in the sun. Corn poppies can grow in dry, moderately fertile soil.

The exquisitely beautiful Himalayan blue poppy (*Meconopsis betonicifolia*) belongs to the same family. An Englishman, Frank Kingdom Ward, when travelling in the Himalayas in 1924, describes his find thus: 'Suddenly I looked up and there like a blue panel dropped from Heaven a clump of blue Poppies—as dazzling as sapphires—gleamed in the pale light.' Later he returned, collected the seeds and sent them to London where they were planted in Hyde Park. Unfortunately, in the tropics, only those people living above 6000 ft can grow this lovely flower.

California poppies (*Eschscholzia*), also belong to the same family as other poppies. The four orange-gold petals are satiny and form a shallow cup. These will grow in most garden soils and flower over a long period. They like the full sun. The finely-cut foliage is green-grey and the flowers are borne on tall stalks.

In the hills, poppies are summer flowers; in the plains they are grown as winter annuals. Poppies should not be watered heavily—they detest damp conditions. Poppies generally do not take well to transplanting, though if you are careful and plant the seedlings on a cool day, preferably in the evening, most will survive. Oriental poppies are tall, shirley poppies and corn poppies are medium-sized, whereas California poppies don't grow above 1.5 ft high. Hybrid California poppies come in many colours—creamy white, red and a deep but clear wine-red.

Marigold (*Calendula*)

Known more simply as golds, these flowers (not to be mixed with the African and French marigolds, both of which incidentally come from Mexico), are natives of Southern Europe and have been grown by Europeans for a very long time. They were mainly grown for their medicinal value and their use as a pot herb, which is why they were called pot marigolds. Medieval housewives used their petals as a cheap substitute for saffron. The petals were also used to flavour cheese, stews and broths. Fresh petals can also be eaten in salads and used to make marigold pudding.

This hardy annual can be used effectively in beds or grown in pots. Most varieties are a bright gold in colour, but modern cultivars come in shades of orange and orange-bronze. The plant grows 15-18 inches high. In beds, the seedlings should be planted 8-10 inches apart.

William Turner, father of English Botany, used the flowers to make a dye which turned hair yellow.

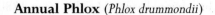

Annual Phlox (*Phlox drummondii*)

These are very important garden plants. They can be used in borders, as edging, grown in pots or in the rockery. The flowers grow in crowded cymes. The individual blooms all have five petals, five sepals and five stamens. Almost all the species are natives of North America but the splendid cultivars are largely the work of British and European hybridists. Phlox come in a wide range of colours—white, cream, crimson, peach, flame, mauve, purple and pink. The plants grow upto 14 inches high but there are dwarf varieties which are only 8 inches high. There is a creeping variety, Moss Phlox (*phlox subulata*), whose trails can cover upto 3 ft of ground. When in bloom, they form a heavy carpet of flowers. Phlox grow easily from seed. Plant directly in pots or in beds and thin out.

Phlox drummondii

Pinch back the leaders when the plants are about 10 inches high to form side shoots. Phlox like light, rich soil and a sunny situation.

Everlasting flowers (*Helipterum* [*Rhodanthe*], *Helichrysum*)—These are grown for the 'everlasting' texture of the flowers which when dried retain their colour. The loveliest are the Rhodanthe from South Africa and Australia which are strawberry-pink. Helichrysms are found in Asia, Europe, Africa and Australia. They come in many colours. Rhodanthe grow upto 12 inches high and the Helichrysums can be up to 3.5 ft tall. There are dwarf varieties available. These are hardy plants that will grow in normal garden soil.

FLOWERSPEAK

Every woman, whatever her age or status, loves to be given a bouquet or posy. A few flowers is all it takes to make her feel desired, appreciated, admired. This is not strictly a European custom; the ancient Japanese, Chinese and Indians all gave their ladies flowers. In Kalidasa's *Meghadutam*, the poor, lovelorn Yaksha, separated from his wife, longs to give her the beautiful flowers that the cloud-messenger sees as he drifts over the forests and mountains.

In England, particularly during the nineteenth century, when interaction between the sexes was stilted and formal, flowers were used to convey the subtlest of messages. Lady Mary Wotley Montague lived for a while in Turkey in the early 1700s. She wrote to a friend, describing how Turkish women sent messages to their lovers not in words but in flowers, silk skeins and gems. Each flower, silk thread or gem had a meaning, and Turkish girls knew them by heart. When her letters were published in 1763, it was the language of flowers which attracted the readers. From very early times, flowers have had allegorical significance and have symbolized many things. In the East, the lotus has long been a symbol of purity; the orchid, in China, was a symbol of chastity and austerity; in India, jasmines were associated with the beloved. But in Victorian England, the language of flowers was so important—thanks to the lack of social interaction between the sexes—that even books on practical gardening included a section on the meaning of flowers.

Flowers and Their Meanings

African marigold—vulgar mind

Almond blossom—hope

Amaryllis—splendid beauty

Apple-blossom—preference

Basil—hatred

Blue violet—faithfulness

Bluebell—constancy

Carnation (streaked)—refusal

Coriander—hidden worth

Heather—solitude

Hop—injustice

Hyacinth—playful

Lily of the valley—return of happiness

Musk rose—voluptuousness

Narcissus—egotism

Peony—bashful shame

Single rose—simplicity

Sweet alyssum—worth beyond beauty

Sweet violet—modesty

Sweet williams—gallantry

White jasmine—amiability

White lily—purity

White rosebud—a heart innocent of love

Yellow carnation—disdain

Yellow jasmine—grace and elegance

Yellow lily—falsehood

Yellow rose—jealousy

Yellow tulip—hopeless love

Bulbs, Corms, Tubers and Rhizomes

I asked the yellow crocuses:
'Where do you spend the winter?'
'Dervish what are you asking us?
We spend the winter underground.'

—Pir Sultan Abdal

All bulbs once grew in the wild and were brought into the garden for their scents and flowers. Some bulb plants were grown for their medicinal properties but most were grown for the beauty of their flowers. The ancient Chinese grew lilies, peonies and irises. As early as 1800 BC, colchicum (a plant from Colchis in West Asia) and scilla (the Greek name for the sea squill), both from the lily family, were cultivated in South Europe for medicinal uses. We know ancient Egyptians grew lilies, narcissi and anemones, as remains of these flowers have been found in some tombs. Narcissi were used to make funeral wreaths and there are remains which are 3000 years old. Pliny the Elder says the plant was named for the narcotic properties of its scent, but many believe it was named after Ovid's beautiful youth Narcissus, who saw his reflection in a pool and fell in love with it, thinking it was a nymph. He stayed by the pool and pined away for this love that could never be reciprocated. When he died, the gods turned him into a beautiful flower with its head drooping down to gaze at its own reflection. The Assyrians and Minoans are known to have grown the madonna lily. Lilies are seen in the wall paintings and friezes

Bee, you fly so far around:
Tell me, have you ever found,
Seen, or ever heard men tell
Of a flower to match the grace
Speak, and do not fear to tell
Of the gentle lily's face?
—Anon, 4-10th century
Sanskrit poem

of these ancient cities. In ancient Persia and China—most bulbs are natives of these lands—people had beautifully-designed gardens in which they grew tulips, hyacinths, lilies, narcissi, irises and peonies. Bulbs have been travelling for a very long time. Theophrastus, in his *Enquiry Into Plants*, written in about 340 BC, describes narcissi, saffron crocuses, lilies, ranunculuses and gladioli. The gladiolus is a native of Southern Africa and appears to be a seasoned traveller. Many bulb plants such as the iris and lily are native to the Himalayas but very few are mentioned in ancient Indian literature. In a rare instance, in *Meghadutam*, Kalidasa likens a sorrowing woman to a Day lily:

> 'Veiling her eyes with lashes heavy-laden with tears
> she will seem to be hovering uncertain
> between waking and dreaming
> —a day-lily on a cloudy day neither open nor shut.'

Many varieties of lilies, irises, fritillaria and a tulip, *Tulipa stellata*, are natives of the Himalayas, but they were not cultivated or imported into other parts of the country. Later, Muslim conquerors brought many bulbs from their Central Asian home to India and popularized their cultivation.

The crusaders took Central Asian and Mediterranean bulbs West into France and Britain, though tulips, which are natives of Turkey and Central Asia, went eastward more than 2000 years ago. When Babur went to Kabul and travelled through the countryside around the city, in one sub-division, the foothills were covered with tulips. 'I once counted them up; it came out at 32 or 33 different sorts. We named one the Rose-scented, because its perfume was a little like that of the red rose.' The tulip went to Europe only in the sixteenth century, and thus began the Tulip Mania, equalled only by the Orchid Mania of the nineteenth century. In Holland, huge sums were spent on acquiring any unusual bulb, and everybody who had a square yard of land grew tulips. The mania spent itself out, but hybridists are still trying to produce a blue tulip.

Almost all the bulb plants we see in the garden come from temperate and cool temperate regions. Oxalis, freesias and gladioli come from Southern Africa; irises and lilies are found from Japan to Europe; and cyclamen are found from coastal Mediterranean to north-west Iran.

Bulbs, corms, rhizomes and tubers are a very important group of garden plants with something for every type of garden. They are a great advantage in small gardens and pot gardens, their beauty so much brighter because they are viewed from up close. In large gardens, unless grown in huge drifts or massed clumps, they get blurred by other flowers and garden features.

Bulbs—A bulb is made up of fleshy scales, which in fact are modified stems. At the base lies the compressed stem, set in like a plate. The centre of the bulb contains the embryo shoot, and in the mature bulbs also the embryo of the flower. Some bulbs are covered with an outer layer called the 'tunic'.

Corms—A corm is a swollen stem covered with a papery tunic. During the growing period, the original corm shrivels up and a new one forms above it.

Tubers—These can be swollen stems or roots. The stem tuber, as in the begonia, produces growth buds, whereas a root tuber, such as the dahlia, does not produce buds; the new growth comes from the 'crown' above the tubers.

Pleione

Rhizomes—Rhizomes are modified stems which store water and food for the plant. Rhizomes grow below, or just above the surface of the soil, rooting as they spread. New shoots are produced at the ends.

All bulbs, corms, tubers and rhizomes are the plant's storage organs. They contain the food it will need when it is dormant. Most lie fairly close to the surface.

HOW AND WHERE

🌺 Many bulbs of the dwarf genera are ideal for rock-gardens and are a boon to any small garden. Anemone, crocus, dwarf iris, grape hyacinth and wood sorrel are some.

🌺 Many bulbs such as daffodils, zephyr lilies, snowdrops and narcissi are very effective when naturalized in grass.

🌺 Some bulb plants like hot, dry areas. Belladonna lilies and Mariposa lilies have very beautiful flowers and are great additions to gardens in hot, dry areas where most bulbs will not grow.

🌺 Most members of this group need dappled shade and like their soil moist.

🌺 In the hills, bulbs can be planted in spring beds or allowed to grow in clumps, but in the plains they must be lifted and stored. Zephyr lilies (hippeastrums) which are mistakenly called amaryllis and spider lilies, are exceptions.

GENERAL CARE

All the plants mentioned in this section usually have 3 phases each year—growth, flowering and dormancy. Some flower before the leaves develop, some after the foliage is well-grown, and all these plants rest after growth and flowering. The length of the dormant period varies; much depends upon humidity and temperature. Bulbs that are summer-flowering in the hills will flower at the end of the cold season in the plains. All bulbs do well in the hills, but only the hardy species thrive in the plains. Many bulbs get crotchety in the plains and refuse to flower in the second year; the narcissus, for instance, is very whimsical.

With most plants in this group, the foliage should be allowed to die down naturally after flowering. It should not be cut off as the plant needs it to build up the storage organs. As a general rule it is good to feed these plants with a liquid feed after they have flowered. This helps build up the storage organs. Liquid-feed once every ten days and water until the foliage browns and dies. Then withhold water, easing off gradually. It is a sound practice to remove flower-heads when they are withered unless you want seeds. There's little point in letting the plant dissipate its energy on seed production. With flowers like dahlias, deheading will give you more flowers.

Most plants in this group are delicate in some aspects. They will not survive severe heat or frost. If left in the ground, they must be mulched properly in extreme conditions. Dried twigs, leaves and straw can be piled up where they lie. Tie down with a nylon netting to make sure it is not blown away.

In the plains, most bulbs must be lifted and stored except for hardy bulbs such as zephyr lilies, spider lilies etc., which should be repotted every two to three years. Stop watering gradually and let the plant rest for two to three months before resuming watering again when the growing season begins.

When you plant your bulbs depends upon the plant and the climatic zone.

Bulbs should be stored in a cool, dark and dry place. If kept in boxes, make holes so that there is air circulation.

SOIL PREPARATION AND PLANTING

All members of this group are relatively easy to grow but need soil that is prepared well in advance. The soil should be well drained, rich in humus and light in composition. The bulb will rot if the soil gets water-logged. On the other hand, if the soil is too sandy and lacking in humus and leaf mould, the bulb will shrivel up and die, so get the mixture right.

When preparing a bed for these plants, dig deep and open up the soil to ensure good drainage. Then dig in well-rotted leaf mould and garden compost—about 5 kg per square meter, and more if the soil is poor.

Bulbs are usually planted two to four months before they are due to flower. The depth at which they should be planted depends upon the species. Few are planted more than 6 inches below the soil.

Bulbs can be grown in pots and in the ground. A great many bulbs are ideal for pot cultivation and can be brought indoors when they begin to flower. A couple of bowls of freesias are enough to perfume a large room.

Bulbs are usually planted after they show some sign of life by sprouting. Do not water soon after planting; if watered before the roots form, the bulb could die. A light sprinkling of water once every other day is quite enough until the first leaves appear. After that they should be watered copiously. Many like a sunny position, but some grow best in the shade.

PROPAGATION

Few beginners will wish to propagate bulbs by division. Some permanent subjects such as clumps of a hippeastrum or zephyr lily can be lifted when dormant, and the clumps split up. They should then be replanted with enough room for new bulbs to grow in. Plants such as the bearded iris can be divided after flowering, or when the clumps become too large. Each division should consist of a piece of the rhizome with a few leaves.

PESTS AND DISEASES

Some hardy members of this group are disease resistant and generally free of pests. But many are prone to fungal rot and can be attacked by slugs, snails and other garden pests.

Slugs and Snails

These usually have to be picked off and destroyed. Look for leaves with missing bits.

Fungal Rot

Fungal rot can attack bulbs when in the soil or when stored. This usually occurs if the conditions are humid and damp. If the disease has not spread, the bulbs should be dipped in a fungicide before planting. Throw away all the rotten bulbs.

Soil Pests

Leatherjackets, cutworms and the larvae of some flies will attack bulbs in the soil. If your soil has been cleaned and cultivated, you should have no soil pests. Symptoms are poor growth and wilting foliage.

Viruses

Many plants become infected by viruses. Symptoms are stunted or distorted growth, leaf mottling or streaking. There is no cure. The infected plant must be destroyed.

Aphids

Aphids infest the tender tips of plants and weaken them by sucking the sap. Destroy the creatures as soon as you see them, and spray with an insecticide.

Soil mixture for bulbs, corms and rhizomes

One part well-rotted cattle manutre
One part leaf mould
Two parts well-drained garden soil

If the soil is heavy, add more leaf mould or compost, *not* sand.

SOME BULBS FOR SMALL GARDENS AND POT GARDENS

Zephyr lily (*Zephyranthes*)

Zephyranthes literally means 'flower of the West Wind'. In Greek mythology, Zephyrus, god of the West Wind, was the gentlest of the sylvan deities. It was he who carried Psyche to Cupid when Venus separated them. In India, they are often called thunder lilies because they bloom with the onset of the monsoon, and oddly enough, these winds come from the south-west.

These small bulbous plants come from the warm parts of America. The leaves are narrow and grass-like, and the funnel-shaped flowers can be pink, yellow or white. The flowers appear in summer. The plants grow quite happily in most parts of the country and can be grown in pots or in the ground. The flowers are always single. The bulbs should be planted in February/March and can be left undisturbed for years. They are excellent pot plants though most effective when grown in drifts in grass. They need no fuss and little care, to thrive. When potted bulbs become too crowded, divide and repot.

Soil mixture for tubes

One part well-drained garden soil
Two parts leaf mould
Two part well-rotted cattle manure

When potting, place a layer of coal directly above the pot shards.

Amaryllis belladonna

This lily is a native of South Africa and is the only species of the genus. The flowers which appear on the top of the stem are rosy-red to pink, and have a delicate perfume. The strap-like leaves appear after the flowers have withered. There are a number of hybrids, one of which is white, and all do well in pots. They are very effective when placed against a dark background.

The bulbs need repotting only once every two to three years, or when the roots become pot-bound. The flowers appear from March to May in the plains and a couple of months later in the hills. The bulb retains its leaves if grown in warm regions. Even so, it should be rested. The bulbs should be planted 2-5 inches deep in humus-rich soil which is porous. The top of the bulb should rest above the surface.

The amaryllis looks pretty striking when grown in clumps or irregular borders with smaller plants in the foreground. Whether the latter are foliage or flowering plants depends entirely upon you. If grown in small pots, they may need to be thinned out every year. Reduce water in October/November until none is given. The bulbs are dormant in winter. Resume watering when new growth appears. In temperate regions, the leaves die down naturally.

Amaryllis belladonna

Lily (*Liliaceae*)

Lilies belong to one of the largest families of flowering plants, and are found in most temperate regions. There are 250 genera and more than 3700 species. One of the most important genera for gardening purposes is *Lilium*. True lilies are all bulbous plants with leafy stems and large flowers. They are among the oldest cultivated flowers, and all belong to the northern temperate regions. The madonna lily was grown by the Egyptians and Cretans more than a thousand years before Christ. The flower is depicted on vases and other objects which date back to 1750 BC. It is believed that Mithradates, King of Pontius, used the juice of the madonna lily bulb as a cure for snake bite.

Lilies can be white, pale pink, orange, flecked or streaked, depending upon the species. The Golden-rayed lily (*L. auratum*) from Japan, often called the queen of lilies, is a spotted-white, with petals that curl back. A ray of gold runs down the centre of each petal and the plant bears more flowers on one stem than any other lily.

All lilies flower in late summer (in winter if grown in the plains), and all like soil that is well drained and rich in humus. Few lilies will tolerate lime. In the hills, bulbs should be planted in spring; in the plains, in October.

The madonna lily has breathtaking moon-white flowers and a honey-like fragrance. If given the right climatic conditions and soil, the bulb is hardy and prefers to be left undisturbed for years. This lily has a brief resting period—the stem and leaves die down naturally and new growth appears not long after. Lily bulbs should be planted 2 inches below the soil. If potted, one bulb should be planted in a 10-inch pot. The tall spikes need staking. When the leaves start to dry, withdraw water gradually and store the pots in a cool, dry place until planting time.

Eucharis (*E. amazonia, E. grandiflora*)

These South American bulbs make excellent pot plants. Plant four to five bulbs in a 12-inch pot. *E. amazonia* has Chinese-white flowers which are very fragrant. While growing, the plants need plenty of water but should be dried out after flowering. The bulbs do not like lime or heavy soil. Grow them in partial shade in soil that is rich in leaf mould.

Eucharis (Spider lily)

E. grandiflora is one lily that will flower during the summer months in the plains. Often called the spider lily, the bulbs are very hardy and can be left undisturbed for years. If grown in pots, divide the bulbs only when they become very crowded.

Sprekelia formosissima

This lily is known as the Jacobean lily. The flower is a native to Mexico and Guatemala. These curiously shaped flowers can be up to 6 inches across and are a deep crimson in colour. Three petals are arranged arching in the rear and three thrusting forward to form a sheath for the stamens. This plant likes a warm situation but does not like the hot sun; it should be protected from severe heat. Pot in normal soil mixture.

Sprekelia
(Jacobean lily)

Freesia

These are among the loveliest of all scented bulb plants. They come from South Africa and were taken to Europe by the Dutch. The highly scented flowers come in a variety of colours— yellow, pink, mauve, white, red, bronze, blue, cream and crimson. The modern hybrids, though they have larger flowers, are not as heavily scented as the old cultivars. In the hills, the flowers appear in late spring and summer; in the plains, they must be planted in November. Plant five to six corms in a 10-inch pot or a shallow earthenware bowl if you want to bring them indoors when they flower. They should not be planted too deep—the tips should lie just below the surface of the soil. The growing shoot is very tender and can break if the corms are exposed, so make sure they are covered. Withdraw water when the leaves turn yellow and dry, and store the bulbs.

The plants usually flower twelve weeks after planting. They like a sunny position but not the midday sun. Mix the corms to create a rainbow effect.

Guernsey lily (*Nerine sarniensis*)

These bulbs from South Africa are usually autumn-flowering. The plant got its English name—Guernsey lily—because it is grown in the Channel Islands where it is cultivated for the flower trade. Long ago, a ship was wrecked on the shores of Guernsey and the bulbs that were washed ashore rooted in the sand. People thought the ship came from Japan and mistakenly assumed the plants were Japanese. Only later did botanists discover that they were native to South Africa. On the Table Mountain, where they are found in the wild, the bulbs flower in March.

In the plains, plant the bulbs in November; in the hills, in spring. Nerines like well-drained soil, rich in humus and leaf mould, and a sunny situation. Plant the bulbs 3 inches deep. This elegant plant has trumpet-shaped flowers which are a deep rosy-pink, with frilly petals. Modern hybrids are available in a range of colours—white, pale-pink, purple-magenta and orange-scarlet. The leaves develop after the flowers have faded.

Damp with dew
The iris is still fragrant
Listen, the cuckoos
Are calling . . .
—Fujiwara no Yoshitsune

Iris (*Iridaceae*)

This is a very large family of plants that can have corms or rhizomes and are among the best-loved garden flowers. There are about 300 species, all native to the temperate parts of the northern hemisphere. *I. florentina* has been cultivated for more than 2000 years. The rhizomes are the source of the violet-scented 'orris-root' powder. The rhizomes must be at least two years old before the scent is fully developed. The Egyptians, Greeks and Romans used orris-root powder in perfumery and medicine. *I. germanica* has a rich, fruity scent and the rhizome is used in the making of some liqueurs. Known as Bearded iris and Flags, these irises are very popular with gardeners. *I. reticulata* from North Persia and the Caucasus is a violet-scented beauty with grassy leaves and deep purple or blue flowers. *I. xiphium*, from Spain and Portugal, has flowers which come in a wide range of colours—white, yellows, orange, bronze and blue. Dwarf irises which come from Southern Europe and Asia Minor have small flowers which are excellent for rock gardens. If conditions are right, irises can be grown in the ground in clumps; when grown in the plains, they need to be potted. There are literally hundreds of hybrids available. The corms and rhizomes are usually very hardy and need little care. Most irises dislike lime-rich soil; some will not tolerate any lime at all. They like loamy, well-drained soil. Plant about 2 inches deep and if potted, divide after every three to four years. In the plains, the bulbs must be lifted and stored after flowering. Irises like a sunny position, though some, like the Siberian iris, like to grow in the shade.

Narcissus (*Amaryllidacea*)

This is a large family of bulbous plants which are found in the wild from Europe through Central Asia, China and Japan. They are grown for their scented flowers which appear in spring in the hills, and at the end of the cold season when grown in the plains. Of this genus, daffodils are the most widely grown in Europe, though in Iran the Pheasant Eye is greatly appreciated. Most narcissi are highly scented, *N. jonquilla*, is probably the sweetest smelling. The old Tazetta is another. The Triandrus group, commonly called Angel's Tears, has some dainty little blooms which are very suitable for rock gardens. Narcissi can be naturalized in the hills; in the plains they have to be grown in pots.

If given the right conditions and soil, the Narcissus increases prolifically. The plant likes rich, well-drained soil, and can be grown in the sun or dappled shade. The bulbs should be planted 3-4 inches deep in late summer or early autumn in the hills, and in November in the plains. The leaves are narrow and strap-like, and the flowers appear in bunches on the end of the stem. The flower consists of a corona and a cup. Some have small cups, others like Angel's Tears have very large ones. In a few, the segments curve backwards. When grown in pots, the plants must be fed every two weeks once the leaves appear. In the plains, the bulbs must be lifted and stored.

Canna (*Cannaceae*)

This has just the one genus and about 55 species, all native to tropical America, and have been naturalized in many parts of Asia and Africa.

> *Life is colour and warmth and light*
> *And a striving evermore for these.*
> —Julian Greenfell

C. indica (Indian Shot) is actually from Brazil, not India, and is found in marshy areas. The hot, splendid colours of the garden cannas owe much to years of hybridization. In Colombia and Ecuador, the fleshy roots are a staple diet of the Indians.

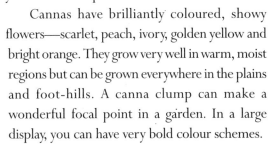

Cannas have brilliantly coloured, showy flowers—scarlet, peach, ivory, golden yellow and bright orange. They grow very well in warm, moist regions but can be grown everywhere in the plains and foot-hills. A canna clump can make a wonderful focal point in a garden. In a large display, you can have very bold colour schemes.

Canna

The plants are easy to grow but have definite requirements. Don't give them what they need and the flowers will be poor and tattered. Cannas cannot abide frost.

Beds—Cannas are greedy feeders and, in this respect, need a lot of attention. The soil must be dug deep—at least 2 ft, and turned over. Spread a layer of well-rotted cattle manure—6 inches thick—and mix well. For a good display, raise the bed in the centre. If the bed is against a wall or fence, make a gentle slope. In the right conditions, cannas can be grown all the year round. For most places in the plains, it is best to plant with the onset of the monsoon. In tropical regions, cannas, after flowering, should be lifted and then replaced immediately. Divide the clumps when they grow too big.

To divide, cut the stems off to within an inch of the ground. Dig up the clump and divide. Each piece should have a good-sized rhizome and a stem. Replant, leaving the stem above the ground. Water and shade the beds with leafy branches till the new leaves appear.

Cannas can be grown in large pots and like rich soil (one part garden soil, and two parts manure). Divide when the clumps become too big.

Crocus

This is an important genus of small bulbous plants, the most famous being the saffron crocus, much prized for the stamens. A native of Asia Minor, the saffron crocus was well known in the ancient world. Saffron was used in medicine, as a dye, and in cosmetics. In Italy, during the Middle Ages, the ladies, envying the blond tresses of their northern sisters, used saffron to dye their hair, but the wrath of the Church fell upon their golden heads and they were compelled to stop. Henry VIII of England passed a law that forbade the dyeing of linen sheets with saffron on the ground that the dyed sheets were not washed frequently enough!

The saffron crocus grows very well in Kashmir where it has been cultivated for centuries. Most crocuses are found in the wild in Asia Minor and parts of the Mediterranean region. They do well in the hills but can be grown as spring flowers in the northern plains. There are several species and innumerable varieties—some flower from late winter to early spring, others from autumn to early winter.

Crocuses like good, well-drained soil that is not too rich. Most grow in full sun but some prefer a shady situation. The corms should be planted 3-4 inches deep in October for spring flowers and in early summer for autumn flowers.

Crocuses can be naturalized in the hills; in the plains one has to settle for potted plants; flowering can be erratic.

Crocus

Gladiolus (*Iridaceae*)

Gladioli are sun-loving plants from Central and South Africa. They grow wild in the mountainous areas of the tropical rain forests which fringe Victoria Falls. These are hardy and highly adaptable plants but cannot tolerate frosts or extreme dry heat. They must be lifted and stored in the hills as well as in the plains. Only in cool, moist regions can they be left to multiply in the ground. Most of us are familiar with the unscented gladioli which are stocked by florists, hybrids grown mainly for the cut-flower industry. Hybridists seem to specialize in scentless blooms. But some old cultivars are sweetly-scented, and if you're lucky, you may be able to get corms from a gladiolus enthusiast. *G. alatus* smells like sweet briar; *G. carinatus* and *G. gracilis* both have a violet scent. The flowers of these are modest in size compared to the gigantic gladioli grown today, but are infinitely more fragile and have an understated elegance.

A pilgrim during the regin of Edward II went to the Holy Land and returned to England with a crocus bulb which he had hidden in his stave. This was done 'with venture for his life, for if he had been taken by the law of the country . . . he would have died for the fact.' The pilgrim started growing crocuses in Wolden Essex and they were grown there for centuries until the arrival of a cheap substitute.

One variety, G. tristis, *has soft, creamy yellow flowers. The flowers have a clove-like scent which is released in the evening. Three or four flower stems are enough to perfume a room. Outdoors, they scatter their perfume with great abandon.*

Planting: Plant large corms 4-6 inches deep; small corms, 2-3 inches deep. The soil should be well drained, rich in humus and rotting organic matter. They should be planted in the full sun, in September/October in the plains, and in spring in the hills. Water lightly if the soil is very dry, until the leaves appear; then water generously. After flowering, withdraw water when the leaves begin to yellow, till none is given. When the foliage has died down completely, lift the bulbs and store. It is wiser to stake gladioli—that prevents twisted or slanting stems. They can be used to great effect in the garden, and when grown in pots, can be extremely striking.

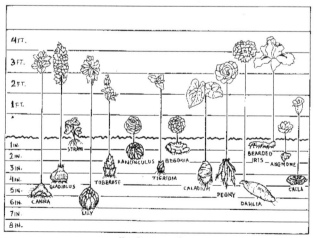

Bulb Planting Chart

Haemanthus (*Amaryllidaceae*)

In some parts of India, this South African lily is called the Football lily because of its round, ball-like flower-head which can be 7-9 inches across. More often they are known as blood lilies for the red colour of their flowers. The flowers appear in spring.

The semi-hardy bulbs must be rested after flowering, and repotted. The flowers appear before the leaves and are densely packed on the stem. The plant likes well-drained soil and a sunny position. If in the ground in the hills, the bulbs must be heavily mulched in the cold season.

Haemanthus coccineus

Japanese Day lily (*Liliaceae*)

These are good garden plants from Europe and Asia (especially Japan). They thrive in the tropics but can be found growing even in arctic Lapland. The bulbs are hardy and dependable in temperate regions. They can grow in the sun or shade and in practically any kind of soil. They will grow quite happily at the edge of a shrubbery or herbaceous border, or sometimes even in shallow water. The flowers don't last long but modern hybrids produce a succession of blooms and the plant remains in flower for weeks.

This lily has graceful arching foliage and the long trumpet-shaped flowers come in colours from pale lemon and pink to a coppery-orange. The flowers appear in summer on spikes that can be upto 2 ft tall.

The flowers can be successfully grown in pots and need repotting only when the pot gets crowded. Use humus-rich, well-drained soil, and liquid-feed before the flowering period.

Cyclamen (*Primulaceae*)

These flowers are native to all countries with a Mediterranean coastline, except Spain and Egypt. They are also found in Switzerland, Austria, Bulgaria, Central Asia and north-west Iran. Greece, Italy and Yugoslavia have the largest number.

These are tender plants with drooping, lovely flowers. The petals turn back giving an impression of being upright. Some can live to a great age—a hundred years or more! The huge tubers carry scores of flowers; some varieties are scented.

Cyclamens like a constant temperature (16°C) and need a greenhouse even in the hills. High temperature or a dry atmosphere can be fatal. The tubers like lime-free soil rich in leaf mould and humus. Some varieties have interesting marbled leaves.

The Chinese use the dried flowers in soups and various meat dishes. The flowers are sold as gum-jum (golden needles) or gum-tsoy (golden vegetables).

Potted Plants and Indoor Gardens

How many days must pass
Before we can go forth
And pluck the young pot-herbs? . . .
When will the cherry flowers open?
—Keichiu

Humans have been growing potted plants for more than 3500 years—probably even before. In 1495 BC, Queen Hatshepsut of Egypt sent an expedition to the land of Punt (probably Somalia or Ethiopia) to procure the incense tree, Boswellia, from which we get the much-prized, aromatic gum frankincense. The plants arrived in pots. A stone bas-relief in her palace shows a row of Boswellias growing in small, ribbed pots. The trees appear healthy, luxuriant and quite happy in their adopted country, a sure sign that the palace gardeners knew their business. The Queen of Sheba gave King Solomon many rare gifts but the most prized was the gum tree from which myrrh is obtained. It was potted and looked after on its long journey to Solomon's kingdom, a sure indication of the excellence of the gardening skills of her people. King Chandragupta I imported flowering trees to plant in his palace gardens. Megasthenes, who was in India during his reign, describes the garden: 'And these trees, from the unusual benignity of the climate, are ever in bloom . . . some are native to the soil, others are with circumspect care brought from other parts.' They were certainly potted before transporting. He also describes indoor gardens with pools—the plants were in pots.

Paintings from early China show azaleas and lilies in ornate pots. The Babylonians were highly skilled gardeners and one of the wonders of the ancient world, King Nebuchadnezzar's Hanging Gardens, had trees growing in large earthenware containers. Ancient Greeks too, knew the art of growing plants in containers. During the festival of Adonis (the god of plant fertility),

'Adonis gardens' were grown. The seeds planted were usually the quick-germinating species like fennel, barley and lettuce. These were carefully tended and, at the end of eight days, were thrown into springs or the sea, symbolizing the young god's seasonal death and rebirth. In India too, during the Navaratra festival, spring and autumn, women grow barley in clay pots and on the eighth or tenth day, the seedlings and pot are cast into a river, stream or pond. This ancient tradition goes back thousands of years and one cannot help but note the striking similarity.

In Rome, pot gardens were seen in town houses more than 2000 years ago; plants were grown in pots because garden space was limited. The Chinese were growing whole landscapes in pots (*pun-ching*), complete with rocks and miniature trees, 2000 years ago. Potting plants is a very ancient art.

Today's cities are more congested than Rome ever was, and gardens are shrinking or disappearing with frightening rapidity. Many 'gardens' are composed solely of potted plants—all one can have in small paved areas and balconies. More and more people are growing plants indoors, and indoor gardens are created almost solely with potted plants. Whether you have an indoor garden or a balcony garden, you need to know how to pot a plant if your garden is to flourish.

POTTING

A potted plant has four vital needs: one, the pot must contain a good drainage hole; two, the soil should be well-drained, rich in humus and soil nutrients; three, regular feeding; four, transplanting when the roots become pot-bound. Potted plants depend entirely upon you for their needs. You must know when and how much to water and feed them. You must also know what type of soil your plant likes. Healthy plants need nutrients, sunlight, air and water and it is you who must give it to them. Your potted plant's roots cannot go foraging for food. If you are new to the art, don't be discouraged if some die; few people get it right the first time. The success or failure depends upon

I saw a busy potter by the way
Kneading with might and main a lump of clay
And lo! The clay cried 'use me gently, pray;
I was a man myself but yesterday!'
—Rubaiyat of Omar Khayyam

the position of the plant (you can't plant a sun-lover in the shade and expect it to thrive), the degree of sun and shade, the soil, and the quality of care. The safest bet for beginners is to buy hardy plants that grow well in the area. Go to the local nursery and find out what will grow easily and what it needs. The expert needs no advice.

In a pot garden, the star is undoubtedly the plant, but the pot plays a very important, supporting role. Even when there is a garden, some plants are put into containers because we wish to single them.out, others because we wish to bring them indoors or have them grouped around the house. So choose your pots with care.

Pots

There are all sorts of containers available today—clay, ceramic, plastic, cement and polystyrene. The ideal container for most plants is an earthenware pot. Being porous it allows the soil to breathe, it doesn't retain heat, and it is inexpensive and easily replaced. Well-fired terracotta pots can be very durable, and when the pots break, you can use the shards as drainage crocks. Clay pots have another advantage over others

Boswellia on Queen Hatsheput's tomb

such as ceramic and plastic. If you happen to overwater your plant, the clay will absorb some of the excess water; in the case of plastic or ceramic, the plant will get water-logged and could die. Clay pots come in all shapes and sizes and usually have nice large drainage holes, so necessary for the health of a plant.

Plastic, Stone, Cement and Polystyrene: Plastic or polystyrene pots can be—and many say should be—used for window ledges and window boxes. Plants in these pots can be easily shifted. Plants in a window-space receive a limited amount of sunlight, and during the monsoon, could be lashed by the rains. In these circumstances they will need to be moved, sometimes quickly if a storm is brewing, as the pots could break. In such cases, plastic makes more sense. Plastic containers tend to retain moisture and watering time is considerably reduced. And if the pot does drop off the ledge, it won't break.

With a stone and cement pot, you must know where the plant fits into the scheme of things. You can't move these pots around frequently as they are much too heavy. You must decide on the effect you wish to create before placing the pot, and you must also know whether your plant is sun-loving or shade-loving; the situation must suit the plant. Cement pots are ugly but you can camouflage them by placing small potted plants around them or growing plants that trail and hang down, such as the wandering Jew. During summer, if your cement or stone pots stand in the full sun, the plants may need watering twice a day. Cement, unlike clay, can get very hot.

Wood: Wooden containers are a boon for gardeners in very hot or very cold climates. They insulate the roots from the extremes of temperature and in hot places don't allow the soil to get bone-dry. Half-barrels and wooden troughs can be used in outdoor gardens. Wooden crates can be used as window boxes, and can be made to fit snugly into a nook, corner or alcove. Some hardwoods will not rot if well-seasoned, but other woods will need protection. Teak, rosewood or mahogany—all hardwoods—can be pretty expensive; you may not want to invest in them. Poorer quality wooden containers are cheap but require a coating of some waterproof material. Use a wood paint that does not contain creosote as it is harmful to plants. Wooden containers have a softness about them that harmonizes with plants, unlike hard cement pots.

Marble: Marble pots can be very beautiful and it has a texture and translucency that makes it ideal container material. Also, it is a 'cool' stone—a boon in hot regions. Marble does not have the harshness of stone or the non-resilience of cement. And it is not static—there's a fluidity in its texture that is not present in other stones, which makes it so very right for plants. But large marble pots on pedestals are opulent and suitable only for formal gardens. Exercise restraint when buying marble pots for small, informal gardens.

Others: You can make a container for plants out of anything that is a receptacle—bird cages, old porcelain sinks, cracked jugs or teapots. Just make sure they have a drainage hole.

Preparing a pot: Cover the drainage hole with crocks, the concave side facing down. Cover the shards with a layer of granular sand or dry moss. Now fill in your soil mixture.

Hanging Baskets

Hanging baskets look charming in any garden, particularly in small patios or terrace gardens but it is where there is no question of a garden that they can be put to best use. They will give you the garden you can't have.

Preparing baskets: Wire baskets do not need pot-shards to line the base; coir fibre or dry mosses are used to prevent the earth from falling out. First line the basket with a thin plastic sheet and puncture small holes in the base of the lining. To prevent the lining from slipping, tape or glue it to the rim. Place a layer of coir fibre or dry moss and fill half the basket with your soil mixture. Now make slits in the sides of the lining, large enough to insert a young plant. Gently poke the root ball of the plant through the slit into the soil. Make sure the roots are entirely covered by soil. Now firm down from the top.

A hanging basket allows you to experiment with a variety of plants though the trailing ones are the most effective. Many plants come into their own only when suspended in front of a window or against a wall. A good display has plants spilling out from all around. To create this effect, you must trim the young plants and shape them. Hanging succulents like the burro's tail don't need anything done to them, nor do strawberries, but some plants, like trailing lantana, will get straggly if left untrimmed.

INDOOR PLANTS

If you don't have even a tiny balcony and still want a garden, you will have to resort to the great indoors. There's one thing you must remember, however, it's harder on the plants than on you, and having said that, let it also be said that there are literally hundreds of plants that will grow indoors quite happily. Many are not at all fussy. Give them their basic requirements—food, sunlight, air and water—and they will thrive even if you are an absolute greenhorn. Plants are very adaptable and there are many that will positively 'bloom and grow' in indoor conditions. Plants from mountain deserts, tropical jungles, pine forests or Pacific islands can be found growing quite happily in London, New Delhi or Beijing. But this does not mean you can throw selection to the winds—you still need to be selective if you want a good indoor garden. Unless you have the expertise, you can't grow an Amazon rain-forest orchid in the blistering heat of Delhi. Choose plants that like the climate you live in and there will be few plants to mourn—none at all if you choose hardy varieties.

Choose plants according to the conditions you can give them. Most house plants come from tropical and sub-tropical jungles. They grow on the forest floor and are accustomed to filtered sunlight. These plants are usually evergreens, and though they have a dormant period, they are never denuded of all their leaves. But they do need high levels of humidity. So, mist their leaves at least three times a day when the weather turns dry.

House plants can be capricious—even the hardiest of them. If you completely neglect and ignore them, they will wilt and die. But give them the attention they need and they will thrive despite the alien conditions, sometimes a little too well.

Check the space you have and the amount of light your windows let in before choosing your plants. What you can expect of them will be in direct proportion to what you can give them in terms of time, care and climatic conditions.

Using Indoor Plants Effectively

Plants cannot invade and take possession of your house; few potted plants can get rampant. Their size is limited because of the confined space they grow in, but if you want a little jungle, you can have one. Just choose the right plants and give them what they need—the right soil mixture, water, light and temperature.

Don't just plonk a plant in any bit of empty space; place it strategically. Use it as a focal point, a dramatic feature, to enhance another feature or to cover up an unsightly spot.

Ask yourself what you want indoors. Will it be in harmony with the rest of the surroundings? Do you want a theatrical specimen or a poised one? Is it grace that you seek, or something more solid and robust? Will it complement your decor? Will it add a certain charm to the ambience? The more certain you are about what you want, the easier it will be for you to make a choice, and with so much to choose from, the task can be exacting. For you can't have all you want.

Choose the right plant for the right spot. Don't try to grow a maiden-hair fern on a hot, dry, indoor ledge, or an African violet in a cold, damp corner. Sooner or later they are sure to die. Understand your plants and sympathize with their needs and they will reward you; fail to do so and they will die without a protest.

Use your plants aesthetically, to their best advantage, but without compromising on their needs. There are plants for every situation, soil type and climate; just choose the right ones. Go to local nurseries and talk to the nurseryman if you are unsure of what will grow in your house.

If you are a beginner, stick to hardy plants that do not require expert care. Experiment only when you are better acquainted with plants. There are plants for even the most unskilled gardener.

The Survivors

Some plants will survive anything, even the clumsy handling of a novice. They are hardy, require little care and even less attention. And they won't disrupt your lifestyle. They will go on with their business while you go about yours. Then there are others that can and will make unreasonable demands on your time and energy, so unless you are an expert, don't try to grow delicate, fussy plants however beautiful they are. Stick to the die-hards. The ones listed below are easy to grow, very pleasing to the eye and will cheerfully take some neglect.

Spider plant (*Chlorophytum comosum 'Variegatum'*)—This plant has fresh green and white-edged leaves which arc out gracefully. It is especially attractive when the plantlets begin to grow on the tips of the long flower stems. It is particularly effective when planted in a hanging basket. Keep the soil moist and place it in semi-shade. Use normal soil mixture for planting.

Bromeliads—Most species do very nicely indoors. Some specimens will need a sunny spot; others like shade. Many are flowering and the flowers last a long time. Check with your nurseryman what conditions a particular bromeliad likes before you buy. They grow in light, highly porous soil which has plenty of leaf mould. One part soil, two parts leaf mould will do very nicely for them. They need very modest attention. (For more details see 'Orchids and Other Exotica'.)

Swiss Cheese Plant (*Monstera delicioca*)—This makes a very good indoor plant, and if used singly can be very effective. Don't clutter it up with other foliage plants. (For further details see 'Orchids and Other Exotica'.)

Phoenix Palm (*Phoenix canariensis*)—These lovely, delicate palms have long fronds of arcing, graceful leaves. Most are from South-East Asia and North Africa. They are slow-growing plants and like being in pots when young. *P. dactylifera*, the date palm, is a large plant and the fronds are bluish-green with fewer leaflets. The plants like a bright, sunny position when young, but don't put them out in the hot midday sun. Water freely in summer; use well-drained, loamy soil. In the winters, use tepid water if you live in the northern plains, and water sparingly. In a mild climate, it can be left out all the year round. *P. roebelinii* is a dwarf variety.

Dumb cane (*Dieffenbachia*)—This is a slow-growing, very hardy evergreen shrub from tropical America. The stem is thick and fleshy and the plant bears clusters of large variegated leaves which are its main feature. If the sap should touch your tongue, your tongue swells up impairing speech, hence the name, 'dumb cane'. Use a soil mixture that is fairly rich in organic manure. Don't allow it to get dry. Water generously and keep the plant out of the summer sun.

Cabbage palm (*Cordyline*)—This is a genus of small trees and shrubs from South-East Asia and Australia. *C. terminalis*, or the 'good luck tree', is a very attractive specimen with large, glossy, oval leaves which may be red, red/maroon or red/green. Some are streaked with cream. It likes a semi-shaded situation, out of the hottest sun. Water moderately in summer and sparingly in winter. Don't overwater and don't let the root ball dry out. The soil should be porous and rich in humus.

Crotons (*Codiaeum*)—This is a family of very colourful evergreens. The leaves come in a wide range of colours, shapes and sizes. Originally from Polynesia, these plants can be seen in tropical and subtropical gardens all over the world. The leaves may be marbled or veined, spotted or splotched in all the shades of green, yellow, pink, red, white, orange and cream. There are countless hybrids and most are very vividly coloured. They like a bright situation but not direct midday sun, except where the summers are mild. Water the plant deeply but don't let the soil get water-logged. The soil should be rich in loam.

Miniature fan palm (*Rhapis excelsa*)—This lovely dwarf palm is a native of China. Though widely grown and appreciated in China, it is in Japan that it is treated with something just a little short of reverence. Imported from China about 300 years ago, it soon became a favourite of the imperial family and synonymous with power and position. Today this unassuming, quiet palm is owned by the rich and collected by enthusiasts who see a special beauty in its form and leaves. More often than not, it is grown in fine handmade porcelain pots decorated with gold.

The soil mixture should be light, but rich in humus. It likes plenty of light but only filtered sunlight. Water well in summer but sparingly in winter. This hardy plant does very well indoors. The leathery leaves, blunt-edged and ribbed with prominent veins, are a rich green.

Syngonium: These trailing plants are extremely easy to grow and can be used very interestingly in the living area. The leaves change shape and increase in number as they grow older. The leaves are usually bright green, but coloured hybrids are now available. The plants like plenty of light, but if outdoors, keep out of direct sunlight. Don't stick the plant in any dark corner; it will be most unhappy. The potting mixture should be rich in humus. The plant is easily grown from cuttings.

Maranta: This genus of plants comes from the rain forests of Brazil. These are low-growing evergreens with unusually-marked, oval leaves, some finely striped with cream. The colours are no less unusual—dark greens, deep purple/brown and maroon/green. These plants do not like direct sunlight but like a light, airy situation. They don't grow well in hot, dry climates. Mist the leaves if the indoor environment is dry. The soil should be rich in loam and manure. Water sparingly in winter.

Cyperus: Cyperus belongs to a genus of grass-like plants which includes the papyrus reed. It is a popular plant as it is very easy to grow, likes the indoors and has a fine, linear beauty. *C. flabelliform* is commonly known as umbrella grass, has tall, dark green stems topped with long, narrow leaf-like bracts which radiate outwards. The greenish- white flowers grow above the bracts. The plants need heavy watering and soil rich in humus and nutrients. As they are fast growing, they may need yearly repotting.

The Great Indoors

Any interior, whether a small bedroom or a well-lit, airy apartment, can be improved with a few well-chosen plants. You can enhance an archway, disguise an unsightly architectural feature, change the look of a room or an unused alcove with plants. There are few spots in a house that do not make a suitable home for some plant or another. Most indoor plants available in nurseries are hybrids and not found in the wild, and many have been developed not only for their particular features but also to make them more suitable for indoor cultivation.

Foliage plants are the most popular indoor plants, and many require little care. Given the right treatment, they can become permanent indoor features. The most successful are the semi-shade-loving evergreens. Many are slow growers and there is no danger of them becoming too large for the room. There is a very wide range of plants available and they should be chosen according to the light and temperature of the room. One should consider how much and for how long there is direct sunlight in the room, and which plants like a semi-lit corner. Room temperatures vary throughout the year, humidity levels increase greatly during the monsoon and are low in winter. These facts should be considered before buying plants.

Visual impact can be made by juxtaposing shape, form, colour and texture. Leaves are no more uniformly green than the sky is uniformly blue. Textures range from velvety softness to shining gloss. Some plants look best when solitary; others do better in a group. By grouping plants, you bring the garden indoors. The number of plants you can have depends upon the space you can give them; don't pack them in like sardines in a can. Groups can be used to make a leafy divide; fill in awkward niches or placed on a window sill.

Some Plants for Shade

1) Arrowhead (*Syngonium*)
2) Philodendron
3) Snake Plant (*Sansevieria*)
4) King of Hearts (*Homalomena*)
5) Aglaonema
6) Golden Pothos (*Epipremnum aureum*)

Some Plants for Semi-Shade

1) Boston fern (*Nephrolepis exaltata* 'Bostoniensis')
2) Crotons (*Codiaeum*)
3) Dragon tree (*Dracaena draco*)
4) Dumb cane (*Dieffenbachia*)
5) Dwarf azalea (*Rhododendron simsii*)
6) English Ivy (*Hedera helix*)
7) Moth orchid (*Phalaenopsis*)
8) Peace lily (*Spathiphyllum*)
9) Spider plant (*Chlorophytum comosum*)
10) Schefflera (*Brassaia*)

Some Plants for Semi-Sun

1) Aloe vera (*Aloe barbandensis*)
2) Flamingo flower (*Anthurium andraeanum*)
3) Areca palm (*Chrysalidocarpus lutescens*)
4) Reed palm (*Chamaedorea seifrizii*)
5) Boston Fern (*Nephrolepis exaltata* 'Bostoniensis')
6) Christmas Cactus (*Schlumbergera bridgesii*)
7) Easter Cactus (*Rhipsalidopsis rosea*)
8) Gerbera
9) Lady Palm (*Rhapis*)
10) Weeping fig (*Ficus benjamina*)
11) Dendrobium
12) Phoenix
13) Begonia
14) Rubber plant (*Ficus elastica*)

Rockeries, Cacti and Succulents

The charm of a rock garden is essentially Lilliputian . . . Climb in your
mind's eye, the mossy stones and grow dizzy on their steep escarpments.
—Beverly Nichols

It is difficult to have a traditional rockery in the hot, dry plains of India. The scorching sun will kill all the tender succulents which usually grow among rocks in higher altitudes. Don't let that deter you. There are some succulents with brilliantly-coloured flowers, like portulacas, which do very well in the plains. Or, with a little effort, you could create a tropical rockery with small shrubs, ferns and a creeper or two, imitating a rocky outcrop in the forest. There will be many wild plants growing in your region and they can be included to create a highly unusual and lovely rockery. You could even have a rockery planned solely for shade plants like begonias, ferns and zephyr lilies to create a thing of rare beauty. But that will require some doing and a fair amount of maintenance, especially if the area is hot and dry. A careful choice of rocks and plants and some imagination are basically all that is needed to make a rockery.

Rocks—Get a variety of weather-beaten rocks in different shapes and sizes, the more scarred and pitted the better. Small rocks are only suitable for *pen-jing* which is the Chinese art of creating a landscape in a pot or on a tray. The ideal thing to do would be to make a trip to the countryside and collect your rocks, but if that isn't possible, you'll have to ask a building contractor to procure some for you. Don't use dressed stone or symmetrically-shaped rocks— your rock garden will be a piece of supreme ugliness.

Planning—To plan and execute a rockery is not as simple as it appears. You cannot get hold of any old stones, jumble them in a heap, plant some shrubs and flowers and call that a rockery. An

esia

Iris

Petrea

A rock garden can be made on a flat site by using a mound of rubble. Firm the mound and cover with a layer of finer rubble. Now cover with soil 18 inches thick. Sink the rocks into the soil. Incline the rocks backward and make sure strata lines run in the same direction.

Dry walls can be made from dressed or random stone or even broken paving slabs.

Constructions: A 6-in (15-cm) trench should be made at the base of the soil terrace and the stones should be bedded into cement on the floor of the trench. Walls above 2 ft (60 cm) in height should be given a slight backward tilt for added strength. As the wall is built up, insert those plants which will grow in it as building progresses. The stones are bonded as are bricks and a thin layer of soil is used instead of cement.

aesthetically pleasing rock garden is essentially naturalistic—a mountainous coastline or a rockery outcrop on a hillside. A large rockery should seem like a range of mountains with little bays, valleys and jutting headlands. A well-constructed rockery with appropriate plants can take away the tedious monotony of a flat expanse.

Making—Dig up the site for the rock garden to a depth of 8-12 inches, fill with gravel or bits of brick and firm down. Cover with a layer of soil at least a foot deep, and arrange the rocks on this surface. The broadest surface should be embedded in the soil. The rocks should tilt back slightly rather than sit forward. Once the largest rocks are in place, build upwards, packing plenty of soil between the stones. Avoid an even, symmetrical appearance; the slope should rise in irregular shelves to the summit. Don't make the ascent too steep, the soil will get washed away. Use the large, bold surfaces effectively, and whatever you do, don't scatter small stones on a heap of earth. Naturally-shaped rocks at different levels will form pockets, cliffs and shelves which will hold the plants. Fill the hollows and crevices with soil suitable for the plants you have chosen. Bulbs, ferns, small shrubs and succulents all need different types of soil. A vertical face on a rock can be used to set off plants which will grow tall. Keep in mind the maximum height the plants will reach—what's the point of having a rockery if the plants obliterate the rocks! Plenty of rock surface should be visible at all times.

If you have the space, you can make a little sunken pool in the rockery, reflecting the plants and rocks, with a feathery-leafed shrub growing out over it. It's easy enough to make— sink an earthenware basin and fill it with water. Don't let the water get murky and rank. Keep the basin clean. The foreground should look as natural as possible (eg. a gentle slope with a few scattered rocks and small shrubs) and ideally, the pool should merge into the rockery. There should be no joint or line of demarcation visible to the eye. In a formal garden, you can plan colour schemes and shape the shrubs to suit the rest of the garden. A wild rockery simply will not fit into a formal garden design.

You can make a small rockery with five, seven or nine main rocks, arranged with smaller ones. Avoid even numbers in the large rocks.

CARE

Thin out unruly plants and trim shrubs with the onset of the rains. Feed permanents like bulbs and small shrubs with well-rotted manure and leaf compost. Good rockeries are usually well drained. During the summer, the plants will need to be washed daily. If you have lifted some plants, make sure that the soil in the pockets is not washed away. Keep the plants clean and snip off dead twigs, leaves and flowers. If the area is dry and dusty, spray the plants every evening to remove dust and grime.

THINGS TO REMEMBER

- The rockery should have five times as much earth as rock.
- Choose large stones with large surface expanse.
- If using stratified rock, the strata lines should run in the same direction.
- Avoid symmetry in design. Break the lines.
- If you have the space, use the height and width of the background to maximum effect with suitable trees and large shrubs.
- The incline of the slopes should be gradual.

PLANTS FOR A ROCKERY

Ferns look best when grown in a cleft in the rocks. Fill the pocket with leaf mould and some sand; ferns need little else. Check nurseries for what is suitable. There are many hybrids available now—annuals and perennials—that are suitable for a rockery.

Annuals for a cold-weather rock garden

Freesias, anemones, alyssum, flowering succulents, dwarf lantana, candytuft, phlox, azaleas etc.

For a shady rockery

Violets (in the hills only), zephyr lilies, terrestrial orchids, ferns, dwarf bamboo, oxalis, maranta, begonias and asparagus varieties

CACTI AND OTHER SUCCULENTS

Succulent plants are found all over the world. They form a separate group because they differ so greatly in habit and form from the rest of the plant world. Succulents grow in areas with low rainfall, high temperatures and dry porous soil. It is these conditions that have shaped them—they are designed to store water and prevent evaporation. They have thick fleshy stems and leaves, and unusual shapes, a direct result of their struggle to exist in a harsh, unfriendly environment. Over time, these plants developed fantastic shapes and habits and conquered their hostile surroundings by not only surviving, but thriving. These plants can withstand heat and drought without a problem. Cacti are essentially succulents except that they have areoles (shiny hairy spots) on them.

Most of the world's cacti come from South America and Mexico, especially those which have spectacular flowers. When the Europeans first conquered the 'New World', as they call it, they came across deserts covered with plants of a strange and unusual beauty. Some were enormous columns dressed in spines, others were squat and globular. Some grew in the low-lying deserts, others grew high in the Andes mountains. Some had small inconspicuous flowers but a great many had fabulous brilliant blooms. The finest species (read flowering) come from Bolivia, Peru, Chile and Argentina. A large number of succulents are native to Africa, but they are also found in other parts of the world which have the same climatic conditions.

Collecting Cacti and Succulents

These plants are very easy to cultivate; even a beginner should have no problems. Choice of plants will be determined by personal taste, space and climate of the area. Few will survive the monsoon if not sheltered during the rains. Many are ideal for a rockery but can't be left to face the elements during the monsoon months. Unless you live in a dry area, it is best to pot them. Don't attempt a large collection if you don't have the time.

The first step when starting a collection is to decide whether they will be grown indoors or outdoors. Many varieties can withstand the worst summer and can usually be grown outdoors.

Shelter them if you see signs of scorching or discoloration. Most succulents, except the alpine varieties, do not like extremes in temperature. Some, like the epiphytes, need a moist, semi-shady location. But all succulents depend upon soil, moisture, light and temperature for their needs.

Soil

It must be light and very porous. The texture should be loose. Succulents dislike tightly packed soil. Some species like a lime-rich soil whereas others like soil rich in leaf mould. Find out what your succulents need before potting them. For those that like calcareous soil, add crushed limestone to enrich the soil. Tiny quantities of bone-meal can also be added. An ideal mixture is three parts lime-rich soil and one part leaf mould. Water this mixture and leave it for a few weeks before using. A small quantity of crushed charcoal will keep the soil porous and sweet and prevent root infection. If the soil remains moist or a green crust forms on it, throw it away and repot the plant with fresh porous soil. This soil mixture can be used for cereus varieties, harrisia, mammillarias, opuntias, lithops etc. Experts vary these proportions to suit specific needs, but don't experiment if you are a beginner, however enthusiastic you may be. Succulents such as epiphytes and rhipsalis need soil rich in leaf mould. For these plants, the soil mixture should be two parts leaf mould and one part garden soil. They do not like lime, so do not add limestone.

Planting

Many hardy specimens can be grown in the ground or in rockeries. Make sure the soil is aerated, porous and rich in calcium. If clayey, add a mixture of sandy soil, powdered limestone and some well-rotted manure in the ratio of 4:1:1.

The best time for planting is just before their flowering season, but they can be planted any time except in the winter months. If you damage the roots while potting, withhold water for a few days to allow healing. Don't plant small cacti in large pots; they should be just large enough to hold the plant. If too large, there is water rentention which causes root damage and growth is retarded as the roots take a long while to fill up the pot.

Potting

(See 'Potted Plants and Indoor Gardens' but use the soil mixture recommended in this chapter.) When the roots get pot-bound, remove the plant carefully without causing any damage to the root structure, and transfer to a larger pot. You'll be able to remove the root ball very easily if you dry out the plant first. Small plants and cuttings should be planted closer to the sides, enabling the young roots to spread quickly. They stay closer to the surface and are less likely to rot if there is too much water. Moisten the soil before planting and thereafter don't water for a couple of days. Spray lightly and keep them in the shade for a week or two before moving them into the sun.

Watering

Succulents and cacti are adapted to grow in areas of drought. Water frequently in the summer when the plant is growing. Small plants must be watered daily since they will be in small pots which hold little soil. Make sure the drainage hole is not blocked and the water runs out freely. Water sparingly in the cool months as the plant is inactive. Don't let water accumulate in the hollows and depressions where the leaves join the stems.

Some Flowering Succulents

Some of the plants mentioned below have very spectacular flowers, but all have flowers which are extremely attractive. Most people think that cacti are weird plants, prickly and thorny, and without flowers. Most amateur gardeners want flowers and may not grow succulents, especially cacti, since they (mistakenly) think there'll be no flowers. In fact they *should* grow cacti for they are terribly easy to grow, need little care and don't wilt and die if you forget to water them for a couple of days.

Mammillaria—This is a huge genus of about 150 species, mainly from Mexico. The plants are globular, oval or cylindrical, with branches or clusters. The woolly or hairy axils bear the flowers. The flowers may be purple, creamy-white, red, pink, yellow, or a green-white depending upon the species.

Nopalea cochenillifera (*Opuntia cochenillifera*)—These are tall plants, almost tree-like, with flat jointed stems. The flowers are red, tubular and with long stamens. Suitable if you have the space.

Mammillaria bodlii

Notocactus—This is a genus of very lovely plants mainly from Brazil and Uruguay. The stems may be cylindrical or globular. Many are hardy and free-flowering. The flowers are in shades of yellow, yellowish-white or red-yellow.

Opuntia—One species of this genus, *O. megacantha*, is a very common cactus in India, often called the prickly pear because the flat jointed stems are sort of pear-shaped. The genus has large and small plants, and the stems may be flat, cylindrical or globular. They are easy to grow and the flowers are usually red or yellow.

Opuntia basilaris

Some species of Opuntia have edible fruits and the plant is cultivated in Central America. O. megacantha *has large fruits of excellent quality. They are eaten fresh or dried and cooked. A favourite liquor of the people,* coloncha, *is made from these fruits.*

Parodia—These are small plants which can be globular or have elongated stems. These plants look like ordinary shrubs, not like cacti at all. They are considered a primeval form of cacti which link the cacti of today with their ancestors. The flowers are very lovely and can be golden-yellow, orange-yellow or a deep blood-red. *P. sanguiniflora* is one of the prettiest of the Parodias.

Parodia aureispina

Peireskia—Native to tropical America, some species have very large, showy flowers. The plants have woody rather than fleshy stems.

Rebutia—All the species are well worth growing. They are small, easy to grow and have beautiful flowers. The flowers may be orange-red, golden or a clear crimson. A must for pot gardens. Most grow well in semi-shade or full sun.

Cereus—This is another large genus with about 200 species. The large, funnel-shaped flowers are very showy and mainly bloom at night. They come in brilliant but delicate colours. The plants may be tree-like, shrubs or climbers.

Rebutia albiflora

E. hookeri *is a common household plant in Indonesia where it is known as Vidjaya Kusuma, meaning fragrant prosperity. The flowers bloom at night exactly at 10 pm! All the buds bloom on the same night. Owners invite friends and relatives to watch the blooms open. When they close at midnight, it's a signal for the guests to leave.*

Epiphyllum—In their natural state, these plants grow on trees in tropical jungles. The flattened leaf-like stems are long and jointed. They bear beautiful trumpet-shaped flowers, 3-7 inches across. The hybrid species are a wonderful sight when in flower.

The plants usually flower in May. Epiphyllums need rich soil with plenty of leaf compost. The soil mixture should contain one part rich soil, three parts leaf mould, one part sand and a sprinkling of bone-meal. Repotting should be done after the rainy reason is over. When grown in pots, the plants require support.

Rhipsalis—These epiphytes from South America have beautiful flowers and red or reddish berries. They require soil very rich in compost, a shady situation and humid conditions. They enjoy being frequently sprayed with water. The flowers are yellowish-white, white or greenish-white.

Zygocactus—Commonly known as the Christmas Cactus because the flowers appear around that time, this genus has just the one species. It is very popular with window-sill gardeners. They require soil rich in leaf mould, the same potting mixture used for epiphyllums. The long, glossy green spines are jointless and the flowers vary from rich carmine to white.

Glossodia

Bamboos, Grasses and Reeds

A child said *what is grass?* fetching it to me with hands full
How would I answer the child? I do not know what it is any more than he.
—Walt Whitman

A debutant gardener rarely appreciates the graceful beauty of bamboos and grasses. ('Bamboos aren't showy enough and grass is what cows eat.') But those inured to the discipline do not disregard them; they know their value. Poets and painters have found inspiration in their subtle, unobtrusive charm, and for the gardener with vision, grasses and reeds are an integral part of the garden design. He sees the loveliness in their slender form and resilient strength. No Chinese or Japanese gardener worth his salt will have a garden devoid of bamboos, and if space is constrained, more likely than not, he'll sacrifice a showy camellia to make place for the bamboo.

Grasses, bamboos and reeds belong to one of the largest plant families in the world. Some are scarcely 2 cm high, others are well over 90 ft such as the giant bamboo. And cows are not the only ones who eat grass; so do we. Man's basic food requirements—rice and bread—come from grass. Rice, wheat, oats, barley, corn and rye are all grass seeds. Without grass, life would not be half as sweet either, for sugar too, comes from grass. Grasses are also used in the paper, perfume, edible oil, fibre and adhesive industries. Even land reclamation needs grass if it is to be successful. Certain grasses like manna grass prevent soil erosion by binding loose sand with their roots.

For the newly-initiated, grass in the garden begins and ends with the lawn. There is no doubting the role of grass in lawn-making but there are other grasses besides those used

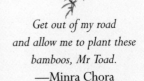

*Get out of my road
and allow me to plant these
bamboos, Mr Toad.*
—Minra Chora

in lawns. There are beautiful ornamental grasses which, like bamboos, can be used as separate garden features. They can be effectively used in island beds, to make hedges and windbreaks, for edging and to provide the contrast in mixed plantings. Many grasses bear lovely feathery plumes and some can be extremely stately. But the most impressive of all grasses are the bamboos. Airy, graceful and elegant, their supple, pliant stems arc with every gust of wind and few people are untouched by the music in their rustling leaves. Our earliest musical instruments come from grasses—Pan's reed pipes and Krishna's flute couldn't have been made without grasses. There's grass, and then there's grass, as every good gardener knows, and lawn grass is the least of them.

All grasses are fast-growing plants, but the bamboo's growth rate is truly marvellous—some species can grow as much as 50 cm a day! Each shoot produces a sharp point that thrusts upward, forcing itself though the thickest masses of branches until it reaches its ultimate height. Only then will it begin to branch and produce leaves. Bamboos are invaluable to the people of Asia and in many areas supply all their basic needs. Homes are made from the stems; tender shoots are eaten as a vegetable; hats and baskets are woven from spliced bamboos; and even utensils are made from them. Bamboos are used to make furniture and boats, paper and pickles. In Java, the black filaments found in the joints of certain species were used to execute criminals. These filaments, when mixed with food, get caught in the throat, causing inflammation which results in death.

SOIL

Some bamboos can grow in the poorest of soils; others require rich, moist soil. In general, a rich, deep, cool, moist soil is suitable for almost all species of bamboos. On the whole, bamboos dislike extremes of temperature and dry heat, but there are many hardy species that thrive even in the northern plains with their harsh summers. Reeds and grasses can grow and thrive in soil sorely lacking in nutrients. Some reeds need

All flesh is as grass, and the glory of man as the flower of grass. The grass withereth and the flower thereof falleth away.
—The Bible

wet, soggy soil like that of boglands, others grow quite well in dry, sandy soil. There are bamboos and grasses for every type of climatic condition and soil.

CARE

All but the giant varieties of bamboos can be potted. Ornamental reeds and grasses also do well in pots.

Some grasses and reeds grow in the full sun; others need shade or partial shade. But there are many varieties that are not particular at all—hot sun, semi-shade, it's all the same to them. Some bamboos and ornamental reeds can be finicky, but you don't have to grow them. If you're not familiar with the various types of reeds and bamboos, take a walk in the parks and gardens of your region; you'll get an idea of what grows best in the area.

Bamboos, long grasses and reeds must be thinned to keep the clumps manageable. In a small garden, huge clumps will eat into the space, but in a large garden, ornamental grasses can bring in the wild, open prairies.

WHAT TO GROW

This will depend entirely upon the space you have, particularly with bamboos and giant grasses.

BAMBOOS

There's an incredible range of bamboos to choose from, most of which come from East Asia. But there are many species which are natives of South America. Being evergreens, they can be used very effectively in gardens.

Golden Bamboo (*Phyllostachys aurea*)

This ornamental bamboo is very popular among the Japanese. It has deep golden stems, sometimes veined with green. Suitable for a small to medium-sized garden. It can also be grown in large pots. If watered deeply and planted in soil rich in compost, it will thrive even in the northern plains. Plant where it can be sheltered from the midday sun.

Black Bamboo (*Phyllostachys nigra*)

This is a tall bamboo which can grow over 20 ft tall. The young stems are a dark purplish-black. Does best in cool wet regions.

Oriental Bamboo (*Bambusa Siamensis*)

This is a very graceful bamboo with feathery plumes. It grows about 30 ft high.

Dwarf Bamboos

These bamboos rarely grow more than 3 ft high and can be grown in shady balconies or terraces. They are very suitable for ferneries and shady banks in the garden. *B. pygmaea* grows only about

Bamboo

11 inches high. Other varieties of dwarf bamboos include fortunei, aurea, striata and ruscifolia. *Shibataea kumasasa* is a highly unusual dwarf bamboo. The stems are not straight but zigzag to a height of about 3 ft.

> *Summer grasses,*
> *all that remains*
> *of soldiers' dreams.*
> —Basho

GRASSES AND REEDS (TALL)

Clumps of grasses can be very attractive near ponds or pools. Don't allow them to get too thick if the garden is small. They will not do for a handkerchief-sized garden.

Pampas Grass (*Cortaderia selloana*)

This grass can grow up to 8 ft tall. It bears lovely silvery-white plumes. In South America, its native land, it is used to manufacture paper.

Elephant Grass (*Saccharum arundinaceum*)

This is a tall, coarse grass which has white plumes and blue-green leaves.

Giant Reed (*Arundo donax 'Variegata'*)

This grass can grow upto 8 ft high and likes full sun and light, sandy soil.

SMALL GRASSES

Job's Tears (*Coix lacryma-jobi*)

This is a delicate-looking grass which bears hard, white seeds that hang down like teardrops. The Chinese thought they had miraculous powers and made necklaces and rosaries with them. The Burmese eat them and use them to make flour.

Greater Quaking Grass (*Briza maxima*)

This lovely grass bears several pearly, heart-shaped flower-heads which dangle from thread-like attachments on the stem. It likes a cool climate.

Feather Grass (*Stipa pannata*)

This is a very pretty grass with feathery, white flower-heads. It grows well in the hills, and in the cool season in the plains.

Bamboo & Grasses

Among the prettiest small grasses are Hare's Tail (*Lagurus ovatus*) and Squirrel Tail (*Hordeum jubatum*). The common names describe the flower-heads.

- Visit your nursery before you plant grasses. They may have species and varieties not common to the area.
- Bamboos and grasses are propagated by division. Many grasses can be grown from seeds. Best time for division is during the rains.
- When planting in containers, the soil should be rich in compost, light and porous. Do not bury the root ball too deep. As most grasses and bamboos have fibrous roots, wide and fairly deep containers are most suitable.
- Clean bamboo clumps and cut out the old stumps. Bamboos take a long time to flower after which the parent clump dies.
- There are hundreds of varieties and species of bamboos, and good nurseries stock at least a dozen unusual varieties, so you have plenty to choose from.

Roses

And if you was to see my roziz,
As is a boon to all men's noziz—
You'd fall upon your back and scream—
'O lawk, O crikey! It's a dream!'

—Edward Lear

Roses are probably the oldest flowering plants known to man. There are fossil remains in museums, some truly hoary, which remind us that they were there long before nature thought of us. The ones found in the Oligocene deposits in Colorado, North America, are all of 35 million years old! Oddly enough, all rose fossils have been found only in the northern hemisphere; apparently no roses grew in the wild in the southern hemisphere.

Roses are one of the earliest flowers grown by man, purely for their beauty, and because he could eat them or use them in medicine, both of which he did later. Roses were being grown in China and Babylon as early as the third millennium BC, and by 500 BC, the library in Beijing had 500 books on roses alone. Sargon, king of Babylon (2845-2768 BC), is said to have sent rose trees to his capital at Akkad and in the ceremonial buildings, roses were carved on the sills. Nebuchadnezzar's principal palace had roses carved on the columns and, though there is no proof, surely there were roses growing in his famous Hanging Gardens. The earliest painting of a rose is from Bronze Age Crete, depicted in a fresco in the palace of King Minos at Knossos. It is a six-petalled rose, probably *R. richardii*, the holy rose of Abyssinia, complete with hips and leaves. The Medes and Persians were cultivating roses as early as twelfth century BC; the flowers were used in rituals and religious ceremonies. Egypt was famous in the ancient world for her cultivated roses and nurserymen who were highly skilled and experts at grafting. No wonder Cleopatra could have the floor of her barge inches deep in rose petals and the sails drenched with scent made of rose oil when she set out to meet Mark Antony.

Ancient Greeks and Romans too set great store by the rose. Sappho (600 BC) put the rose at the pinnacle of flower hierarchy:

> If Jove would give the leafy bowers,
> A queen for all their world of flowers,
> The rose would be the choice of Jove,
> And blush the queen of every grove.

The Romans' passion for the rose was nothing short of excessive. According to Seneca, Romans constructed special greenhouses, heated by pipes filled with hot water, to get out-of-season flowers. During their ceremonies, roses were used on an astonishing scale. At banquets, roses were worn in extravagant garlands and wreaths; rose petals were strewn on the couches and floors and were floated in cups of wine. When insufficient, shiploads of roses were imported from North Africa. Cicero writes that Verres, the governor of Sicily, was carried about in a litter, the cushions of which were stuffed with rose petals. This extravagance was due to the belief that the rose was a protection against drunkenness, a chronic ailment of that society. At one lavish banquet during the reign of Emperor Elagabalus (218-222 AD), showers of rose petals were poured through apertures in the ceiling in such quantities that many of the guests literally drowned in rose petals. In Sybaris (from which we get the word sybarite), the inhabitants were so given to luxury that people slept on mattresses filled with rose petals—literally a 'bed of roses'!

The ancient Persians too, were great lovers of the rose. When Cyrus the Great conquered Babylon in 539 BC, he did not destroy the rose cult and was often found tending the plants in his garden. Sixth century Persia was a land of roses, and not surprisingly, the word 'Gul' in Persian means both 'flower' and 'rose'. In Persia, the rose motif is seen everywhere—in their carpets, paintings, architecture and tapestries.

Today, wherever a rose can be grown, it is. There are about 250 species of roses—about 150 in the wild—and tens of thousands of cultivars. Roses are as varied as the regions they come from. Some can be as large as saucers, others so tiny they can be slipped through a ring. There are climbers and ramblers, shrubs and miniatures. Some rose species can even be called trees. There are scores of old cultivars and hundreds of modern hybrids. Roses may be white, red, pink, yellow and every shade of these colours. Today we even have mauve and green roses but a true blue has escaped the hybridists. In Australia they have been trying to produce one for years. There's a fortune to be made for anyone who can produce a blue rose.

Wild roses grow true from seed and all the roses we know have come from these 150 wild species. All roses, except the damasks, are summer flowering. The damasks, which flower in summer and autumn, were highly regarded by the people of the ancient world. All these old roses are disease-resistant and almost all have single, five-petalled flowers. Their colours range from white and pale pink to deep pink and crimson. The flowers have a delicate charm and the hips are brightly coloured. The old shrub roses are natural hybrid species roses and occur when a wild rose gets pollen from another species. Rose-breeding began when man collected these natural varieties and cultivated them. And he's never stopped since.

Rose oil or 'attar', also called 'otto' of roses (a corruption of the word attar), is one perfume which still has no satisfactory synthetic substitute and is one of the world's most expensive oils. Avicenna or Ibn Sena, the Persian philosopher and physician (980–1037), first extracted rose oil by distillation. Today, most of the world's attar comes from Bulgaria. East of Sophia lies the Valley of Roses, 20 miles wide and 100 miles long, and it is filled with rose gardens. It takes one ton of rose petals to produce one pound of rose oil!

The history of the rose is long and convoluted. In the ancient world, roses from the Middle East were bred with European roses. They travelled with the conquering Persian, Greek and Roman armies, but earlier civilizations too saw an exchange of roses. *Rosa alba,* one of the oldest cultivars, was grown in ancient Greece. A thirteenth century writer, Albertus Magnus, describes it as a white garden rose which often has as many as fifty or sixty petals. The Medes and Persians were cultivating *R. gallica,* sometimes called *R. rubra,* as early as the second century BC. The Greeks grew it in Miletus in the fourth century BC from where the Romans imported it. The Chinese were cultivating their roses such as *R. chinensis* more than 2500 years ago, and these roses travelled along the caravan routes into Central Asia.

The roses we know today come from breeding four Chinese roses with European cultivars. The first China stud arrived in Europe in 1790. By 1860, Japanese seeds reached France, leading to the dwarf rose that flowers repeatedly. In the 1920s, the first hybrid Polyanthas were produced. The diligence of gardeners over the last 3500 years have given us the thousands of cultivars we have today. We owe them more than a heart-felt prayer.

There are only two roses native to India—the Himalayan Musk Rose (*R. brumonii*) and *R. webbiana*—though many experts think the latter is a naturalized rose. Roses are not mentioned in any ancient Indian text, from the Vedas to Kalidasa. Sanskrit has no word for the rose. Some claim that *shatapatri* refers to the rose, but Apte says it is a lotus. Monier-Williams however, says it is a 'flower, a kind of rose' but also goes on to say that it's a lotus that opens in the day. Had roses been cultivated in India, Kalidasa, that great

> The word rosarium *is the Roman word for a rose garden. A rose nursery was called a* rostum.

poet and passionate lover of flowers, would have eulogized them as he did the lotus, siris, hibiscus, jasmine and a host of other flowers in his poems. He most definitely wouldn't have left the rose out. Rose cultivation in India truly began after the Mughal conquest. By Jehangir's time, they were all the rage because the Emperor and Empress favoured the flower above all others. Nobles and courtiers filled their gardens with roses but there were not too many varieties seen in their gardens.

Roses come from a family that has 200 genera and 2000 species. They come from the same family as plums, apples, pears, strawberries and raspberries—*Rosaceae.* Roses are found in the wild in all the cool temperate regions, and grow best in a temperate climate but are also widely grown in the tropics. Roses fall naturally into 2 groups—the roses from West Asia and Europe, and those from East Asia, especially China and Japan. All the former, except the damasks, are summer flowers; the latter, like the damasks, flower from summer through autumn. From the crossing of the Eastern and Western cultivars come the perpetuals, which are free-flowering and robust.

> *O how much more doth beauty*
> *beauteous seem,*
> *By that sweet ornament which*
> *truth doth give!*
> *The rose looks fair but fairer*
> *it we deem*
> *For that sweet odour which in*
> *it doth live.*
> —Shakespeare

Almost all the old roses, cultivars and hybrids, were very sweetly scented, but the modern hybrids are showy, beautiful blooms without a trace of fragrance. The hybridists have sacrificed soul for appearance. Today in most Indian rose gardens, it is these showy, scentless blooms that are grown. A great pity, since there are literally hundreds of scented roses available and the modern hybrids, for all their beauty, are poor substitutes. A rose, like the jasmine, is synonymous with scent, and these scentless blooms really ought to be called something else—anything but a rose.

In the northern plains, roses bloom from the end of January to early April. But if kept in semi-shade, will continue to bloom till the monsoon arrives, though the flowers are poorer in quality. In the hills and more temperate regions in the plains, they will flower from early summer upto the onset of the cold season. The best roses for the plains are Teas, Hybrid Teas and Bourbons. Hybrid perpetuals, which are comparatively new roses, also do well in the plains and come in many shades and colours. The old summer roses do not like the heat of the plains but in the hills you can grow any rose you like and it will thrive.

A radish for the stomach
A rose for the nose
That's what's good for all
As everybody knows.
—Anon

SOIL AND MANURE

Roses like rich, loamy soil which is unlikely to dry out in summer, especially if the plants are in pots. Do not overmanure the plants as they will produce more leaves than flowers. The plants should be manured just before the flowering period. If your soil is dry and sandy, you will have to enrich it with farmyard manure and compost to get good results. Dig in large quantities of manure to make the soil water retentive.

Potting mixture for roses

Two parts soil, one part well-rotted farmyard manure. Good garden centres stock sheep manure. Add one heaped tablespoon bone-meal.

PREPARATION OF BEDS AND PITS

Good drainage is very essential for the well-being of roses. Dig a hole 3-4 ft deep and 2 ft across. Mix the soil with well-rotted cattle manure in the ratio of two to one and refill, raising the bed 3-4 inches above ground level. When planting, remove the topsoil, leaving enough to cushion the root ball of the plant. Fill in the pit and press firmly around the base of the shrub.

PLANTING

When planting, the most important thing to remember is that the soil is dug deep and well-loosened, in and around the pit. The plant should be firmly pressed down. There's nothing a rose dislikes more than being buffeted by the endless winds which blow during the monsoon months. There are two planting seasons but the main one is in the rainy season. The smaller season is from November to early December. In the hills, roses are best planted in March/April. If planted when the weather is very cold, the plants will bloom only in the following season.

It is far simpler to go to a good nursery and buy a young plant than to grow one from cuttings or layers. Many roses need to be grafted on a sturdier stock, and that is something most beginners and experts with little time would like to avoid. When buying plants, make sure you chose healthy ones. Look out for leaf spot or leaf curl. The leaves should have a healthy glow.

Remove the plant from the container and cut off weak straggly roots. If the soil around the root ball is very sticky and clayey, remove it gently without damaging the fine roots. Soak the root ball in a bucket of water before you remove the soil. If the soil is fine, do not disturb the earth around the root ball. Place it in the pit and cover with soil. The top-most roots should lie a couple of inches below soil level. If the plant is grafted, the joint should be at least two inches above the level of the soil, so that you can remove the suckers easily.

Roses in the ground should be at least 6 ft apart, especially the hybrid perennials. If you are growing them in pots, get the largest pots available, unless they are miniature roses. After planting, keep the bed clear of weeds, and reasonably moist. Shade the plants for a few weeks until they recover from the shock of transplanting. Keep an eye on the young plants, and remove all suckers growing below the root level, if grafted. Do not allow the plant to flower for at least five months; allow it to build up its strength. Pick off buds as they appear. If planted in February, the plant will grow steadily until the monsoon and be ready for pruning in October.

RESTING

Roses have a definite dormant period and this is very essential for roses grown in the plains. In the hills, temperate plants naturally shed their leaves and become dormant; in the plains, one has to induce dormancy. If not allowed to rest, the plant will keep growing, weaken and die much before its allotted time. Given the right conditions, roses can live

> *What's the use? I look for roses*
> *but the thorn bed's all I find.*
> *To a garb of life in tatters I must*
> *be it seems, resigned.*
> —Ahmed Pasha

for more than a thousand years—and that is no exaggeration. There are two contenders for planting the oldest living rose tree. Some claim Charlemagne planted it in the Cloisters of Hildesheim Abbey in Germany. Others say it was planted by Kaiser Ludwig. Either way, this rose tree is over a thousand years old. The Cathedral and most of the town were destroyed in 1945, but the root stock remained undamaged, and though many shoots were burnt, some survived and the tree is now 30 ft high! When examined in 1950, experts found it was a Dog Rose (*R. canina*).

> *A rose bush lives five years, after which its prime is past, unless it is pruned by burning. With this plant, the flower also becomes inferior as it ages . . .*
> *If the rose if burnt or cut over, it bears better flowers; for then, they say the roses ar improved.*
> —Theophrastus
> (Father of Botany)

Prune your roses in October if in the plains, and expose the roots. Remove 6 inches of topsoil; less if it is in a pot, and bare the roots. Withhold water for a few days. After that, the soil is mixed with well-rotted cattle manure and replaced. Begin watering when the new shoots appear, which is usually in ten days. As the buds begin to appear, feed the plant with a good organic feed every two weeks.

WATERING

In dry climates where the weather is hot, roses should be watered every evening. Give the plants a thorough soaking. In cool or moist regions, they need to be watered twice or thrice a week. Potted plants may need more frequent watering. In wet areas, water only when required, which is when you see the soil drying out.

DISBUDDING

If you want large, showy blooms, you have to disbud the shrub. This is usually done to plants which are grown for flower shows. You will have fewer blooms but they will be healthy and much larger. A stalk usually carries three buds. Keep the healthiest (usually the centre one), and remove the others. Modern hybrid shrubs often produce just the one bud. If there are two, cut off the lower one. If on the other hand you prefer a profusion of smaller blooms, don't bother to disbud. The flowers will be smaller but they are a far lovelier sight, and you're saved the bother. If it is a scented rose, it will be criminal to disbud. Large is not necessarily more beautiful.

ROSE PRUNING

Pruning roses gives beginners the willies. Pruning requires a certain skill, and knowledge of the plant and its habits—all roses don't behave in the same manner. If you have doubts, the best would be to go to a nursery and ask the nurseryman what you should do. But pruning is not all that difficult and there is nothing esoteric or mystical about it. Understand and observe your plant to see whether the buds appear on the previous year's growth or the current year's growth and you'll do fine. Shakespeare summed it up nicely, 'Superfluous branches we lop away, that bearing boughs may live.'

   In the wild, roses constantly throw out new shoots—all the plant's energy goes into the production of new shoots. The pruner's job is to hasten the rejection of older wood *before* it dies naturally. The pruner must encourage the plant to make more healthy limbs. First arm yourself with a pair of secateurs or a sharp pruning knife. Stand in front of your plant and study it. You cannot hack and hew as you please. Ask yourself: does it flower on new wood or the previous year's growth? does it flower on the main stem or lateral shoots? Is it vigorous in its growing habit?

   There is all sorts of conflicting advice about pruning. Stick to the basics and you won't go wrong. The fine-tuning will come only after some experience, when you have more intimate knowledge of the art.

When

In the plains, the best time for pruning is October; in the hills it is in March. If pruned earlier, the plants tend to produce more foliage.

How

When pruning roses, wear a long-sleeved blouse unless your don't mind being viciously scratched. The October pruning is severe—only four to five branches are left on a two to three year old plant. The numbers increase as the plant grows older. Cut the branches back to the third or fourth 'eye' or leaf bud. The new branches will develop from these. Choose an eye that is pointing outward. For climbers, remove all damaged and dead branches. Remove blind shoots, new growth that the plant keeps throwing out.

Retain only three to four main branches. The rest should be cut back to the base. Cut off all old wood that does not produce healthy shoots. The cuts should be at an angle of about 45°.

If your plant is grafted, remove all suckers from below the graft. Get to the end of the suckers—if cut at soil level, they will strengthen and multiply rapidly, and your plant will revert, that is, become like the stock. The grafted scion will die out. Trace the suckers right down to the roots and then pull them off.

With young plants, one has to build a strong and sturdy frame. Only then can you decide how you want to shape it. The same methods are used for pruning a hedge or bush. The difference lies in how severely you apply the secatuers.

Pruning Tips

   ✿ Most climbers flower on the previous year's growth.
   ✿ Hybrid Teas and Floribundas flower on new wood, that is, the current year's growth.

A BRIEF CLASSIFICATION OF ROSES

Rosa gallica, R. damascena, R. centifolia—These and all their natural cultivars are old world roses which flower in summer. The Provence roses are usually red, though there is a white variety. The heavily perfumed cabbage roses are natives of Asia Minor and Caucasia and they flower profusely. Moss Roses (*R. centifolia muscosa*) are related to the Provence roses and look like them except for a moss-like growth on the stems. Damask Roses which are the offspring of *R. gallica* are very old roses. They are semi-double, white, striped or blotched pink. These are hardy roses and need little pruning.

Hybrid Chinas, Bourbons, Damask Perpetuals

Hybrid Chinas are the result of crossing China Roses with their European cousins. These are not as free-flowering as the Bourbons, but the Bourbons are not quite as robust. The Damasks are very heavily scented and remain in flower for a long time.

Briar Roses

There are many species of Briar Roses and most are summer flowering. Natives of Persia, Austria and the Himalayas have been around for a very long time. Some, such as the sweet briars, have fragrant foliage as well. These roses are usually single and have pink or white flowers.

China Roses

These are perpetuals and very popular with the hybridists. They are semi-scandent, very hardy, and their flowering season is long. They are used for hedges, or allowed to ramble over walls and banks.

Teas

These are sweet-scented perpetuals. The plants are slender and free-flowering and the blooms richly coloured. They were very popular until the Hybrid Teas came on the scene. They come in a lovely range of colours—blush, apricot, apricot-yellow and a pure yellow.

Musk Roses (R. Moschata)

The ones seen in today's gardens are hybrids of the old cultivars and are usually climbers.

The old cultivars were grown extensively in China, Persia and North Africa, and are related to the Himalayan Musk Rose. The flowers are borne in clusters and have a musk-like scent.

Banksias (R. banksiae alba)

These are vigorous climbers and bear pendulous trusses of small fragrant flowers which grow on lateral shoots. A double variety from China has a wonderful violet-like scent.

Bourbons

These perpetuals form a species which evolved from crossing a Damask with a China Rose. The flowers are not large and come in shades of pink, blush and white. The roses have glossy leaves and the flowers are very fragrant. Bourbons were grown extensively in India a hundred years ago but are hardly seen today.

Hybrid Perpetuals

Many crossings have been made to produce these varieties. They flower marvellously in the hills, where it is not too wet. The branches have fewer thorns and many varieties are scented. They may be white, pink, crimson, yellow or a clear red.

Hybrid Teas

These are extremely popular roses. These hardy plants can take aridity and heat, and they flower profusely. The plant's habits resembles its Tea parent. The flowers may be white, cream, yellow, copper-rose, pink, flame, bright red or crimson.

The 'Omar Khayyam' is a subtle rose with pink flowers and a delicious fragrance. In 1884, seeds from Omar Khayyam's grave in Nishapur were taken to the Royal Botanical Gardens in Kew. From the raised seedlings, a cutting was planted on the grave of Edward Fitzgerald who translated the Rubaiyat.

The rose very early became a symbol of love (red), peace (white), beauty, pain (the thorns), and secrecy. The term sub-rosa which literally means 'under the rose', implies a conversation held in secrecy not to be repeated. People noticed how the petals enfolded the centre, and the term was adopted as a political symbol in fifth century BC when Greece was attacked by Xerxes, the Persian king. The generals discussed their strategies in a rose garden and were subsequently victorious. Whenever secret matters were discussed, a rose was suspended from the ceiling. In Rome, when people wore rose wreaths on their heads and the halls were festooned with roses, it meant that nothing said was to be divulged—not even if inebriated! Later, carvings of roses took the place of the flowers. The Roman Catholic Church adopted the symbol and carved a rose on the confessional to signify that what was said was said in confidence.

Polyantha (*R. Multiflora*)

'Poly-Pom-poms'—These miniature roses occurred after years of crossing. As their name indicates, they bear many clusters of blooms. The plants are free-flowering, hardy and very suitable for pot cultivation. They do not like a moist climate. The flowers come in shades of pink, red, yellow and white. Some may be a vivid orange-red.

Few nurseries or *maalis* will know a rose by its classified name. You can't ask a *maali* to give you a Tuscany Superb or a Quatre Saisons. All you'll get is a blank stare. Some good nurseries will be able to give you a Bourbon or a Tea but not any particular Bourbon such as Mrs Bosanquet, or a Marie Van Houtte which is a Tea Rose. The safest bet would be to ask him what roses he's got, whether they are shrubs or climbers, their colour and form, and whether they are scented or not. Then make your choice. In cities like Calcutta, Bangalore and Chandigarh, it is quite possible to get what you want; the nurserymen there are better informed.

Feeding

Just before flowering, roses plants must be properly manured and fed with some liquid feed every eight to ten days. There are many organic rose feeds available in the market.

The gooseberry, respaberry, and roses, all three,
With strawberries under them truly agree.
—Thomas Tusser

SYMBIOTIC ROSE

The rose, in general, dislikes plants growing around it. But there are some plants that do it a world of good and, in return, get something from it.

Garlic and roses are mutually beneficial. The garlic prevents black spot, keeps aphids away, and increases the scent of the rose. Roses also enjoy a compost made of garlic and onion plants.

Chives, a member of the onion family, is a good companion for roses.

French marigolds, when grown near roses, keep nematodes and eelworms away, and the plant becomes healthier.

Parsley too, is good for roses. Gardeners in Europe have known this for a long time.

Roses like *mignonette* and *lupins* growing near them. Their collective scent is unforgettable.

Many *herbs* make good companions for roses. The roses seem to be the better for their presence, perhaps because these medicinal plants repel a number of insects. Lavender, rosemary, origanum and thyme are all good for roses.

EAT YOUR ROSES

One of the nicest things about roses is you can feast your eyes on their beauty, inhale their heady perfume *and* eat them. Their taste is as exquisite as their scent. Roses are not used in traditional Indian cooking, and rose water, which is used in some sweets and Avadhi cooking, owes its presence to the influence of Islamic culinary traditions. But Greeks, Persians and Romans knew the unique taste of roses. The Chinese are said to have used roses in ragouts and at a famous feast in China, whole flowers were dressed and served. Modern palates are unfamiliar with the taste of roses and the loss is ours.

Roses are not only good to eat, they are good for your health as well. Culpeper, the seventeenth century English herbalist rated them highly: 'Red roses do strengthen the heart, the stomach and the liver, and the retentive faculty. The white and red roses are cooling and drying, and yet the white is said to exceed the red in both properties.' In early times, roses were as much admired for their beauty as their medicinal and cosmetic properties and during World War II, rose-hip syrup was a valuable dietary supplement. Today we know that rose-hips are a rich source of vitamin C.

The only preparation needed is to 'heel' the rose petals, that is, to remove the white portion at the base of each petal. Needless to say, the petals must first be washed and rinsed carefully.

For all the following recipes, use scented red or pink roses.

Rose-Chicken Patties

This recipe is based on a medieval English one.

    350 g cooked chicken
    50 g rose petals
    2 eggs
    50 g bread crumbs
    Salt and pepper (to taste)
    A few drops of Worcestershire sauce
    3-4 teaspoons of milk
    A pinch of sugar
    10 crushed almonds
    A few strands of saffron

Mince the chicken and blend the rose petals in a mixer or pound them in a mortar. Beat the eggs and mix with minced chicken, rose petals and bread crumbs. Season with sugar, salt and pepper, and mix in the almonds, Worcestershire sauce, saffron and milk. Shape into patties and fry in a vegetable oil till golden brown on both sides. Serve with French fries and a crisp green salad.

Rose-petal honey

Prepare 50 g of rose petals and put them in an enamel pan with 250 g of honey. Boil for about 10 minutes and then strain the honey while still warm into an air-tight jar.

Rose-petal sandwiches

Use rye or wholewheat bread. Cut the slices very thin. Mash some cream-cheese with a couple of teaspoons of milk, and salt and pepper to taste. Add 50 g (or as much as you need) of finely chopped scented red rose petals. Blend together and spread on the bread. Close the sandwiches and remove the crusts if you wish. Cut and serve with a scattering of rose petals on the sandwiches.

Rose pancakes

These are utterly delicious and can be served like crepe Suzettes. They make a truly epicurean finale to a dinner.

    4 egg yolks
    100 g flour
    150 ml cream
    50 g castor sugar
    3 tablespoon rose water
    A pinch of nutmeg
    Chopped rose petals

Blend all the ingredients in a liquidizer, then add the petals to make a thin batter. Cook the pancakes, making them nice and thin. Serve hot with lemon and sugar.

Crystallized rose petals

Garden-fresh roses are the best, but if you don't have them, get three or four scented red roses in full bloom. Remove petals from the flower-heads and discard any that tear. Wipe each petal carefully and lay it on a tray on greaseproof paper.

Lightly beat the white of one egg and coat each petal with it. Both sides must be perfectly coated. Now dip the petals into castor sugar and place them on the tray, making sure they don't touch each other. Put them out in the sun, and when they are absolutely dry, store in an air-tight container with a sheet of waxed paper between the layers. Use them to decorate cakes, ice-creams and deserts.

Rose-petal ice-cream

    2 egg whites
    175 ml rosé wine
    2 tablespoons fine white sugar
    150 ml double cream
    30 g icing sugar
    1 large cupful scented red rose petals (heeled)
    40 g icing sugar

Put the rose petals, wine and sugar into a blender and make a smooth paste. Beat the cream with icing sugar until it is thick, and stir in the rose mixture. Beat the egg whites until stiff and fold into the cream. Put into a container, cover and freeze. Serve with a garnish of crystallized rose petals.

Rose-petal vinegar

Take 300 ml white wine vinegar. Prepare 50 g of scented red rose petals put both into an air-tight glass jar and set it out in the sun for three weeks. Then strain into a bottle and keep in a dark cupboard.

Rose-petal jam

    1 kg rose petals (heeled)
    1 kg sugar
    1 litre water
    Juice of 4 lemons
    A pinch of nutmeg

Simmer the rose petals in water until they are tender. Add sugar, lemon juice and nutmeg, and boil rapidly until the jam sets. Put into clean air-tight jars and store.

Roses can also be used in salads and fruit salads.

Rose water

Fresh rose water lasts only for a couple of days but is very easy to prepare.

Gather your roses early on a fine morning—this is the time when they are most aromatic. You will need about 500 gm of petals.

Put the petals in an enamel saucepan and cover with water. Don't use hard water as it has too many chemicals. Put the pan on the stove and bring it slowly to boil. If you have an oven, put the petals and water into the oven (450° F) and bring to boil. This method draws out more scent from the petals. Simmer for 15 minutes. The water will turn a lovely pink if you use red or deep pink roses. Allow the liquid to cool and strain into a bottle. Store in the refrigerator.

When roses are not in season, you can make rose water from the dried petals. Use three-fourth the quantity given for fresh rose petals.

> *Red rose water is well-known, it is cooling, cordial, refreshing, quickening the weak and faint spirits.*
> —Nicholas Culpeper

Orchids and Other Exotica

In my garden
Side by side
Native plants, foreign plants
Growing together.
                    —Emperor Meiji

The 'Exotic' is that which is unknown, unfamiliar, from another land. Many will consider the Bird of Paradise an exotic flower, but in South Africa, where it grows in the wild, it's almost a weed, prosaically known as the Cranebill. On the other hand, something familiar may still be remarkably strange and exotic like some orchids. Orchids are exotic flowers even in Sikkim or South America, familiar or not, though they are native to these places. People eat them, wear them, grow them by the hundreds and yet they remain exotic. Some are outlandishly beautiful.

ORCHID

'You may have my head but not my orchids!'
                    —Cheng Ssu-hsiao

Cheng Ssu-hsiao is one of China's most revered painters, and lived when the country was being systematically raped by the Mongols. Chen was arrested and imprisoned, but when the warlords forced him to paint, he famously said, 'You may have my head but not my orchids.' Later he made an exquisite painting of uprooted orchids, one of the most subtle expressions of political protest.

Of all the flowers in the world, orchids probably head the list of exotica. The Chinese

Coelogyne nitida with *Gloriosa lily*

Fuschia with Sweet Pea

have cultivated them for 5000 years and tomes have been written about them. The earliest comprehensive text is *A Treatise on Orchids of Chin-Cheng* by Chao Shih-keng, published in 1233. But many earlier books mention orchids.

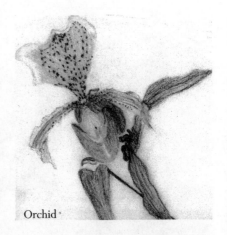

Orchid

The ancient Greeks were familiar with some orchids. *The Herbal of Dioscordes* mentions several Mediterranean orchids. Many orchids have swollen bulbs which lie above the soil, and the Greeks seeing the resemblance between testes and the bulbs proclaimed these orchids aphrodisiacal. Ancient Greeks believed in the Theory of Signatures which states that the shape of the plant indicates its medicinal use. *Vanda tsselata* in ancient India was eaten by women who believed that by doing so they would have sons. In eighteeth century Europe, men and women ate the tubers, and farmers fed them to rams, stallions and bulls to encourage them to copulate. Dioscorides called this orchid Satyrion, after the lustful beast-men. In fact the word 'orchid' comes from the Greek word *orchis*, meaning *testis*. In the Middle Ages, people in Europe believed that orchid bulbs aroused unholy satyric passion. Legend has it that Orchid was the son of a nymph and a satyr, a fellow of unbridled passion. During the festival of Bacchus, drunk on wine, Orchid attacked a priestess and the crowd tore him limb from limb. His father pleaded with the gods to restore him and the gods turned him into a flower which was imbued with his nature. Oddly enough, the notion is not so wild for now we know that in the plant kingdom, it is the orchid that produces the largest number of seeds—millions of them per plant!

To the Chinese however, the orchid is the symbol of the scholar—unassuming, chaste and ascetic. Orchids were symbols of beauty, love, grace and refinement. There is scarcely a Chinese painter who has not painted orchids. 'Paint bamboo when you're angry, orchids when you're happy,' was the advice given to painters. Orchid cultivation was a popular pastime of the scholars and nobility in tenth century China. The ancient Chinese grew flowers for themselves, for their beauty; the Greeks grew plants for their uses, which says much about their respecive natures.

The ancient Mayans and Aztecs used the pods of the vanilla orchid to flavour their chocolate drink. Emperor Montezuma was served 'chocolatl' (the Indian word for chocolate) in a golden goblet before he visited his wives. And the drink was always flavoured with vanilla.

Orchids have been been around for quite a while, but the gorgeous, exotic blooms of South America and the far East made their way to Europe only after colonization. The nineteenth century saw the speed of orchid-mania throughout England and Europe, much like the tulip fever that had gripped Holland earlier. Plant hunters braved high mountains, deep jungles and cannibals in their quest for exotic orchids. Fortunes were paid for some species and orchid collecting became big business. Hunters searched in secrecy and risked their lives to find new species. Orchids were the most expensive flowers in the market. They were the aritocrats among flowers. Fortunately they don't cost an arm and a leg now; easy hybridization and cloning have made them relatively inexpensive, but by no means cheap. The mad scramble may be over but they are still everyone's idea of an exotic bloom, and still fairly expensive.

Orchids come from the second largest family in the plant kingdom. There are 20,000 known species, and at least 80,000 hybrids and clones have been registered. Orchids grow almost everywhere—on high mountains, deep in the tropical jungles, in semi-desert regions and even in the freezing Arctic zone. Some orchids bear blooms the size of a man's palm; others are so tiny, the whole plant is no larger than a thumbnail. They bear flowers in all colours except black, and the shapes are as diverse as the hues. Orchids produce vast quantities of seeds and are great colonizers. They are very adaptable and can grow in many climatic conditions. In 1882, when Krakatoa in Hawaii erupted, all life on the mountain was destroyed. The first plant to reappear was an orchid.

Orchids are truly remarkable—some are epiphytes, others terrestrial, some autotrophic (able to make food from simple inorganic compounds), others saprophytic (able to live on dead or decaying matter). Many people mistakenly think that orchids are parasites; they are nothing of the sort.

The majority of orchids come from the tropical and sub-tropical regions of the world. The largest number come from the jungles of South America but there are a great many native to north-east India (especially Sikkim), Indonesia, China and the Philippines. In Malyasia, orchids are used to sprinkle water around the house where a death has occurred to prevent the ghost of the dead person from haunting the living!

Habits and requirements of orchids vary so greatly that there are no hard-and-fast rules to guide the grower, and only broad outlines can be laid down. Anyone who wants to know more about orchid-growing will have to pursue the subject by reading, consulting an expert or by trial and error.

Where to Grow

Orchids do well in most parts of the country except the hot, dry regions. Even there they can be grown in greenhouses where the level of humidity is artificially maintained. Experts though, manage to grow them even in the most inhospitable regions.

Types

Orchids may be divided into two main groups—terrestrials (ground orchids) and epiphytes (those that grow on trees or rocks). The terrestrial orchids usually have a tuber or rhizome, and the roots grow underground. The epiphytes have thick, fleshy roots which hang in the air. All orchids are perennials and have a dormant period. When growing orchids, select varieties which will be comfortable in the climate you live in. It would be a pity to grow the wrong type and have it die on you. Orchids grow during the rainy season and are dormant during the cool months. Some species flower in spring, others in summer.

Climatic Conditions

Orchids vary considerably in the amount of heat and humidity they require. Some like cool, moist conditions, some favour a moderately dry climate, and others like it warm and steamy. Find out what your plant needs when you buy it.

Propagation

Most orchids reproduce from seed but that requires more than a bit of expertise. The simplest way with terretrial orchids is to divide the root stock or pseudo-bulbs with some roots attatched. Some species produce plantlets which can be removed and rooted in sphagnum moss. Use coir fibre if you don't have moss. The best time for propagation is at the end of the dormant season or during the rains, after the plant has flowered. A vigorous and healthy root system indicates good growth. The compost must be highly porous so that the roots are well supplied with oxygen.

Growing Epiphytes

Epiphytes can be grown in hanging baskets, on logs, or in bamboo boats which are made by splitting a large bamboo lengthwise. The boat will hold the potting mixture when hung. Make sure the water drains out freely.

> **Compost for Epiphytes**
> *One part coarse bone-meal*
> *Two parts pieces of charcoal*
> *One part bits of brick*
> *Two parts leaf-mould compost*
> *Two parts sphagnum moss*

Planting Orchids

Place a layer of pot shards over the drainage holes in the container. Cover the shards with a thick layer of dry moss which is available in most garden centres and nurseries. Mix the charcoal, bone-meal, brick and leaf mould and fill the pot, making a small mound on the top. The orchid is mounted on the heap. Make sure you do not injure the pseudo-bulbs and don't bury them in the mixture—they should rest on top of the soil. Apply a layer of peat compost or leaf mould over the roots till the plant is established.

Epiphytes—These orchids grow best on trees with forked branches, a rough bark and a shady crown. Trees that have a very dense crown or a smooth bark are not suitable. The roots of the plant are wrapped around the branch and will eventually clasp it. Cover the roots with a thin layer of moss and bind with any natural fibre such as coir or jute. Do not make the covering too thick—this will retard root formation.

Epiphytic orchids are often attached to small logs, or 'floats' as they are termed. They can be hung on a tree (if you have one), or from a hook in the wall. Make a shallow depression in the log and place the plant in it. Spread the roots over the sides and cover with a thin layer of dry moss. Don't choke the plant with a layer that is too thick.

> **Compost for terrestrial orchids**
> One part decomposed animal manure
> Two parts leaf mould
> One part clean soil
> One part fine sand
> One part small pieces of charcoal

Pots

Clay pots with holes underneath and in the sides are excellent for orchids in a greenhouse or fernery, or basically any situation which provides the same conditions. They are hung to allow air to pass through the holes.

Orchids in general grow better if left undisturbed. Epiphytes may need repotting when the roots become pot-bound, but not otherwise. Most orchids need a high level of humidity. If the weather is dry, wet the area near the pots or grow them near plants whch transpire heavily such as the areca palm.

Watering

Orchids in general are grown on moss or fern roots. Those in pots require more water than those grown on logs or floats. Water everyday during the growing period, from the end of the cool season to the rainy season, even if they

> **Some Epiphytes**
> 1) *Aerides offine*—pink flowers.
> 2) *Aerides odorata*—white flowers with pink dots, scented.
> 3) *Vanda caerulea*—long, bluish sprays.
> 4) *Vanda teres*—pink and yellow sprays.
> 5) *Dendrobium aggregatum*—clusters of deep orange flowers.
> 6) *D. wardianum*—white, purple and yellow.
> 7) *Cattleya*—huge blooms in shades of pink, purple, mauve and white.
>
> **Terrestrials**
> 1) *Arundina bambusifolia*—pink-mauve flowers.
> 2) *Phaius maculatus*—yellow, white, purple, bronze flowers.

are grown under a covering. The best time to water is in the late afternoon. During the cool season, watering will depend upon the type of orchid. Plants with equipment to store water will require only a little direct watering. But if you notice the pseudo-bulbs beginning to dry out, increase the amount of water. Orchids native to warm, humid regions need regular watering all the year round. If they are grown indoors, mist the air and leaves everyday as well. In the hot weather, water your orchids whenever you notice the moss or compost is dry. You may have to water them twice a day if the weather is very dry. Keep the foliage clean and remove grime by swabbing the leaves with a mild soap solution.

Cattleya

This species has enormous flowers which are positively spectacular, especially the cyclamen pink or purple varieties. In fact, to most people, orchids *are* cattleyas. Cattleyas are epiphytes and there are about 60 species all of which are from Central and South America and the West Indies. They come from a wide range of habitats and heights in jungles and mountains. Most grow on forest trees. These are best grown in sphagnum moss mixed with peat or leaf mould compost. There are many hybrid varieties available. All cattleyas have large, showy blooms.

Cattleya

Cattleya crosses, such as *Brassolaeliocattleya*, have large blooms and come in a wide range of colours. They require the same treatment as cattleyas.

These flamboyant flowers are named for a William Cattley, a North London amateur grower who lived in the early nineteenth century. He grew many plants of this species and when he died, his collection went to Joseph Knight and Thomas Perry, famous nurserymen of the time. From there they went to James Vietch and Sons who sent collectors to all parts of the world to procure this rare species.

Pleione

These are beautiful little orchids from East Asia, India, Burma and China. They have flask-shaped pseudo-bulbs which last only for a season. The flowers are showy, quite like cattleyas, and are borne on short stems. The flowers appear in spring, before the leaves. They come in many shades of pink, purple and a pinkish mauve. There are several white cultivars available. These orchids grow very happily in pots. Pleiones should be grown in fern fibre, leaf mould, sphagnum moss and sand. They need to be kept cool but not cold.

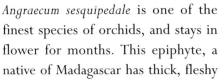

Paphiopedilum

Paphiopedilums

These orchids from north-east India are a great favourite with orchid growers. The flowers are usually solitary. *P. venustum* is a beautiful orchid which has greenish-white or pink petals and sepals striped bright green. The petals are fringed with purple markings and the pouches suffused with purple. *P. Hunters Moon* is an artificial hybrid which is gold and white and green with dark spots on the petals.

Angraecum sesquipedale is one of the finest species of orchids, and stays in flower for months. This epiphyte, a native of Madagascar has thick, fleshy roots and strap-shaped leaves which are long and narrow. The waxy-white flowers are 5-8 inches across and very fragrant. It is very tolerant of potting, and requires cool, moist conditions.

Cymbidium: These are very popular orchids in temperate countries and can tolerate fairly cold conditions. They usually bloom in winter and make splendid houseplants. The flowers remain on the plant for months. There are about 40 species, all natives of Asia and Australia. The cultivars have larger flowers which come in a wide range of colours. They grow best in moss, leaf mould or peat, and they do not tolerate lime. They need plenty of light but not strong sunshine and can be left for years without repotting.

The Lost Orchid

The fairy orchid, P. fairieannum, a lovely white, purple and green orchid, first turned up in a London sale room around 1855, and it was displayed at a show in 1857 by a Mrs Fairie of Liverpool. It is named after her. Collectors tried in vain to find it in the wild and a reward of £1000 was offered to anyone who could procure it. But the lost orchid eluded seekers until 1904, when a party of surveyors rediscovered it in the mountains of Bhutan.

Glossodia major is a delightful little ground orchid from Australia. It has purplish-blue flowers that smell like vanilla when crushed. The plant has only one leaf at the base and grows very well in pots. Use well-drained compost.

Coelogynes come mainly from Sri Lanka and East Asia. These epiphytes have pseudo-bulbs and make a pretty subject for baskets or small logs which are suspended. The flowers are usually white with coloured markings. They may be single or in racemes, upright or drooping, depending upon the variety.

Vanilla Imperialis

Vanilla Orchid

This is the tall South American orchid, *V. fragrans*. Vanilla is obtained from the cured seed pods of this plant which the Spaniards took back to Europe where it soon became popular and was used in confectionery and perfumes. For 300 years, Mexico was the sole supplier of vanilla as attempts to grow it in Asia and elsewhere had failed—the plants simply would not set fruit. Much later people realized that this was because the flowers were pollinated by a certain species of bees and humming birds found only in South and Central America. Then in 1836, a Belgian botanist solved the matter quite simply—he hand-pollinated the flowers and the plant bore fuit! Even today this is done in Madagascar and the Seychelles, which now produce most of the world's natural vanilla.

The vine flowers for a long period and each vine may produce up to 1000 blooms. The plant is propagated by root cuttings. It likes a warm, moist climate, but not too warm.

Vandas

Few oriental orchids have captured the imagination as the Vandas have, particularly the blue orchid, *V. coerulea*, from the Khasia Hills of Assam. It bears upto twenty flowers which are a deep blue with paler sepals. Calcutta businessmen have the dubious distinction of plundering these flowers practically into extinction. Vandas come in many colours and are usually fragrant. The flowers are poised on the slender stems like butterflies. The plants are best grown on logs.

Vanda

OTHER EXOTICA

Peonies

> Farewell! Like a bee
> Reluctant to leave
> The sweet deeps
> Of a peony . . .
>
> —Basho

Peonies belong to a family that has just one genus (*Paeonia*) and about 30 species. All belong to the north temperate regions, from Siberia and China to Europe. Peonies are either rhizomatic or tuberous. The Chinese were cultivating peonies centuries before the birth of Christ. At first they were grown for their medicinal uses, but by 500 AD they were grown for the beauty of the blooms. Both Dioscorides and Pliny the Elder describe peonies in their books as does Theophrastus, in his book *Enquiry Into Plants*. It was a popular flower in Tudor England and had delightful names such as Hundred-bladed rose, Nan Pie and Marmaritin.

The most popular peonies for garden purposes are the cultivars derived from the fragrant white peony *P. lactiflora* which is a native of Siberia, Mongolia, Tibet, China and Manchuria. They are usually called Chinese hybrids because the Chinese were the first to raise them. There are several single and double varieties in a wide range of colours—white, cream, all shades of pink, crimson, red, purple—and even a combination of two or more colours.

Peonies grow well in the hills; in the plains they must be kept in a greenhouse where the temperature is controlled. Peonies do not tolerate heat. Besides having lovely exotic blooms, they possess other qualities of value to a gardener—the plants are sturdy, the blooms appear early and they grow well in most types of soil. They can be grown in full sun or partial shade. The perennials are ideal for permanent planting as they have attractive, deeply-cut leaves and are naturally neat, requiring little or no pruning.

Peonies like rich, well-cultivated soil for the thick, fleshy roots to penetrate deep down. They should be given a yearly mulching of bone-meal, well-rotted cattle manure and leaf mould. Water well during the hot, dry spells. If looked after, they will reward you year after year with masses of gorgeously coloured blooms. Clumps of peonies have been known to bloom even after eighty years!

Peonies are propagated by root divison, which may be done either in Novembr or early February. The crown buds should be near the surface, not burried beneath the soil. Old plants, if disturbed, do not readily produce new shoots.

P. emodi, or Himalayan peony, has lovely, large, fragile pure white flowers and golden stamens. The tree peonies from China are more small trees than shrubs, and unlike the herbaceous kinds, should never be cut or disturbed. An occasional shaping and removal of dead and damaged wood is all the pruning they need.

Bird of Paradise (*Strelitziaceae*)

This is an unusual and rather dramatic family of herbaceous perennials, first cousins to the banana. The flowers are unconventional, very beautiful and vividly coloured. The Bird of Paradise comes from South Africa and gets its name from the inflorescence which bears a striking resemblance to a bird's head. The flower head, poised on a stout stem is about 9 inches in length. The boat-shaped spathe contains the flowers. The sepals are a brilliant orange and the petals a rich peacock blue. It is ideally grown in clumps and does well in warm, wet regions. It does not like the cold or dry heat. It can be grown in large pots. The soil mixture must be rich in loam and compost, and if potted, the soil must not be allowed to dry out. The bird of paradise is the emblem of Los Angeles where it is widely grown.

Camellias

Camellias are named for George Kamel, Latinised to Camellis, a Jesuit priest who collected plants in China and the

> Now having taken warmed water . . .
> The vase welcomes my camellia.
> —Onitusra

Philippines some time in the seventeenth century, though opinions differ as to whether it was he who took the seeds to Europe. Camellias are natives of China, Korea and Japan. This large family consists of 16 genera and more than 500 species, the most important, economically, being *C. sinensis*, the tea plant.

There's a rather interesting legend concerning the tea plant. When Bodhidharma went to China to preach Buddhism, he practised austerities and penances—one of them was wakefulness. Then one day, he fell asleep during meditation. Furious at his weakness, Bodhidharma cut off his eyelids and threw them on the ground and the Buddha caused them to sprout. These were the first tea plants, the dried leaves of which look like eyelids. Tea is also said to keep sleep at bay.

Among the ornamental camellias, *C. japonica* from the mountains of Korea, is probably the loveliest. There are any number of cultivars available. The flowers may be single or double, from a pure white through shades of pink to red. One of the most pleasing is 'Elegans', which can grow up to 10 ft tall and in spring is covered with hundreds of blooms, provided the conditions are right. There are literally scores of hybrids, many of which are very hardy and free-flowering. The Chinese camellias are less hardy, but extremely lovely. The semi-double flowers have crimped petals. The plants must be sheltered from extreme heat, cold and frost.

Camellias are evergreens with glossy, leathery, oval leaves. The plant grows tidily and requires little or no pruning. Pinch back occasionally to induce new side shoots. Camellias dislike lime-rich soil. They need plenty of leaf-mould compost and rich, porous soil. A mulching of used tea leaves is greatly appreciated by them.

Flamingo Flower (*Anthurium*)

Anthuriums come from a family which has more than 2000 species. Some have strange reptilian flowers which possess an unnatural beauty. Most come from the depths of damp forests but some are bog and marsh plants. Arum lilies, which are neither arums nor lilies, come from this family. The most colourful plants, and the most ornamental, are the anthuriums and caladiums, the former prized for their flowers, the latter for their leaves.

There are about 700–900 species of anthuriums, but for garden purposes, *A. andraeanum* and *A. scherzeranum* are the most important. *A. andraeanum* has masses of orange-scarlet or deep crimson spathes, borne on long, slender stems. The spathes are usually flat and shiny; some are puckered and blistered and the cream-coloured spadix rises from the centre of the base. There are countless forms of this Colombian anthurium. The spathes may be white, rose pink, salmon pink or dark red. Modern cultivars have spathes which are smooth rather than puckered.

A. Scherzeranum—Another variable species, this is from Guatemala and Costa Rica. The spathes may be white, yellow, blood-red, pink, scarlet or purple, often striated with another colour. The spadix which twists and spirals up may be white, yellow, orange or red.

Anthuriums must be grown in highly porous soil, rich in leaf mould or peat. The plants like warm, moist conditions. They are best grown in a light, airy situation, out of direct sulight. Mist the leaves frequently during the dry spells. Plants must be protected from the hot sun and frost. They do not grow happily in the northern plains; only an expert gardener will be able to have an anthurium collection. However, if you are keen, get a few hardy varieties. The spathes are pink.

Swiss Cheese Plant (*Monstera deliciosa*)

One solitary plant is enough to create a dramatic impact in any room. The plant is mainly grown for its foliage—the large shiny leaves have holes and tears and no two leaves are identical. The generic name comes from the delicious fruit which look like slim pinecones and take a year to ripen. When ripe, the succulent fruits taste like a cross between a pear and a pineapple and have the aroma of a banana!

Monsteras come from the jungles of Central and South America, and in the forests can grow to a height of 30 ft. But the plant is quite adaptable and grows well in large pots if given some support. In tropical gardens, the plants can be trained up a tree, but they also make excellent indoor plants. They can take all but the lowest of temperatures. In the hot, dry months, the plant must be watered frequently and the leaves sprayed twice a day. The flowers are squat and creamish-white.

Monsteras need a well-lit but shady situation and the soil should be rich in leaf and peat compost and humus. It is propagated by cuttings of a growing shoot with a leaf attached.

Bromeliads

Most of the 1400 species of bromeliads are natives of South America—Brazil in particular—but some are found as far up as south-east USA. Some are terrestrial but many grow on rocks and the

The pineapple belongs to the bromeliad family. Columbus found it growing in the West Indies. It is the world's most canned tropical fruit. Oviedo, a Spanish historian, wrote about pineapples in 1539 and the Spanish called it Pina-las-India which was later corrupted to pineapple. The Latin name Annas comes from the South American Guarini language—'a' meaning fruit and 'nana' excellent.

epiphytes grow on trees and shrubs. Their brilliant flowers and rosette leaf shapes look like perching birds. Some are found on the high Andean plateau while others grow on rotting logs or cacti. Their flowers vary in shape and colour—some resemble lilies while others look like three-petalled violets. Some bromeliads have leaves which have a vase-like formation made up of rosettes of leaves which curve and fit snugly at the base to form a receptacle for food and water. Some species have nondescript flowers and leaves whereas others are quite spectacular and highly unusual. The flowers usually have three petals.

One of the loveliest of bromeliads is *Tillandsia cyanea*. The narrow, graceful leaves arch out from a central point and the inflorescence is striking—the panicle is a deep soft pink and the flowers are a mauvish-blue. The flowers of *T. lindenii* are pink and powder blue and the leaves are reddish. Both these species need a warm, moist climate to flower.

Billbergias, another member of the family, are very popular because they are hardy and grow easily in normal soil and compost. These epiphytes need to be grown on a log or up a small tree. *B. nutans* has dark green, narrow, arching leaves which are pretty ordinary, but the inflorescence is startling. The flower-head drops down with the weight of the red bracts and the violet-blue, green-tipped flowers. This plant is often called Queen's Tears. One of the most beautiful bromeliads is *Aechmea fasciata*. The spiny-edged leaves are a silver-green with grey, horizontal bands. A well-grown specimen can be upto 2 ft across and about 15 inches high. The inflorescence which rises above the leaves has rosy-pink spiny bracts which enclose lavender-blue flowers. A native of Rio de Janeiro, it tolerates low temperatures and reproduces easily from offshoots.

Bromeliads should be potted in porous, leaf-mould compost mixed with plenty of fibre such as dry moss or coir fibre. They like a warm, moist climate and must be sheltered from the midday sun.

Begonia

There are about 900 species of begonias, all with delicate watery stems and asymmetrical leaves one side larger than the other. Begonias are found in the tropics and sub-tropics, particularly South America, from the Andes to Mexico. But there are some which are natives of Africa and the Eastern Himalayas.

The most splendid of all the begonias are the tuberous species which have huge, double, rose-like flowers in brilliant shades of yellow, red, orange and pink. There are many cultivars available with frilled and ruffled petals—some resemble hollyhocks, others look like roses, and yet others like camellias and carnations.

The plants are started from dormant tubers at the end of the cold season. They do not grow well in the plains and they dislike frost. They are best grown in cool temperate regions. In the hills, the plant flowers profusely.

Today, double begonias are available in a huge range of colours and shades—pink, rose, red, clear yellow, salmon-orange, vermilion, cream and white. They may be in combinations— white-edged with deep pink, yellow with a pink border or apricot with rose-pink edges. All begonias produce separate male and female flowers. If they are grown for flower shows, the small, female flowers that flank the large male blooms should be removed. Retain them only if you want the seeds.

Heliconia

This genus of about 100 species belongs to the banana family and come from the humid jungles of tropical America. They are large, often gigantic plants with simple stems sheathed by huge banana-like leaves.

The inflorescences are alternately arranged and zigzag along the stem. Brilliant red bracts shield the tiny flowers. The plants do very well in the tropics if the soil is rich and moist.

The Lobster Claw, *H. humilis* is a commanding plant which can overshadow the others in a garden. The scarlet bracts, edged with gold, are tightly packed and can be up to 4 ft long. *H. bihai* is an imposing giant species which can grow up to 18 ft high. The bracts are a deep scarlet with yellow tips. The plant bears edible fruits.

Heliconias should be grown in the ground but can also be grown in tubs. For the best effect, grow them in a prominent position.

Heliconia bihai

Lotus (*Nelumbonaceae*)

From very early times the lotus has, along with the sun and the moon, been a symbol of the higher destiny that man is forever seeking. It has been venerated in Ancient Egypt, India and China. In India it still continues to be revered. This flower, though so well-known in the East, is nevertheless exotic. There are not many of its kind; there is just one genus and two species.

These large acquatics are found in the warm, tropical parts of Asia, America and Australia. The whole of the leaves are like tea-trays, and grow well above the water. The upper surface is

Crossing the river I pluck the
lotus flowers;
In the orchid swamps are
many fragrant herbs.
I gather them but who shall I
send them to
—Anon
Chinese poem

waxy and raindrops roll off them like globules of mercury. The solitary flowers which grow on the tips of long stems, have four sepals and numerous petals and stamens. The seed pod looks like the rose of a watering can or a large poppy head. The seeds and roots are both edible.

The lotus is portrayed in Ancient Egyptian art and architecture, much as it is in India. *Nelumbo nucifera*, the sacred lotus of the Hindus, was taken from India to Egypt probably after the Persian invasion in the sixth century BC. But *Nymphaea lotus* and *N. caerulea*—the former white, the latter blue—are native to Egypt. *N. nucifere* is the lotus which grew out of Vishnu's navel, in which Brahma was born. Another name for Brahma is Kamalaja, meaning 'lotus-born'. The flowers of this species may be white, carmine, or deep purplish-pink. There are dwarf varieties which have streaked or colour-edged petals. The seeds and roots are eaten in India, China, Japan, and in Indo-China, the stamens are used to flavour tea. Revered by both Hindus and Buddhists, it symbolizes man who can rise above the mire just as the flower rises above the muddy waters it grows into. Buddha too, like Brahma, was born in a lotus.

The whole plant is edible—the leaves, roots and seeds were eaten by Asians and N. American Indians.

You can grow lotuses if you have a large tank or pond, not otherwise. The long, creeping rhizomes can run up to 30 ft in a season. In small gardens they can be grown in pools which have a depth of at least 2.5 ft. The smaller kinds are quite happy in pools but remove the seed pods to encourage new flowers.

Herodotus called the lotus the Rose Lily, and gave this account of the flower which he saw in Egypt: 'When the river is full and has made the plains like a sea, great number of lilies, which the Egyptians call Lotus, spring up in the water; these they gather and dry in the sun, then having pounded the middle of the Lotus, they make bread of it and bake it!

Lotus crowns can be purchased from a good nursery. A better way is to find a lake or pond with lotuses and collect a few. Plant singly in earthernware pots with a soil compost composed of five parts soil, one part well-rotted animal manure and three teaspoons of bone-meal. If the pot has a hole, block it with some waterproof material. Place the pot on bricks submerged in the pool and remove them when the leaves reach the surface of the water. The pots can then be embedded in the soil at the bottom of the pool.

Bonsai

A bonsai, much like a garden, is a living, breathing piece of art which continues to evolve till it dies, quite unlike any other objects of art. Once a piece of music is written, it is fixed for all time, once a painting is done, it stays done, but a bonsai changes with every passing season. It is never static.

Most people think that bonsai is a Japanese art form, but its origin and development lie in China where it is known as *pun-sai* (from which the Japanese word is derived). Both terms basically mean the same thing—a tree in a pot. The Chinese were making *pun-sai* centuries before the Japanese learnt the art, and by the Han Dynasty (206 BC-220 AD), making *pun-sai* was a common practice as was *pun-ching*, a landscape in a tray. *Pun-sai* is first mentioned in a text from the Ch'in Dynasty era (221-206 BC).

Japan inherited a highly evolved artistic tradition from China—calligraphy, painting, pottery, silk and bonsai. It is thought that Buddhist monks carried the art to Japan along with Buddhism. By the eighth century AD, Chinese cultural traditions were well established in Japan due to direct links with the T'ang Dynasty. *Pun-sai* quickly became *bon-sai*, and by the Heian period (eighth to twelfth century AD), was a highly popular pastime of the Japanese nobility.

Bonsai may well have originated in China, but the art form was perfected in Japan. By the fifteenth century, under the influence of Zen Buddhism, bonsai and other forms of miniature gardening acquired a new aesthetic and philosophical dimension, though techniques and skill, were

> *The miniaturization and dwarfing of plants originated in China. The ancient Taoists, in their search for immortality, believed that by miniaturizing an object, they could gain control of its essence and 'magic'. Immortality, to the ever practical Chinese, meant a couple of centuries, not 'forever' as it means to other races. The Taoists were searching for practical magic. They dwarfed and extended the life of trees by slowing the rise of sap, as they did with their own pulse and breathing. Some Taoists are reputed to have lived to a great age, like their bonsais.*

courtesy Chu-Shun-sui, a Chinese official who fled China and Manchu rule around 1644, taking with him his entire collection of bonsai literature. It was his specialist knowledge that made it possible for the art form to spread in Japan.

Initially, bonsai were only grown by the aristocracy, the samurai and the priestly class, but by the end of the eighteenth century, people of all classes were growing them. The Japanese made bonsai their own particular art form. Their bonsai are smaller, spikier, and have fine sense of proportion, quite unlike the Chinese *pun-sai* which are larger and not quite so aesthetically pleasing. But that is a matter of opinion; both have their distinct personalities. This deviation due to the influence of Zen Buddhism and Japanese philosophy influenced every aspect of life in Japan. For the Japanese, the truly great poem, painting, garden or bonsai must have *wabi* (best explained as a sense of moderation; a calm tinged with sadness; simplicity), *yugen* (mystery) and *satori* (the moment of illumination). Without these, no *haiku* or bonsai has any merit.

It is the Japanese who are considered the undisputed masters of bonsai, their natural-seeming styles the result of centuries of thought. But even their most stylistic style, the 'literati', considered by experts to be the highest form, actually came from China. In the fourth and sixth centuries, many artists and scholars in China went to the mountains to distance themselves from the corrupt imperial court. This select group was called the 'literati' and their style grew out of their paintings. These bonsai bear a fleeting resemblance to trees in nature, shaped as they are by imagination and fantasy. The Japanese merely adopted the style, as they did with much else.

All Japanese art is based on simplicity and austerity, but it is by no means simplistic. It expresses what is essentially profound and deep without resorting to elaborate means. So a bonsai must be spare yet majestic, grand without trappings, and like the ancient Taoists, should live to a great age. There are bonsai in Japan that are over five centuries old, still vigorous and strong, and their recorded history can be traced back as far as three centuries. Many of the masterpieces we see today are two to three centuries old, though age is not the main criteria. A bonsai is far more than an old tree in a pot. They are priceless works of art, handed down as heirlooms from one generation to the next and tended with far more care than many family members usually receive. The oldest bonsai in Japan is over 500 years old and belonged to the military ruler of Japan, Shogun Iemitsu of the Tokugawa family. This is one of Japan's greatest treasures, priceless to the Japanese. A poignant Japanese tale tells of an impoverished samurai who was visited by the Shogun in 1383. It was a bitterly cold winter night and there was no firewood in the house. To keep the honoured guest warm, the samurai cut down his three precious bonsai and burnt them. A famous woodblock print shows the samurai, stoic in demeanour, his sad face averted from the bonsai he is about to cut down. One can only hope the shogun was suitably appreciative.

MAKING BONSAI

The most highly prized of all bonsai are those gathered from the wild, often from inaccessible mountain crags. Bonsai made by men are considered slightly inferior but only marginally. Most bonsai that we see owe their existence to human skill, patience and a great deal of care.

Bonsai can be collected from the wild, grown from seed or cutting, or made from a young tree. Trees are not the only plants used; any woody shrub or creeper can be used to make a bonsai. Many plants such as the hibiscus or bougainvillea can be trained to make very beautiful bonsai, but make sure the plant you choose does not have large blossoms or leaves, or else the bonsai will be disproportionate.

Traditionally, Japanese and Chinese bonsai are made from temperate trees like the pine, maple and cherry. But we in India have a wealth of trees to choose from—tropical, sub-tropical and temperate. Many members of the ficus family, bauhiniascassia, lemon, orange, guava etc. make very good bonsai. There are plenty of fruiting and flowering trees to choose from. For many of us who want to make bonsai but the plant doesn't have the required twenty to thirty years of life when the tree will attain form and character, we have a choice of quick-growing shrubs and trees that begin to flower or fruit when fairly young. They may not have the majesty of a mature tree, but they are very attractive when fruiting or flowering. It also helps if you choose a plant 3-10 years old. There are plenty available in nurseries, but remember, the older the plant, the more the expertise required to make a bonsai. For beginners, a readymade young bonsai is the best bet. Good nurseries stock them nowadays.

If growing from seed, plant in tiny thimble-sized containers for a year before transferring to a larger one, where it should remain for the next few years till it is planted in its final pot.

PLANTING

In India, the best time to begin a bonsai is during the monsoon months. In the northern plains, February/March is also a good time, especially for repotting, root-pruning and shaping the plants which have a dormant period. These plants are usually deciduous and shed their leaves in winter. The plant then rests and produces sap for new growth only with the onset of spring.

GROWING FROM SEED

This method has some distinct advantages but requires a fair amount of patience. You can watch it grow and gradually acquire form; shape it as you want and learn about its needs as it grows. Most plants take seven to ten years to get a mature look. If the seeds are large and hard-cased, they should be soaked in warm water for a few hours before planting. If smaller, place them on wet cotton wool overnight. This helps germination. Make little scratches on the case if they are stony hard and leave the seeds in the wet cotton wool for a few days. The ideal seed box is a shallow container, 3-4 inches deep with holes in the bottom. The soil mixture should be 1 part sand and 3 parts well-rotted leaf mould.

Three rules for Tree Selection

1) They should be hardy.
2) The branches should have naturally artistic forms.
3) The plant should alter with the seasons.

CUTTINGS

Making a bonsai from a cutting or a layer is far quicker. Most trees and shrubs familiar to us can be grown this way. Cuttings are best made when the current year's shoots are mature enough for the process. As a general rule, pines and other evergreens should be cut before the new leaves appear in spring. In the case of deciduous trees, cuttings should be made from young, medium-hard stems in summer. (For how to make cuttings, see 'Cultivation and Watering'.)

Dishes form Tokoname, Japan, each complete with maker's signature

Glazed dishes

CONTAINERS

For a good bonsai, it is vital that the container and tree be in perfect harmony. They should form a unified whole. It is very important to choose the right pot for the plant. The type of pot also depends upon the style of the bonsai. The shape and size of a pot for the cascade style will not do for an informal, upright style. In general, the colour of the pot should

Antique bonsai dish from China

Unglazed dishes

harmonize with the foliage, flower or fruit, whichever is the most striking.

Pines and conifers look their best in unglazed or lightly glazed, dark-coloured pots. Deciduous trees look good in coloured glazes. Trees that are delicate and graceful in form and appearance should not be grown in heavy, pompous pots. The pot too, should have a certain grace. Black pines and other majestic trees such as the peepul (*Ficus religiosa*) look their best in strong, heavy pots. The pots can never overpower them.

In a good bonsai, the placing of the tree and the amount of surface cover such as moss should be in proportion to the size of the container and the trunk of the tree. Shallow containers—rectangular or oval—are best suited to upright bonsai. 'Weeping' trees such as the bottlebrush or willow look well in deep square or round pots. If the tree has a heavy crown, it will require a container with weight and depth. The ideal width of the container should be two-third the height of the tree.

If you have a group of trees, the width of the container should be two-third the height of the tallest tree.

The finest containers come from Japan and China, but local potteries also make some, though they are poor imitations. The best are studio-pottery pots if you can get them, but they are not easy to come by or cheap.

Styles that may be planted singly or in groups

Hokiachi—broom, or besom, style

Fan-shaped branches on an upright trunk to look like a giant broom.

Fukinagashi—windswept style

Trunk at an angle with branches and twigs growing only in one direction—as if lashed by the wind.

Bujingi—literati style

Trunk or trunks growing upright or at a slight incline with no branches except at the top. An elegant shape.

Ishitsuki—clinging-to-rock, or rock grown, style

Miniature tree growing above or on a rock, its roots firmly clasping the stone and reaching down into the richness of the soil.

STYLING

The Japanese dislike even numbers in art. The only even number acceptable is two. Symmetry is unwelcome and this has greatly influenced bonsai styles and ought to tell you how many trees you should have if planting in groups.

GROUP PLANTING

In nature many trees are found growing in groups, so it is possible to create a dark forest, light woodland copse or a group of wind-swept trees. You only have to look at trees in their natural surroundings to see the infinite possibilities. You will know you have succeeded when you see that specific quality emerging in your chosen group. You can get the desired effect much quicker than you think; you don't have to wait for decades to see the results. You can either choose old trees (5-10 years old) from a nursery, or collect from the wild.

COLLECTING FROM THE WILD

The older the tree, the more it dislikes being uprooted. Young plants, 10-12 inches high, pose no problem; they can be easily dug up. To remove an old natural bonsai requires patience and labour. First you must cut off the large branches. Then make a narrow trench, a couple of inches wide,

Individual trees:

Chokkan—formal upright
Strong, vertical trunk with pyramidal arrangement of branches stretching uniformly in all directions except forwards.

Moyogi—curved informal upright
Trunk winds round in curves that become smaller towards the top.

Shakan—slanting style
Similar to the windswept style except that a Shakan has branches growing in all directions. Strong roots are exposed in the direction of incline.

Han-Kengai—semi cascade
This style does not cascade downwards from a rock, but juts out horizontally above a cliff.

Kengai—cascade or hanging style
Trunk and branches hang down over the edge of a pot, usually one that has been placed high up.

Trees with several trunks and group plantings:

Sokan—twin trunk
Two trunks of differing thickness growing out of one root (father and son).

Sankan—triple trunk
Three trunks of differing thickness growing out of one root (father, mother, son).

Kabudachi—clump
The term used for all bonsai where several trunks grow from one root.

Ikada—raft style
Trunk buried horizontally in the ground with branches trained to give the effect of individual trees.

Netsuranari—raft from root, or sinuous, style
Severl trunks growing from a root lying horizontally, producing the effect of a group of trees.

Yose-ue—multi-tree or group planting
Several miniature trees of greatly differing ages planted in a flat dish to give the appearance of a wood or forest glade.

around the tree. The diameter should be the same as that of the crown. Dig deep into the trench, cutting any roots you come across with a sharp knife. Cut cleanly. Gradually reach a depth of 12-18 inches. Once that is done, dig underneath horizontally, cutting the ground to make a half-moon and cut off the tap root. Slice the ground off from the other side and lift the tree with the root ball packed in earth. Wrap the root ball in damp newspaper or moss, whichever is handy. Take the tree home and plant in a container. The soil should be well drained and rich in humus. Trim the crown back so that the plant is not overburdened. The tree will be in a state of shock and the roots will take a while to repair the damage done to them. Place it in a sheltered spot, out of the wind, till new growth starts to appear. The tree will take eight to twelve weeks to get used to its new home. After a year, the roots should be cut and the tree repotted in a bonsai dish.

> **Other Bonsai Styles**
>
> *Hoki-dachi*—Broom style. The trunk is upright and the branches fan-shaped.
>
> *Fukinagashi*—Windswept. The trunk grows at an angle, the branches and twigs all growing in one direction, as if lashed by a storm.
>
> *Bunjingi*—Literati style. The trunk of trunks are upright with a very slight incline. The branches are all at the top, none low down. Very stylized.
>
> *Ishitsuki*—Clinging-to-a-rock. The tree is grown on or above a craggy piece of rock. The roots clasp the stone and grow downwards into the soil in the tray.

SHAPING

You can determine the shape of your tree only if you start with a young plant. Training should begin in the second year. Remove all buds and shoots you don't want growing in a particular direction and cut back the growing tip to get another branch. As the tree grows, it will produce more branches; these should be trimmed back to a leaf-axil. The tree will appear more compact if the branches are trimmed.

Most deciduous trees can be shaped quite easily by trimming and pruning. They rarely require wiring. Cutting in the right place, in the right season will determine the height of the trunk and the direction of the branches. The tip of the leaf bud generally points in the direction it will grow. Gradually, in a few years, the tree will acquire shape and form. Only then does one decide the style of the tree.

ARTIFICIAL AGEING

It is with age that a tree acquires character and true beauty. And that can take decades but it is possible to make a young bonsai appear older than it is. There are three basic techniques you can use.

Jin

Jinning involves leaving branches that have been badly lopped off or which have died on the tree. Strip away the bark and smoothen the branch with emery paper. You can sharpen the end of the branch if you wish. If your tree has grown too tall, jinning can make it look more proportionate. In the case of jinning with a live branch, cut off the leaves or needles on the top and peel back the bark to expose the wood. Paint with citric acid to prevent rot. All conifers are suitable for jinning.

Sharimiki

Partially strip off the bark from a branch or the trunk and if there's a prominent root above the soil, strip the bark from the top. Working downwards, peel a narrow strip of bark from the front of the trunk or branch, but first make vertical incisions with a sharp knife. Smoothen the exposed wood and paint over with citric acid. Don't let the acid touch the living bark.

Shabamiki

This ageing technique will not only make the bonsai look older but more impressive as well. Your tree will look like it has weathered many storms. Shabamiki means hollow or split trunk. The wood will have to be split, giving the tree a hoary look. If there is a damaged spot on the tree, remove it and scoop out a hollow. Treat the wood in hollow with citric acid. Some experts rip off a forward-growing branch and enlarge the depression to make a hollow.

- Ageing techniques must be done in summer when the wounds will dry quickly.
- Trees will also appear older if you scratch the bark on the trunk and branches with your nails, and lower the branches by weighing them down.

Wiring

If you want to alter the direction of some branches or shape the trunk, you have to resort to wiring. This is neither simple nor easy. Wiring is done when you want to lower the branches, make a curve in the trunk, or straighten it if it is bent. Copper wire is frequently used, but the best is aluminium as it does not oxidize or get brittle and stiff when exposed to air. Wiring is mainly done with conifers; with broad-leaved deciduous trees you can get the desired shape by pruning alone. However, if you still wish to wire the tree, do it in spring when the sap is running. The wires should be removed after six to eight months. Conifers and other evergreens take a long time to shape, but even with these trees the wires should be removed twelve to fifteen months later.

Don't allow the wires to cut into the bark. If that does happen, use a good pair of wire-cutters and cut the wire and remove it without damaging the bark more than necessary. Repeat wiring after one growing season if required. Keep repeating, with suitable intervals, until you are satisfied. The wiring should always be in the direction of growth. The wire is coiled around in a spiral, from bottom to top. You may have to use more than one wire if the branch is thick. The rule of thumb says use the thinnest wire required to shape. If wiring the trunk, secure the lower end of the wire by pushing it into the soil right down to the bottom of the dish. Then wind it around the trunk, angling it with the line of the trunk. The ideal angle is 40-45°. The distance between the coils should be even; it gets smaller only as it reaches the top. The coil should not be too tight.

The technique for the branches is the same, except that the wire is secured to the trunk or opposite branch. After wiring, bend the branch to the required shape. It is wise to pad the area under the wire to avoid damaging the bark. Thick rubber sheeting cut into narrow strips, is the best. If the branches are too close to one another, wedge a piece of wood between them to widen the gap. After each wiring period, the bonsai must be allowed to recover. Keep it away from the hot sun, wind and rain for a few weeks. Do not repot after wiring.

Other ways to bend branches
1) Fix wires to the container and attach the branches to them.
2) Attach wires to the trunk and tie the branches to it.
3) Use lead weights or sand bags to weigh the branches down.

MYTHS ABOUT BONSAI

The uninformed or those with little knowledge have a great many foolish notions about the art of bonsai. They think it is cruel to bonsai a tree; that the tree suffers greatly and is wantonly treated to satisfy some not-so- noble artistic leanings. They firmly believe that dwarfing a tree causes it anguish and pain, and that cutting back the roots and pruning the branches is akin to chopping off a human limb. 'How would you like to be dwarfed?' they ask. They will think you a shade less cruel than Hitler if you tell them their beliefs are a load of rubbish. But if these people take some time to talk to an experienced gardener, they will be cordially informed that if he didn't prune his fruit trees or rose bushes, he'd have no roses or fruits. They will also be told that a tree which is shy of fruiting or flowering requires root-pruning. His potted plants (most of which, technically speaking, are bonsai) would get pot-bound and eventually die if their roots are not pruned every now and then. And the gardener will privately think these people are abyssmally ignorant.

All potted plants need this treatment, whether bonsai or not. Pruning of roots and branches is an essential part of gardening. Root pruning, as good gardeners know, stimulates the development of fibrous roots which are vital for healthy, vigorous growth. The undercutting of trees and shrubs is a horticultural practice which is more than 3500 years old. Tell the owner of any orchard not to prune his trees and you risk being labelled a fool.

Nature makes bonsai all the time. Seeds that fall into a crevice in a rock will ultimately become bonsai. Some trees grow slanted because of the wind and weather. Some live in inhospitable places such as the high mountains and become stunted. The fact that man-made bonsai live to a great age proves that they like where they are growing and appreciate the care lavished on them. They live on long after the person who made them is gone.

Any plant in a pot is not a bonsai, just as a splash of paint on a canvas does not make a painting. A good bonsai can bring the atmosphere of a forest into a room, and to make one

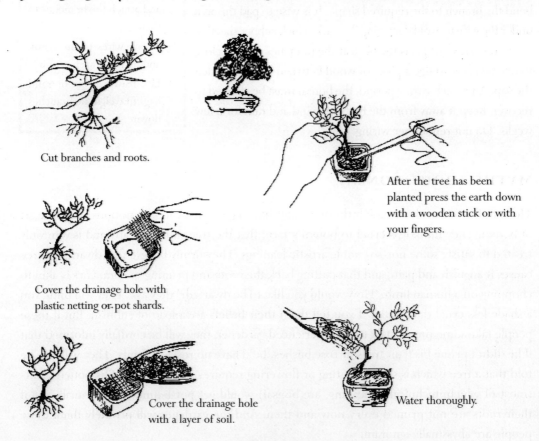

Cut branches and roots.

After the tree has been planted press the earth down with a wooden stick or with your fingers.

Cover the drainage hole with plastic netting or pot shards.

Cover the drainage hole with a layer of soil.

Water thoroughly.

Potting Bonsai

requires a highly developed sense of aesthetics. One must have an eye for colour, form, texture and a sound knowledge of nature and her ways. You must have intimate knowledge of a forest, the wind, rain, storms and the sun. The old tree in your bonsai container must have the same grandeur, majesty and imposing presence of an ancient tree in a forest. For bonsai, you need more than a green thumb—you need an eye for beauty.

India is not a nation of gardeners, and most people don't want to make bonsai because they think that the true bonsai is an old tree and they won't be around to see their tree when it is mature. Age is not what a bonsai is all about. A bonsai as young as six or seven years can be a very good specimen, provided it is shaped and trained correctly. Don't start from seed; get a plant three to ten years old, and in a couple of years, you can have a marvellous tree.

CHARACTERISTICS

A good bonsai has certain definite characteristics. The trunk must have character—it must rise gradually from the base. The branches should be evenly distributed, tapering all the way to the crown. The bark should have an interesting texture. The tree must be planted in the precise position in the pot. Finally, the pot itself must harmonize with the whole composition. To create depth and perspective, there should be slightly fewer branches in the front.

MAKING BONSAI BY AIR-LAYERING AND FROM NURSERY SPECIMENS

Growing a bonsai from seed or cutting takes a fair amount of time. Nowadays, when people want everything almost instantly, the quickest ways to acquire a bonsai which is satisfactory is by air-layering or making one from a nursery specimen. The latter method gives you an 'instant bonsai' if you prune the branches right.

Air Layering

This is an old, well-established method of propagating plants and trees. The Chinese were using this technique more than 1500 years ago. With this method, a bonsai enthusiast can have a very creditable bonsai in an extremely short time. Branches upto 5 cm (2.2 inches) thick can be very successfully air-layered. Remove the bark in a ring or make tongues on the chosen branch. If the branch is more than an inch thick, you will have to cut the underside wood to half the thickness of the branch. Cover with moss or coconut fibre and wrap with a porous natural netting such as gunny-sacking. Tie the two ends, leaving the mouth open for watering. Water very carefully. If you give it a few drops of liquid vitamin B1, it will speed up the rooting process. The vitamin should be given twice a month. The best time for air-layering is during the monsoon. Some plants will root quickly, within a month; others can take up to six months. The thicker the branch the longer it will take to root. Choose a branch with an interesting shape.

Nursery Specimens

Nurseries are a rich source of potential bonsai. The choice of shrubs and trees can leave you bewildered, so look for plants with promise—thick, crooked trunks with branches growing fairly low down. Prod the soil in the containers—often shrubs and trees are planted deeper than they need be and the base of the trunk will be much thicker than you think. The branches should taper interestingly too. Making a bonsai from a nursery specimen will not traumatize the plant as much as digging it up from the ground, because the plant has already adapted itself to growing in a container. A considerable amount of the top can be cropped off without doing much harm to the plant. As a general rule, if you are cutting off one-third of the branches, you must remove one-third of the root ball too, to maintain a balance between root and foliage. When cutting the tap root, cut cleanly, leaving as many fibrous roots as possible. The most suitable plants are slow-growing species, compact, and with small leaves. When choosing a tree, bear in mind the eventual form you are aiming at. Branches should be thick low down and thinner on top.

When you take the plant home, tidy it up—remove all dead and insignificant branches and you'll be able to see what your tree looks like. Observe the flow of the trunk and branches and decide which bonsai style will suit it best. Before removing any of the larger branches, cover them with your hand to see the form you will get when they are cut off. The lower third of the trunk should be free of branches. The main branches should dominate the middle third, and the smaller ones, the top. Prune the roots and plant in a dish. Roots require pruning whenever a plant is potted for the first time. In a young plant, roots need to be pruned every one to two years, especially with broad-leaved trees. Conifers need root-pruning every two to four years as they are slow growers. When pruning roots, keep the inner roots intact. Remove the earth gently and prune back by at least one-third. The older your bonsai the less root-pruning it will require.

REPOTTING

This is a very important part of the art of bonsai. Ideally, a bonsai, when young, should be transferred to a larger pot (one inch larger) every couple of years for about six years, when it is planted in its final dish. Old bonsai should be repotted only when the soil is exhausted

Narcissus

Rose

Orchid

Anthurium

or when the roots have grown so dense that they need pruning and should be repotted in the same dish. The soil mixture depends upon the plant, but in general, all bonsai require porous soil rich in humus. The water should drain out freely. If the bonsai is large and the dish shallow, you have to fix the root ball with aluminium or plastic wires which pass through the drainage holes and are wound around the root ball with the ends twisted and secured in the soil. You don't need to wire the roots if the dish is deep. The wire is removed six months later. Many experts recommend wire-meshing over the drainage holes and covering the bottom of the dish with a layer of coarse sand or gravel. This is not really necessary if your soil mixture is porous; pot shards are enough to cover the drainage holes.

When placing the plant in the dish, the top-most roots should be at the same level as the edge of the dish. If there are any prominent roots, expose them—this will create an impression of age. Cover the roots with soil and press down firmly as you fill the dish. Don't just dump your tree in the middle of the dish; decide which spot will be to its best advantage. After potting or repotting, keep the bonsai in a sheltered, semi-shady spot. It should not be subjected to the hot midday sun, excessive rain or wind. In a few weeks, when it has settled down, move it out. Begin feeding only when it has settled.

Carefully remove the tree from its container.

Cut the roots back by at least one third.

GROUND COVER

In hot, dry regions, one cannot use moss as a ground cover, or have that look of a velvety forest cover. But there are many other ground covers available. A walk around the nurseries will provide you with pretty ground covers if

Using a wooden stick remove about half the old earth from the root ball.

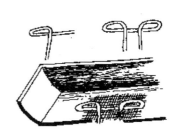

Use a loop of wire like this to secure the mesh over the drainage hole in the dish. Pot shards can be used too.

Repotting Bonsai

you care to look for them. For those who live in cooler regions, moss can be grown easily and you can create quite an effect by growing different kinds of mosses.

All bonsai are outdoor plants; don't treat them like delicate hothouse plants, they will not thank you for it. Let them feel the wind, the rain and the sun, the amount the tree is accustomed to when growing in the wild.

Never allow the soil to get bone-dry.

HARMONY AND BALANCE

These are essential for a good bonsai. These qualities cannot be explained but felt, like the wetness of water or the warmth of fire. The best one can say is that it is the placement of an object in a well-defined space. A painting is two-dimensional, but a bonsai, like sculpture, is three-dimensional and all angles must be considered. It is immobile no doubt, but it has a rhythmic dynamism. To place a bonsai right, you must have an understanding of space and proportion.

Bonsai Aesthetics
1) Composition of a tree as a whole
2) Line and form
3) Harmony and balance
4) Perspective and depth
5) Focal point
6) Movement
7) Rhythm
8) A pot that is in harmony with the composition

FEEDING

As a plant grows, it extracts various elements from the soil. Feeding is vital for bonsai as they have very limited soil to grow in. But over-feeding can be harmful. It may produce branches that are too thick or leaves that are too large. And mainly, overfeeding can cause root damage which will ultimately kill the plant. As a rule, young plants require more nutrients than older ones, fast-growing trees more than slow-growing ones. Do not feed the plant when it is dormant. Begin feeding when the first shoots appear and carry on at regular intervals till leaf-fall. Flowering plants should be fed just before they begin to flower; fruit-bearing plants just as the fruit has begun to form. Water the plant thoroughly before feeding, especially when using inorganic feeds. The Japanese use pellets made of rapeseed, bone and fish meal, but though garden centres don't stock organic pellets, they do stock the ingredients. Finally, you must know what your plant requires. (*See* 'Cultivation and Watering'.)

The Perfumed Garden

Soft breeze, sweet perfumed with the fragrant scent
Of jasmine white and gold, caress her face,
Brush with your breath her breast and bring content,
The scented fragrance of her sweet embrace.

—Bhavabhuti

The most neglected of all our senses is the sense of smell. There's a paucity of words to describe scent; one has only broad similes and even those are inadequate. And yet it is the sense of smell that adds so much to the quality of life. It is the aroma of food that gets the salivary glands working, it is the perfume of a flower that makes it so much more appealing and often, the scent of a woman is remembered long after her face is forgotten. We don't have a special word for the sense of smell perhaps because it is not as important to us as sight or hearing. But it *is* of greater significance than we think since without it, qualitatively, life would be so much the poorer.

And we do pamper the nose whether we consider the sense of smell important or not. People have always appreciated perfumes and gone to great lengths to procure them. Today a good perfume is worth its weight in platinum. The Song of Solomon praises the scented plants in the garden: 'an orchard of pomegranate with pleasant fruits, camphire and spikenard, saffron, calamus and cinnamon, with trees of frankincense, myrrh and aloes with all the chief spices.' The ancient Persians, Indians, Romans and Greeks were inordinately fond of perfumes, and used them as much to adorn

It's people? Ah well!
I know not their hearts,
But in my native place
The flowers with their ancient
Fragrance are odorous.
—Ki No Tsurayuk

themselves as in their rituals. Perfumes travelled the old caravan routes and probably even before that. Perfumes were big business as much then as it is now. The Egyptians imported sweet-smelling plants and spices to make unguents to scent their bodies when alive and to preserve their embalmed bodies when they died. Perfumed oils were extensively used in India more than 2500 years ago. The Yaksha in Kalidasa's *Meghadhutam* is briefly transported to his wife's bower when he smells flowering jasmine and siris in exile.

Aroma therapy, now being propounded by the pundits of natural medicine, is not a new discovery but the rediscovery of a branch of knowledge the ancient world was familiar with. The people would not have gone to such pains to import the 'perfumes of Arabia' had they been used only for their cosmetic value. In Europe and England, people believed that the scent of cloves and oranges kept the plague away. It didn't, but was better than the stench. Cardinal Wolsey carried a pomander of orange stuck with cloves which was called a

'comfort apple'. According to Bullenyn, they were 'to be worne against foule stinking aire'. In ancient Greece, a wreath of rosemary was worn by students as it was said to improve memory. 'The smell of basil is good for the heart and head,' wrote John Gerard the herbalist. In India, perfumed oils were used to soothe the body and ease tension. Men and women twined jasmine, champak, siris and other perfumed flowers in their hair and wore them on their person, as much for their perfume as to keep the body cool. Today, a number of essential oils are used to treat nervous disorders ranging from fatigue and stress to hypertension.

She breaks off playing
Looks out, twines her hands
Wishes for some book and
then, disturbed
She pushes back the jasmine
scent, she finds
The fragrance hurts.
—Rilke

All through the ages, poets have written about perfumed breezes, scent in the air, sweet-smelling flowers, perfumed night air, or the scents in golden sunshine. The sense of smell may not be important to our existence, but life would lack a certain something without it. Scent is soul food, vital not to the stomach but to the spirit. Sit in a garden in the midst of sweet-smelling flowers and somehow, all care seems to slip away. The air refreshes and soothes the weary spirit and we know that it does, though we don't know why. Perhaps scent is far more important to us than we think.

A garden without perfume is like a poem without poetry. In the ancient civilizations of China, Greece, India, Egypt, Persia and Rome, perfumed gardens were the norm rather than the exception, and the famous gardens of eighteenth century Europe and England were merely following this tradition. Flowers were valued as much for their beauty as their scent, and many flowers were cultivated chiefly for their aromatic qualities. The old cultivars of most garden flowers we know—carnations, roses, jasmines, stocks, pinks, and narcissi—are heavily perfumed. Only the twentieth century hybrids are bred more for size, form and colour rather than scent, which is a terrible pity. The flowers are beautifully formed and gorgeously coloured, but their scented cousins would give them a run for their money. It's a mystery why the hybridists choose to ignore scent. It must be something to do with the twentieth century love for packaging. But all gardeners, if true to their calling, prefer the scented flowers of

Come, girl, and stand before now,
If you but knew what no one knows,
You'd let me have a single hair
More fragrant for me than the rose.
—Karacaoglan

an old cultivar to the more showy, modern hybrid. Only the uninformed or those whose olfactory sense is moribund will stock their garden with these scentless, ostentatious blooms.

You can have a garden redolent with perfume if you choose to. It does not matter if the garden is large or small. In fact a small garden, if enclosed, will trap the perfume which would otherwise be wafted away by the breeze. Choose plants suited to your garden and the climate of the area. Plan for year-round fragrance by planting the right annuals, shrubs and creepers, some that will flower in summer, others in winter and those that bloom in the rainy season. If you're living in the plains, it's easy, for most bulbs and annuals which are summer flowering in the cooler regions are part of the winter annuals here. The true aesthete will plan not only for the seasons but also for the day and night. Some flowers release

Upon that rosy cheek bestrew the
hair of violet;
With scented balms perfume the
garden through, gentle breeze.
—Ahmedi

their perfume at night, though most release their perfume during the day. In India, your seasons will include the monsoon—many shrubs and creepers bloom during the rains but very few annuals can tolerate the Indian summer or monsoon as most come from temperate regions.

The sense of smell is the most evocative of all our senses, far more than sight or sound. There is a theory that this is because the olfactory centre is very close to the memory centre in the brain. Science can take away the magic, but a scented garden is nothing short of enchantment.

India has a stupendous wealth of scented flowers and aromatic plants, both indigenous and naturalized. With a small garden, you will have to choose carefully. You cannot have plants which have a short flowering season and look shabby the rest of the time, neither can you have large flowering

At Kandilli, in the old garden,
when Evening drops her curtains
one by one, sadness is tinged
with happy memories.
—Yahya Kemal Beyatli

trees like the siris or champak. You cannot have too many creepers and shrubs either. Making a choice is onerous but it must be done in the case of small gardens. If you have a large garden, you can go to town.

Aromatic Abode:

- If the plants are in pots, place them near doors or windows to bring the scent in. Creepers can be trained up a wall near a door or window. Small beds can be made beneath windows and scented annuals can be planted in them.
- Many plants such as freesias and hyacinths can be brought indoors once they start flowering.
- Buy old-fashioned flowers which are scented rather than the modern hybrids, whether roses, annuals or bulbs.
- In a small space, don't crowd the plants; they need to breathe too. Restrict yourself to a few well-chosen ones.
- Many aromatic plants are not very spectacular but are exquisitely scented, and some release their perfume when bruised. Include them in your plan; they will give great satisfaction.
- The rose has the widest range of scents in the floral kingdom, from the apple-scented *R. wichurianas* to the raspberry-scented Bourbons, and as bonus, the flower petals retain their scent when dried.

SOME SCENTED FLOWERS

Jasmine (*Jasminum*)

> The owner may also set the jasmine tree bearing a fragrant flower . . .
> it yieldeth a delectable smell, much refreshing the sitter underneath it.
> —Thomes Hyll

There are about 300 species of jasmine, most of which are tropical and sub-tropical plants. None are native to North America, but fortunately for us, many are indigenous to India. Jasmines may be climbers or shrubs with white, yellow and occasionally rosy-pink flowers. The ones with white flowers are usually very fragrant; the yellow ones are practically scentless except for *J. parkeri*, the dwarf evergreen, which has scented blossoms. Most jasmines are summer flowering but a few flower in winter. *J. grandiflorum* has snow-white flowers which bloom all through summer. It is a hardy plant and requires no special care. In the northern plains, it is deciduous. In Italy and Spain, this variety is used to produce the famous jasmine oil of the region. In China, the flowers are used to scent tea.

One of the most fragrant jasmines is *J. polyanthum* from China. This too is a climber, and the flowers are used to produce jasmine oil.

J. officinale has sweet-smelling small flowers. It is found in the wild from Iran to China and was grown all along the ancient trade routes, and was introduced into England in the middle of the sixteenth century.

J. pubescens is a bushy shrub which can also be trained onto a low trellis. The long sprays of flowers appear during the monsoon and last well into the cool months.

J. pubescens var rubescens is a winter-flowering jasmine. The flowers appear on the tips of the branches—the outer petals are pink and the inner petals white.

There are too many varieties to enumerate. Check your local nursery and see what is available before you buy.

Jasmines are propagated by cuttings or layerings. They should be pruned after the flowering season is over.

Queen of the Night (*Selenicereus grandiflorus*)

This is a popular shrub and widely grown in the plains. It does not do well in the hills. The plant flowers twice a year—spring/summer and again before the onset of winter. The small, greenish flowers have a heady perfume and open at night, drenching the air with scent. A few shrubs can fill a fairly large garden with perfume. The shrub can grow to a height of 12 ft but should be pruned during the rains or whenever you think necessary. Don't allow it to get straggly. It makes an excellent hedge plant and can be trained on a trellis. It is easily propagated by cuttings.

Brunfelsia

See 'Small Trees and Shrubs'.

Gardenia

This shrub from South China has large, beautifully scented white flowers which resemble the camellia. The plant blooms profusely when mature, and the flowering period lasts several months. It does not like heavy pruning. The soil should be rich but not clayey.

Curry-leaf Tree

This is a small tree, grown mainly for its leaves which are used in Indian cooking, but it bears umbels of scented flowers in March/April. The flower-heads appear on the tips of the branches and have a sweet, heady fragrance.

Ixora

These are outstandingly ornamental plants which grow in the tropics, from Madagascar to India and China. The only scented one is from Madagascar. Like other ixoras, it is hardy and flowers right through the summer and rains. It is a neat, slow grower and extremely effective. It has huge clusters of white or pinkish-white flowers which are very sweetly scented, but look dirty with age. Ixoras like moderately rich soil and grow best in warm moist regions but can be grown in the northern plains if sheltered from the summer sun. It is a large shrub, so plant more than one only if you have the space.

Oleander (*Nerium*)

Oleanders are a very popular species of Mediterranean shrubs and grow well all over the country. They are very ornamental, very pretty and very poisonous. The Borgias, especially Lucrezia, are said to have used the oleander to get rid of their enemies. Almost every part of the plant is poisonous, so if there are children in the house, don't let them nibble on a leaf or twig. The lovely pink flowers have a vanilla scent and release their fragrance at night. It is also a useful plant for patios or terraces as it makes a good pot plant. The plant can grow upto 12 ft tall but is much smaller when confined in a pot. The flowers may be white, deep pink, pale pink, crimson or purple—single or double. The variegated forms are usually double. Not all oleanders are scented. Check with your nursery before buying a plant. Oleanders, if shaped and trained, can be made into small trees and used as a focal point in a small garden. They need plenty of sunshine, air and water duing the growing period. Oleanders do not need rich soil; they grow well in fairly poor soil, so they are a good choice for those who do not want to improve the soil conditions in their garden.

Olea (fragrans)

This is a slow-growing shrub with dark green leaves. The creamy flowers are not very conspicuous but are delightfully scented. The perfume is rich and penetrating but not in the least cloying. Needs good garden soil to thrive. This plant does not propagate easily. It's best done by layering or cuttings.

Trachelospermum jasminoides

This creeper is also called *Rhyncosperum jasminoides*
in some gardening books. It is a useful climber as it
grows well in semi-shade. It does not like the full sun of
the northern plains, especially in summer. It has neat,
attractive foliage and the small, scented flowers are a sparkling
white. It flowers profusely in the hot months. This plant was
very popular in colonial America, especially in the southern
gardens. Many think it is a native of America but it is in fact
indigenous to Malaya and China. This creeper should be grown in
the ground as it does not take well to potting, but the expert manages
quite well. It can look straggly in the northern winters when it sheds
its leaves. It is easily propagated by cuttings or layers.

*Trachelospermum
jasminoides*

Honeysuckle (*Lonicera*)

This is a large genus with about 200 species. They are found in North and Central America,
Eurasia, the Himalayas, Philippines, China and Malyasia. Most are shrubs but the ones we are
interested in are the climbers, *L. periclymenum* and *L. p. var' belgica*
and *L. japonica*. All bear very fragrant flowers. Honeysuckles do
very well in the hills and cooler regions of the plains. They can
get rampant and invasive if left uncontrolled. They are very
effective when trained over an arch, a pleached walk or onto an
arbour. Honeysuckles require fairly rich soil and are propagated
by cuttings. All these honeysuckles flower in spring/summer.
Among the shrubby honeysuckles, there are several that bloom
in winter, particularly the two Chinese species, *L. fragrantissima*
and *L. standishii*. They have a compact form and masses of white flowers which are very sweetly
scented. The flowers appear on naked branches.

> And bid her steal into the
> pleached bower,
> Where Honeysuckle, ripened
> by the sun,
> Forbids the sun to enter.
> —Shakespeare

Creeping Tuberose (*Stephanotis floribunda*)

This is a very handsome creeper with umbels of large, tubular waxy-white flowers which are very
fragrant. It is a native of Madagascar and is often called the Madagascar jasmine. The fleshy leaves
are smooth and oval in shape. It can grow up to a height of 12 ft. It flowers throughout the
summer and the rains. It likes soil rich in humus and soil nutrients, and must be grown where it
will not be exposed to the strong midday sun. Water copiously during the growing period. It likes

a warm, moist climate but can be grown in the northern plains if sheltered from the summer sun.

It grows well in tubs or large urns. If grown in a container, thorough drainage is essential.

Rangoon Jasmine (*Quisqualis indica*)

Also known as the Drunken Sailor, this splendid creeper is from tropical Asia. It's generic name, literally translated from Latin, means 'Who? What?' It got this name because of its odd growing habit. It starts off shrub-like, erect for the first three feet. Then it produces a new basal shoot which is a climber, and the original stem dies. The Rangoon Jasmine is grown extensively for its showy racemes of five-petalled flowers which open white, change to pink and finally become a deep crimson towards the end of their lives. The flowers release their perfume at night, a light jasmine-like scent. It blooms throughout the summer months and often again after the rains. It is a vigorous creeper that does well in fairly poor soil once it is established. The best time to prune is in January. It is propagated by cuttings.

Rangoon Jasmine

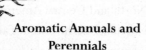

Aromatic Annuals and Perennials
Alyssum
Stocks
Sweet Sultanas
Sweet Williams
Dianthus (carnations and pinks)
Tobacco plant
Nasturtium
Sweet peas
Mignonette
Pansies
Lupin
Violets

Aromatic Plants
Lemon balm
Lavender
Lemons
Marjoram
Patchouli

Cowslip Creeper (*Pergularia odoratissima*)

This is a creeper that should be trained up a tree or grown as a backdrop for other plants. The yellowish-green flowers are not particularly attractive but they are very fragrant. Another plus point is that it will flower several times a year and will grow well in normal garden soil. The creeper likes warm, moist conditions. Water frequently during the hot months.

Snow-wreath (*Porana racemosa*)

This is an evergreeen perennial climber from India and Burma. It bears many funnel-shaped white flowers in a loose, leafy panicle. Bridal-wreath (*P. paniculata*) has masses of pure white, scented flowers that appear in November/December. It should be severely pruned after flowering.

Aromatic Bulbs
Madonna lily
Freesias
Hyacinths
Grape hyacinths
Iris
Narcissus
Spider lily
Eucharis lily
Crocus
Japanese day lilies

Midnapore Creeper (*Rivea hypocrateriformis*)

This creeper from west India has large, fragrant, white flowers that open at night. The flowers have a clove-like scent, somewhat like the old-fashioned carnations.

Aromatic Small Trees
Coral Tree
Temple Tree
Mandarin Orange
Bauhinia

Moonlight Garden

Even in the rain come forth
O midnight moon!
But first put on your hat.

—Basho

In a climate where it is far more pleasant to linger out of doors after nightfall, it would be a shame not to create a garden designed to be seen by the light of the moon. As the brilliant colours of the day fade leaving a chirascuro of light and shade, scents are more heightened as they linger softly in the night air. A moonlit garden has a magical quality. It is pensive and subtle, mysterious and romantic. The ancient Chinese and Japanese, passionate lovers of the moon, created gardens which were used and viewed only on moonlit nights. The court calendar of Heian Japan (eighth to eleventh century AD) marked the fifteenth day of the eighth month for The Great Moon Viewing, a ceremony imported from China. Ivan Morris writes in *The World of the Shining Prince*: 'To the sound of lute and zither music, men and women spend the night in boats on artificial lakes of the palace and private residences, viewing the moon and composing poems in its honour.'

In ancient China, before the Christian era, moon-viewing nights, especially the night of the August moon, were celebrated by the aristocracy. Later the custom spread among people from all walks of life. Commoners and nobility alike went moon-viewing and made offerings of dumplings to the moon retiring only when the moon had set. The August moon was regarded as the most beautiful of all full moons and the night was reserved exclusively for its viewing. This was no religious ceremony such as the Greek offerings to Selene; the Chinese simply

It seemed odd that the Mughals, especially Jehangir and Shah Jahan, did not create gardens for the moonlight. Both had a great love of beauty and pleasure and surely among the many gardens that they built, there were some to be enjoyed only by the light of the moon. But none of the known ones are. It is reassuring to know, thanks to recent excavations, that Shah Jahan, for one, did create a garden to be enjoyed by moonlight. Opposite his beloved Taj Mahal, on the other bank of the Yamuna, he created Mehtab Bagh (Moon Garden). The Emperor had a grandstand view of the Taj from the crescent-shaped grassy bank. The garden had white plaster walkways, two pools, one square and one octagonal. There were fountains in the water courses and delicate, colonnaded pavilions where the Emperor sat to view his white marble Taj awash in moonlight. Back in the seventeenth century, when the air was unpolluted, the gardens must have been absolutely magical in the light of the moon.

celebrated the beauty of the moon. Ma Yuan, one of China's greatest painters, painted the famous 'Plum Blossoms by Moonlight'. A scholar sits on a rock, raptly viewing the moonlit plum blossoms, while a pageboy stands silently behind. There is an ancient legend about an old gardener who, loathe to leave the garden at dusk, stayed in the moonlit garden and met the Willow, Plum, Peach and Pomegranate fairies who were in trouble, and rescued them. The fairies rewarded him with magic flower petals which gave him back his long-lost youth and when he died, the flower fairies made him an immortal. Painters and poets alike were inspired by the moonlight. A monk artist during the Ming Dynasty was inspired by a shadow of a branch of plum blossom on a moonlit night, and his painting was the first of many of this genre.

The ancient Greeks and Romans worshipped the moon—Selene, Cynthia, Diana—and temples to them were erected in sacred groves. But they did not create special gardens purely to enjoy the moonlight on rippling water or flowers drenched in moonshine. Their poets and writers, however, like those everywhere throughout the ages, have waxed eloquent about the beauty of a moonlit night. By the seventeenth century, England, France, Italy and Holland were creating gardens of great vision and beauty, and by the eighteenth and early nineteenth centuries, gardens of unsurpassed loveliness were created by artists such as Capability Brown and Thomas Wright, and many garden features were designed to be used and enjoyed specifically on moonlit nights. Arbours, grottoes, and cupolas were covered with jasmines and roses, some of which bloomed during the day and some which bloomed at night.

How sweet the moonlight sleeps upon this bank!
Here we will sit and let the sounds of music
Creep in our ears.
—Shakespeare

❧ The ideal setting for a moonlit garden is where the moonlight can come into full play, where artificial lighting will not dim it or blot it out altogether. But even in the neon-lit urban landscape, you can create a garden all silver, black and luminous white with an ethereal loveliness, equalled only by a garden at dawn when the dew lies thick on the flowers and scent begins to drift in the air. All colours change when darkness falls—reds, dark greens and deep purples turn to black; the pale greens turn to grey; and the blues, the last to fade out, also turn to grey. But the yellows remain bright; the lemons turn to white; and white turns luminescent. If the plants have been chosen after careful deliberation, rich scents will fill the air. If there is water, it will be the final touch to a garden which even Titania would not scorn to grace. A small balcony which receives only a few hours of moonlight can be, for those few hours, a place of pure magic.

❧ The most effective flowers in the moonlight are white, yellow, lemon or cream. The flowers should be planted where they can create a dramatic effect, but this deliberate planning should not be evident—it should look as natural as possible unless the artifice is a part of the garden plan, as it can be in a formal design.

❧ You can have water even on a balcony, though in a garden or patio, you can have a proper little pool or fountain. In the balcony you can have a shallow basin of water surrounded by plants so that the container is not visible. The plants should not obstruct the water. Small plants with a few leaves or flowers hanging over the water are ideal. White and yellow zephyr lilies which bloom in summer and other such bulbs are well suited to this. If properly planned, you can have something blossoming almost all the year round. If you have a little pool, plant white flowers near it along with some rushes or reeds. Choose ones that bear silvery-white plumes. The effect can be quite theatrical.

❧ Plant banks of plants with yellow or white flowers against a wall or against a backdrop of a dark shrub or hedge. If there is a large tree, or even a small one, train a creeper with white blossoms up the tree.

❧ Some plants have insignificiant flowers but are very sweetly scented and release their perfume at night. Plant them in any quiet spot, leaving the prominent places for those flowers that have visual impact.

❧ When planting, check which areas in your garden receive moonlight. If you're lucky and have a garden which receives the light of the rising moon, the moon in mid-heaven and the setting moon, you can have a field day. Don't limit yourself.

- If you have a garden seat, plant white or yellow annuals in beds on the opposite side, where they can be viewed. No point planting them behind the seat.

- In a flat, cut out the light of nearby buildings or street lights by enclosing your balcony.

- If you have a lawn, plant yellow or white flowers on the edges surrounding it to create a rather dramatic effect of light and dark.

- Train appropriate plants on a trellis or pergola. Do the same if you have an arch. For flowers all the year round, plant two species on either side of the arch, one to flower in summer, another to flower in winter. The choice of creepers is almost limitless. If there is a seat under the arch, include a creeper with scented flowers which bloom at night, even if the flowers are not white or yellow. Jasmine will give you both perfume and flowers which open at night. If in the hills, you can have roses entwined with honeysuckle.

- Create a play of light and dark at different levels. Plant some low beds with a flowering shrub in the background or a flowering creeper against a wall or a post. If there is a large tree, train a creeper up the dark trunk. If the creeper has drooping flowers, so much the better.

- Unless you have a large formal garden, make the low beds informal in design. Blur the outlines and have irregular shapes.

- Don't choose plants that close at night. There are some which bloom only at night, but there are many which bloom during the day and remain open at night such as roses, phlox, petunias and lilies. In India, there's no dearth of flowers to choose from. Find out what grows best in your area from your nursery or garden centre.

- Keep short, bushy shrubs in the foreground and the larger ones in the background.

- In a small space, go vertical. Use the walls which get the moonlight or train a white flowering creeper up a dark wall. Break a flat expanse, even if it is small. Grow a creeper in a large pot and train it up a bamboo pole—the height will depend upon the size of the area—which has been sunk into the soil, and place the pot in a strategic spot. In a small garden, you can have a pergola or trellis, or you can make a frame and train a creeper on it. Creepers with pendulous flowers or ones with salver-like forms are the most effective.

🐚 In a large garden, the shrubs should gradually vanish into the background—their blossoms should seem to recede into the distance. Grow lower shrubs in the front and taller ones behind, the height increasing gradually. It will give you the effect you desire. Plant irregularly, but not haphazardly.

PLANTS FOR EARLY HOT WEATHER

Beds

Yellow coreopsis, white cosmos, yellow marigolds, white flowered tobacco plant, (fragrant) yellow sunflowers, white balsam, white and yellow zephyr lilies.

> *Thou loved of lovers, Bee, buzz off—*
> *what zestful petals wait your tupping!*
> *Such news to me was never new*
> *whose honey's long been mixt with rue.*
> —Meleagir

Climbers

Yellow alamanda, white antigonon, white ipomoea (moonflower—opens at night), white *Rhyncosperum jasminoides*, white solanum (potato creeper), white thunbergia, white bougainvillea.

Shrubs

Non-scandent jasmines, white oleander (double), white lantana, white lagerstroemia (Ragged Robins), white hibiscus.

For scent

Lemons and China oranges, white ixora, white ipomoea, Queen of the Night (jasmines), *Pergularia odoratissima* (Cowslip Creeper), Rangoon Jasmine (*Quisqualis indica*).

Flowers that stay open at night

Asters, petunias, Sweet Williams, jasmines, lilies, gladioli, chrysanthemum, Sweet alyssum, candytuft, panises, freesias, mignonette, bougainvillea, roses, begonias, orchids, narcissus.

PLANTS FOR THE COLD WEATHER

Beds

White snapdragons, white phlox, yellow snapdragons, white asters, white petunias, white candytuft, white sweet alyssum, white hollyhocks, white lupins, Lady's Lace, white verbena.

Shrubs/Small Trees

Coral Tree, yellow cassia, callaindra, roses.

Bulbs

White iris, narcissus, yellow and white freesias, eucharis lily, spider lily, white and yellow zephyr lilies, arum lilies, white canna, Japanese day lilies, white gladioli.

Note: Many plants that flower in winter in the northern plains are summer flowering in the hills and other temperate regions. Magnolias, azaleas and rhododendrons can be grown in the hills, not in the plains, as with other flowering plants such as honeysuckle, lily-of-the-valley, snowdrops, daffodils and briar roses.

A Mini Vegetable Garden

Most people think that in order to have a vegetable garden, one must have a huge plot of land. One does if the vegetables are being grown for commercial use or if you have a huge family, but you can grow fine vegetables even if you have no land. Naturally you'll have to restrict yourself to a few, but vegetables, and certainly herbs, can be grown in pots and containers. There's scarcely a city-dweller who knows the pleasure of eating freshly plucked vegetables he's grown himself. Today, organically-grown vegetables are highly regarded, and highly priced. The health nuts in the West won't eat any other, and though fanatical, they are quite right in doing so. The whole world has suddenly woken up to the fact that chemicals are unwelcome in our food, something that has been known all along. But this does not stop the growers from using them. Profits would shrink substantially. But the vegetables you grow in your yard, tubs or window-boxes will be totally free from chemicals—unless of course you use them—and you will have the added pleasure of watching them grow and ripen.

It's surprising, the number of herbs and vegetables you can grown on a tiny terrace, a little yard or in a pot garden. A lot of edible plants don't require much space—onions, lettuce, garlic, ginger, coriander, okra, chillies, strawberries, small radishes, carrots, mint, aubergines and many more. There are many hybrid dwarf varieties available today—okra,

> Ammianus, the Greek poet who lived during Emperor Haridan's reign, seems to have had an acute dislike for vegetables. Few share his sentiments, but one doesn't need to dislike vegetables to appreciate his humour:
>
> Supper at Appeles'
> Was a garden butcher's work—
> Feeding time not for men
> But a herd of cattle.
> Radishes, chicory, fenugreek,
> Lettuce and onions, leeks,
> Mint, basil, rue
> And asparagus—
> I was afriad he would then
> bring out the hay,
> So I left
> After the soggy lupins.

aubergines, tomatoes, etc. can be obtained from a good nursery or garden centre. A strip of balcony or a small paved area is quite sufficient to grow a few vegetables, many of which are very decorative plants. The one thing they do need is plenty of sunshine, so if the area receives no direct sunlight, scrap the idea of a vegetable garden and grow some shade-loving plants. But if you're determined to grow some all the same, you can have window-boxes—miniature and dwarf varieties are ideal for them.

If growing in a small plot, cultivate and enrich the soil. The soil must be rich in nutrients— nitrogen, phosphorus and potassium, the last especially if you want large, luscious vegetables and fruits. The plot must be prepared a month before you plant. Water and remove all weeds as they spring up.

Containers for vegetables must have good drainage. Since the plants have a limited amount of soil to grow in, the mixture should be rich. You can use the most unlikely objects to grow vegetables—broken buckets, a baby's old bath-tub, wooden crates, old plastic basins—anything that will hold soil and accommodate a heavy root structure. Remember, most vegetables have vigorous root growth, so the container must be reasonably deep.

Most vegetables are annuals and you can have a constant supply of quick-germinating vegetables such as lettuce and radishes if seeds are planted at three-week intervals.

- Vegetables grown in small containers will naturally be smaller than those grown in the ground, but those grown in large containers will achieve their full size provided they are well fed.
- As with any kind of gardening, the soil mixture will have to be right for the plant. The plant should have enough room for growth, sufficient light and water, and must be fed at regular intervals, especially if grown in containers.
- What you grow will depend largely upon the climate you live in. Even so, a shaded area in the plains or a sunny patch in the hills will give you vegetables other than the local produce. Out-of-season plants can be grown if they are provided the right conditions, but that can be a bother and eat into your time. There are vegetables and fruits for almost any climatic condition, and even the amateur, with a bit of effort, can have quite a respectable vegetable garden.
- Most vegetables grow easily from seed, but if you don't want the bother of thinning and transplanting, get seedlings. Seeds and seedlings are both inexpensive and worth experimenting with.
- Vegetables are energetic growers and require daily watering and a weekly dose of

good liquid feed. Some, like lettuces, are ready to be plucked after sixty days; others take upto four months to produce a crop.

✤ When the fruits and vegetables begin to appear, feed with potash. You may have to resort to inorganic chemicals such as wood-ash, which is very rich in potash, and not readily available.

✤ Don't grow the same vegetable in the same spot the following year. It is more prone to being attacked by pests and diseases. Also, different vegetables take varying amounts of essential foods from the soil. There are roughly three basic crop categories— brassicas, root crops and what might be termed as 'others'. The chief among the brassicas are cabbage, cauliflower, radish, turnips, Brussels sprouts and parsley. The most popular root crops are carrots, beetroot, potatoes, onions, garlic, leeks and spring onions. Among the 'others' are aubergines, okra, beans, peas, capsicum, lettuce, spinach and other greens, tomatoes and sweetcorn. For best results, make three divisions in your vegetable garden, growing each type in a specific area, changing the crops around the following year.

✤ Root vegetables prefer a light soil mixture because they grow and swell underground. Vegetables like cabbage and cauliflower should have their feet firmly planted in the ground, as heavy gusts of wind can uproot them. The soil mixture should be heavier. Peas and beans too, prefer heavier soil. These are academic points because in a tiny urban garden, the soil composition will not vary. But it will if the garden is extensive. Soil mixture in containers however, can be made to suit the plant's requirements.

✤ Planting time for seeds and seedlings can be tricky. Some areas get the monsoon rains quicker than others. In the northern plains one must make sure the seedlings are fairly mature before the real summer begins or they will be scorched by the sun. The same applies to the monsoon. Seedlings must be mature before the onset of the rains or they can suffer from water-logging which only a mature plant can withstand. When planting winter vegetables, and this is especially true of the northern plains, the vegetables should be ready to eat before the weather gets too hot.

✤ In a fair-sized vegetable garden, the beds should be at least 4 ft wide with small paths running between them. The soil should be dug at least 2 ft deep, bulk manure added and mixed thoroughly, and another thin layer added on top.

✤ Peas and beans need stalking. Root vegetables

> *Samuel Johnson had no use for cucumbers. 'A cucumber should b sliced, and dressed with pepper and vinegar, and then thrown out as good for nothing.'*

should be allowed to grow at least to a fourth of their ultimate size before being thinned out, as they are very sweet and delicious when young.

- Many of us have developed a taste for vegetables that are not part of our traditional cuisine, such as Brussels sprouts, artichokes and broccoli, which are not easily available even in the most exclusive markets. And when available, the quality isn't too good. You have little or no choice and have to take what you get. However, you can grow them quite easily in your vegetable garden. They will be superior in quality and infinitely cheaper.
- Nowadays there is an emphasis on quality in the vegetable garden, as it is in other areas. Many seed varieties ensure bumper crops, but to achieve this, flavour is often sacrificed. Whether it's to be quality or quantity, only you can decide. Many hybrids not only produce more vegetables but they are also better looking. The old strains however, are far tastier. Try and get local seeds or seedlings rather than the hybrid ones.
- When sowing seeds of root vegetables, they should be directly scattered into the beds and plots and later thinned out. Beans and peas are generally dropped singly into shallow drills. Small seeds such as cabbage, cauliflower and lettuce are sown in seed boxes or sheltered beds, and the seedlings are transplanted later.
- Plants such as cucumber, marrows and gourds can be trained onto frames or a trellis or allowed to ramble on a fence or low wall.
- In most parts of India, particularly the northern plains, certain vegetables are grown in the cool months, others in the hot, dry season. But in those areas where temperatures are moderate, most vegetables may be grown all the year round.
- Buy good quality seeds or seedlings. Do not sow in wet, soggy soil but in moist soil. Do not apply much fertilizer, especially inorganic chemicals.
- To simplify crop rotation, not planting the same crop in the same spot, plant similar kinds in one bed. For instance, plant leafy vegetables such as spinach, lettuce and cabbage in one bed, fast-growing vegetables among slow-growing vegetables.

SOME WINTER VEGETABLES

Globe artichoke (*Cynara scolymus*)

Sow seeds anytime between the end of August and October. A perennial in the hills, it's usually grown as an annual in the plains. Sow in seed boxes and transplant when six leaves appear. If seedlings, plant directly in the beds or containers. Ready to eat in six months.

Asparagus (*Asparagus officinalis*)

This is a perennial. Sow seeds in a seed bed, and when the ten to eleven months old, transplant into well-drained beds or large containers. The plants should be at least 12 inches apart. Feed it once a year with rich compost and a sprinkling of salt. The plants will be ready to cut after the third or fourth year.

French beans (*Phaseolus vulgaris*)

Sow seeds from August to October. There are several dwarf varieties available. Climbing French beans on scarlet runners do better in the hills, but if provided light, shade and protection from inclement weather, they can be grown quite successfully in the plains. Pinch off the growing tip when flowering begins.

Beetroot (*Beta vulgaris*)

Sow in light soil which is a bit sandy, between August and October. Scatter seeds in beds or large-mouthed containers, which are at least 1.5 ft in depth, and thin out later. If seedlings, plant directly, 10 inches apart. Ready in twelve to sixteen weeks.

Brussels sprouts (*Brassica oleracea*), **Cabbage** (*B. oleracea var. grossum*), **Cauliflower** (*B. oleracea var. botrytis cauliflora*)

Seeds should be sown in September/October in seed boxes, and when the first pair of true leaves appear, they should be transplanted. The soil mixture should be rich and a bit heavy. Ready to eat in twelve to eighteen weeks.

Capsicum (*Capsicum longum var. grossum*)

Sow seedlings 2 ft apart or one in a 12-inch pot. The soil should be rich and light. Ready to pluck in sixteen to eighteen weeks.

Capsicum

Carrots (*Daucus carota*)

Sow seeds in October in light, rich soil. There are two types—the long-rooted and short-rooted varieties. If planting in containers, get the ones with short, stubby roots.

Lettuce (*Lactuca sativa*)

There are many types available, but the most nutritious are the Romaine and the least are the Iceberg lettuces. Sow seeds in rich soil that is not too light, 12 inches apart. There are basically

Persian kings ate lettuce around 500 BC according to Herodotus. A century later, Hippocratus stated it was good for people.

two types of lettuce—compact with broad, rounded leaves and cos, which has slender, rather pointed leaves. There is also the loose-leaved lettuce. Seedlings may be sown from September to November. Ready to eat in eight to ten weeks.

I love tomatoes, hot from the sun, and the crisp feel of lettuces with the dew on them . . .
—Beverly Nichols

Onions are native to West Asia. The slaves who built the Pyramids are said to have subsisted on bread, onion, garlic and radishes. When the children of Israel fled Egypt, they bitterly missed the onions they were deprived of. In ancient India, they were grown before 1000 BC. The tale goes that when Vishnu cut off the asura Rahu's head as he was drinking amrit *(the elixir of the gods), a few drops of blood and nectar fell onto the earth. From the blood, the red onion sprang up and from the* amrit, *the white onion.*

Radish (*Raphanus sativus*)

The small, red table radish is the best for growing in containers. Radishes vary in shape, size and colour. Some are mild flavoured, others are peppery.

If you want a constant supply, sow at weekly intervals from August to January. They are ready to eat in about five weeks. Radishes like rich but light soil. The turnip-shaped radishes can be grown in containers. The long, cylindrical-shaped ones are best planted in the ground or in large tubs.

The Chinese and Japanese were eating radishes more than 2000 years ago. C'hu Yuan wrote of 'minced radishes in brine' in the third century BC. The ancinet Egyptians and Greeks too ate them. Radishes in Egypt were eaten before the Pyramids were built. Today, most radishes we eat are the oriental ones.

Onion (*Allium cepa*)

Sow seeds in October/ November or plant seedlings 8 inches apart. Sow in rich, light soil. They are ready to eat in about fourteen weeks.

Onion

Tomatoes (*Lycopersicon esculentum*)

This 'berry' (botanically the tomato is neither a fruit nor a vegetable), belongs to the deadly nightshade family, and was not eaten in many parts of Europe until the eighteenth century. Earlier, tomatoes were grown as ornamental plants.

Tomatoes

Tomatoes are said to be natives of the Peruvian and Bolivian Andes and were eaten by the Aztecs and Toltecs. In fact, the word 'tomato' comes from their word for the berry—*tomatl*. The soil for tomatoes should be light and rich. Sow seedlings in September/October, 2 ft apart. When the plant starts to fruit, nip off surplus leaf shoots at the axils of the leaves. Pinch back the top of the stem when it is about 3.5 ft high. Remove some of the lower branches so that it will grow umbrella-wise over bamboo supports. Thin out bud clusters. Feed weekly with a liquid fertilizer for best results.

Other winter vegetables

Spinach, turnips, leeks, peas, parsley, kholrabi, mustard greens, celery, garlic.

SOME SUMMER VEGETABLES

Okra/Lady's fingers (*Abelmoschus esculentus*)

This vegetable belongs to the hibiscus family. It is hardy and easy to grow. There are many small varieties available. Plant seedlings from April to late June. A 12-inch pot can comfortably hold two plants, if dwarf variety. The plants can grow upto 4 ft tall. Pinch back the leader to induce fruiting. The pods are ready to eat in about sixteen weeks.

Okra is said to have come from Ethiopia and the higher reaches of Sudan. It was grown in the Nile Valley more then 3000 years ago. The Arab raiders and traders took it to South Asia and the Mediterranean where it quickly naturalized.

Aubergine (*Solanum melongena*)

Sow seeds or plant seedlings in March/April. Plant in rich soil about 18 inches apart. There are may varieties available, small, large, round or long. Choose dwarf species for container-growing. The fruits may be purple, white or green. Ready to be plucked in about five months.

Aubergines are said to have originated in India and the neighbouring area. They too, like tomatoes, belong to the poisonous nightshade family. The Arabs took the plant to Spain and the Spaniards took it to the 'New World'.

Chilli (*Capsicum frutescens*)

Sow or plant seedlings in April/May. You will start getting chillies in ten to twelve weeks.

Bottle gourd (*Lagenaria vulgaris*), Ribbed gourd (*Luffa acutangula*), Sponge gourd (*Lufta aegyptiaca*) and other gourds

Sow seeds or plant seedlings from March to May. As all are climbers, they will need supports. A strong support is needed for vines with heavy fruits. They can be trained onto a trellis.

Other summer vegetables

Cucumbers, bitter gourd (*karela*), pumpkins, ginger and greens such as spinach.

A final word

A vegetable garden is not for the lazy or those short on time. These plants are more demanding, and if you want vegetables of quality and size, considerable care is needed. You have to constantly check for pests, feed weekly, water them daily—sometimes twice a day if the weather is dry and hot. If you don't think the effort worthwhile, scrap the idea. But you'll miss out on the joy, and the satisfaction you get when you pluck what you have grown. This is a case of 'no pain, no gain.'

A Gardener's Tale

A gardener couldn't keep his aubergines alive. Every time the seedlings came up, they wilted and died. Very upset, he went to an old, experienced gardener to ask his advice. The old man told him to bury a coin beside each plant. 'And why will that work?' he asked. The old man replied, 'There's an old saying: Those with money can survive anything!'
—A tale from ancient China

Cucumbers are the oldest vegetables to be cultivated. People were growing them more than 3000 years ago. Experts say they originated in India, from where they began their triumphal spread, East and West. They have been mentioned in the writings of ancient Chinese, Greeks, Egyptians and Jews. The Romans ate them in salads or braised. The notorious Emperor Tiberius was so fond of them everyday. They were grown on movable frames and were taken wherever he went.

The Herb Garden

Herbs that sprang up in the times of old, three ages earlier than the Gods,—
Of these whose hue is brown, will I declare the hundred powers and seven.

Be glad and joyful in the plants, both blossoming and bearing fruit,
Plants that will lead us to success like mares who conquer in the race.
Plants by this name I speak to you, Mothers, to you the Goddesses.

The healing virtues of the plants stream forth like cattle from the stall—
Plants that shall win me store of wealth, and save thy vital breath, O man.
Reliever is your mother's name, hence Restorers are ye called.

—Rig Veda

People have been using herbs since the year dot and long before. They were used in medicine, cosmetics, dyes, perfume and clothing. They were practically the only source of medicine we had until synthetic drugs came along and replaced them. Herbs were then dismissed as 'grandma's remedies', 'witch's potions' and the like. The fact that these 'potions' and 'brews' were used quite successfully by the ancients to treat diseases ranging from colds and fevers to brain surgery and rhinoplasty, was disregarded. Nose jobs are not new.

Trepanning, the drilling of a hole in the skull, was performed to treat head injuries and the resulting haematoma, swelling filled with blood. It was practised in Asia and Europe as far back as 6500 BC. Post-operative treatment was mainly herbal.

Ancient civilizations, barring none, had a staggering knowledge of plants and their uses, with India, China and Egypt heading the list. This knowledge was acquired after thousands of years of inquiry, experimentation and application. Our ancestors knew far more than we think they did, which doesn't say anything for our intelligence. Synthetic drugs have permeated every aspect of our lives, even where they have no business being present. Herbs were, until very recently, consigned to the doghouse and only the potty tinkered around with them. Pills, however, were popped at the drop of a hat.

Then we realized we were not so clever after all, in giving herbs the heave-ho. Our new-found 'awareness' (which every grandmother possessed) has made mantras of 'ecology', 'environment', and 'nature', making herbs very respectable again. After decades of contempt and being shunned, herbs are being used as if they're going out of fashion. Food, medicine, cosmetics, soaps, cleaning agents, beauty agents, all made from herbs, are flooding the markets. But these are just the same, age-old remedies in fancy packaging and highfalutin names—'Alternative medicine' (mind you, it's been around all along), 'aroma therapy', 'naturotherapy' and what have you. Manufacturers give you the impression that this is something entirely new—in the same league as Cortez beholding the Pacific.

Herbs, strictly speaking, are soft-stemmed herbaceous plants that die down in winter, but for our purpose, herbs are those plants we can eat and that have medicinal properties to boot. Until a few decades ago, we ate our vitamins and drank our trace minerals. Basil, rose petals or curry leaves were not eaten only because they are aromatic but because they constituted healthy eating.

All cultures have their traditional herbs, herbs that have been in use for thousands of years. When people moved, so did their herbs, and they have been travelling ever since. Today, herbs are moving across the globe at a furious pace, in keeping with everything else. Palates have been re-educated, and Thai, Indian, Chinese, Lebanese and European foods are eaten far from their native shores. Everywhere, people are using a greater variety of herbs than ever before. Fusion-cooking is gaining popularity even in the most conventional households and today, we not only use our traditional garlic, ginger, mint and coriander but also marjoram, galangal, lemon-leaves and parsley. Many European and East Asian herbs are available in the market.

Herbs are best eaten when they are freshly plucked, and for that, you have to grow them. They are so easy to grow, it's a pleasure. There's nothing quite so romantic as a herb garden with a seat (the scents are half the enchantment), a

---

In 400 AD, Susruta, the great surgeon, performed plastic surgery operations such as skin grafting, rhinoplasty and for ear-lobe deformity.

The Charaka Samhita *(100 AD) has a whole section devoted to 'competence in cooking'.*

Knot gardens were very popular in Europe in the 16th and 17th centuries.

Horti serviunt voluptati:
Hortus holitorius utilitati.
The knotte garden serveth for pleasure:
The potte garden for profitte.
—Latin grammar exercise for Eton scholars in 1519, one of the earliest references to a knot garden.

sundial or a bird-bath. If you have the space, design one—it is a marvelous addition to any garden. If you have a small patch, design a herb garden instead of the hackneyed lawn with a border. In a pot garden, herbs come into their own.

Herbs require little space and minimal care (diseases and pests generally avoid them), they look pretty and are so very useful to us. To have a thriving herb garden and to save yourself some heartache, grow only those herbs that will like the climate you are living in. Needless to say, this piece of advice does not apply to the expert.

Most herbs come from the warm temperate regions of the world. European herbs such as 'parsely, sage, rosemary and thyme' do very well in the hills; in the plains unfortunately, they must be treated as winter annuals, even if they are perennials. Unless you have a cool house, they will not survive the summer, but herbs native to tropical Asia will grow quite happily almost all the year round.

Herbs are best grown from seed. Nurseries don't usually stock seedlings or young plants except Holy Basil (*tulsi*). Sow winter herbs in September/October and summer herbs in February/March. If growing in the ground, broadcast the seeds and thin out. If growing in pots, germinate the seeds in seed-boxes and transplant when three sets of leaves appear.

All herbs like well-drained soil that is not too rich, and a sunny position. Few herbs will grow in the shade. Pot-herbs need extra feeding, especially the perennials.

Basil is indigenous to India and south-west Asia, and was probably taken to Greece by Alexander's soldiers where it quickly became popular.

SOME POPULAR HERBS

Basil (*Ocimum basilicum*)

This aromatic plant is very popular both in Europe and South-East Asia. Thai and Indonesian cooking owe much to basil. Thais use all the basils—*O. basilicum* as well as *O. sanctum* (Holy Basil). The plant grows easily from seed. Shelter from the monsoon rains.

Anise (*Pimpinella anisum*)

This herb was very popular with the ancient Egyptians, Greeks and Romans. When planting in the garden, scatter the seeds abroad and cover with a thin layer of topsoil. They will germinate in ten to fourteen days. The plant has a long taproot, so if grown in seed-trays, transplant seedlings after four weeks. The plants will be ready for harvesting in four to five months. Gather when the seeds turn from green to greyish-brown. Cut the entire umbel with a length of stalk, and hang upside-down in a paper bag.

Pot marigold (*Calendula*)

Plant seeds or seedlings in time if you want a good crop. Flower-heads are used in food and medicine when they are newly open.

Caraway (*Carum carvi*)

This is a biennial herb native to central Europe and west Asia, an old herb even in ancient times. It does well in the hills. It has slender, feathery leaves which grow in rosettes. Harvest seeds when they begin to darken.

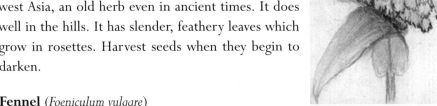

Pot marigold (Calendula)

Fennel (*Foeniculum vulgare*)

The ancient Greeks ate fennel for long life; the ancient Romans to keep their waistlines trim. It is native to the Mediterranean where the tender stalks and leaves are considered a delicacy. The

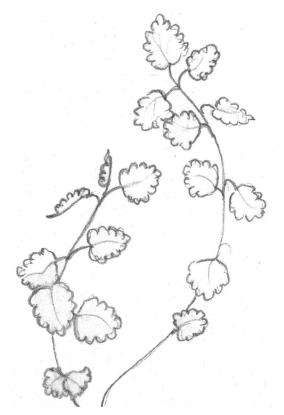

plant grows 4-5 ft tall, has bright green, shiny stems and fern-like leaves.

The bright yellow flowers are followed by the aromatic seeds for which the plant is justly famous. Ready to harvest in four to five months. *F. officinalis* is an annual, and well worth growing.

Burnet (*Sanguisorba minor*)

This bright, pretty plant will add something to the garden and to the table. Though a perennial, it must be treated as an annual except in temperate regions. This is one herb that does not like the sun too much. It likes a moist, shady site and siliceous soil. *S. officinalis* has dark red flowers which are borne in densely packed, oblong heads. The whole plant

Burnet (*Sanguisorba minor*)

has medicinal properties. *S. minor* (Salad Burnet) adds a special something to salads. It has the subtle taste of cucumber. This is one herb that always exceeds one's expectations. The leaves are a greenish-grey with a pink streak and have a curious formation. In the hills, it is one herb that will stay green throughout the winter.

Spearmint (*Mentha spicata*) and Peppermint (*M. Piperita*)

This herb can easily be grown in shallow trays or pots with a minimum depth of 3-4 inches. Give the plant space to spread itself out, though when grown in the ground, it must be severely controlled. Both mints like rich, moist, well-drained soil and do well in partial shade or bright sunshine. In the plains, it must be grown in partial shade. If in pots, shelter during the hottest part of the day. Mints are perennials but their vitality diminishes after 4-5 years when plants should be dug up, divided and replanted in a new situation.

Garlic

Allium

In the herb garden, the most useful species of this family are garlic (*A. sativum*), chives (*A. schoenoprasum*) and the potato onion (*A. cepa proliferum*). Garlic is grown from the cloves which should be planted in October/November or February/March. Chives can be grown in clumps or used as edging. Welsh onions (*A. fistulosum*) are like chives, but larger and evergreen; useful for the winter garden, especially in the hills. All alliums like rich, well-drained soil. Onions of all kinds are easily grown from seed.

Coriander

Coriander (*Coriandrum sativum*)

This is a very ancient herb, so old, it's origin is lost in antiquity. Probably a native of East Mediterranean, it is widely used by Asians and eastern Europeans. The Chinese consider this herb their own and in the West, is called 'Chinese parsley'. It is one of the seeds eaten during the Passover, the Jewish festival celebrating the deliverance of the Israelites from bondage in Egypt. In India, coriander is the most loved of all culinary plants and has been used in ayurvedic medicine for thousands of years.

Coriander grows so easily, it's embarrassing when it fails to do so. A crop can be had with virtually no effort. If grown in the ground, just broadcast the seeds. Do the same if growing in wide containers. It makes a very pretty edging too, and can be used in flower beds.

The Garden for the Gourmet

Your garden need not be a feast only for your eyes and nose. It can give your palate a great deal of pleasure as well. The flowers and leaves used in the recipes below can be found in most gardens during the growing season and the herbs are easily grown.

MARIGOLD PULAO

1 kg chicken (diced)

2 cups rice

15 almonds

5 onions

10 cloves garlic (crushed)

5 tablespoons butter

1 teaspoon thyme (fresh or dried)

1 teaspoon coriander leaves (chopped)

$\frac{1}{2}$ teaspoon cinnamon powder

salt and chilli to taste

5 cups stock (veg or non-veg)

3 tablespoons seedless raisins

5 cloves

4 tablespoons marigold petals

Cook the chicken in the stock till it is just half cooked. Blanch and slice almonds and cut the onions into rings. Wash rice and soak in water. Melt the butter in a *dekchi* and cook the onions and crushed garlic until tender. Do not brown. Remove and set aside. Drain the rice and sauté in the butter till light brown. Then add the cooked onions and garlic, almonds, thyme, coriander, raisins, cinnamon, cloves, chilli and salt. Mix and make a well in the centre and put the chicken in. Add stock and marigold petals. Cover and cook.

If you are vegetarian, omit the chicken and use vegetables.

NASTURTIUM CANAPÉ

Blend 125g of cream cheese with 2 teaspoons of nasturtium leaves. Use only the tender leaves. Spread thickly on cream crackers or toast, and decorate with nasturtium petals. This spread should be used immediately as it turns bitter if left standing.

LIME-LEAF TEA

This is a very refreshing summer drink which also relieves nervous strain.

Pick young leaves, wash and chop. Boil water and remove from heat. Add half a teaspoon of chopped leaves for every cup of water and let them steep for 20 minutes. Serve with honey. The tea can be either hot or cold.

WOOD-SORREL SOUP

1 lettuce head (chopped)

2 tablespoons butter

2 tablespoons chopped wood-sorrel leaves

4 potatoes

1 onion or leek (chopped)

1 litre stock (vegetable or chicken according to preference)

1 tablespoon coriander leaves (chopped)

250g chopped Chinese cabbage (cabbage leaves if you don't have Chinese cabbage)

Salt and pepper to taste

> **Wood-Sorrel**
> *The English poets called it shamrock. It is the national emblem of Ireland though the Irish shamrock in living tradition is the lesser trefoil.*

Sauté the onions in the butter but do not brown. Add sorrel, lettuce, cabbage leaves and sauté for 2 minutes.

Add stock. Peel, chop potatoes and add to the stock. Simmer for 45 minutes. Remove the potatoes, mash thoroughly and return to the soup. Add coriander, salt and pepper, and simmer for five minutes. Serve with hot garlic toast or buttered toast.

WOOD-SORREL SAUCE

This sauce can be served with fried or roasted meats, broccoli, Brussels sprouts or potato dishes.

> 2 handfuls of freshly chopped sorrel leaves
> 1 tablespoon sunflower or safflower oil
> $1/_2$ cup milk
> 1 cup stock (meat/vegetable)
> 2 tablespoons American flour (*maida*)
> Salt, chilli or pepper to taste
> Pinch of sugar
> 6 basil leaves (chopped)

Wash and chop the leaves fine. Heat the oil in a pan and sauté the leaves lightly. Add the stock and boil till the leaves are tender. Blend the flour in the milk, add to the stock and allow to boil till it thickens a little. Season with basil, salt, sugar and pepper, and serve at once.

SORREL TURNOVER

This is a dessert with a difference.

Dry pastry mix

> 125g butter
> 250g flour
> Salt, a pinch or more
> Water

Place the salt in a bowl, sift the flour and add it to the salt. Mix the butter in the flour until it resembles breadcrumbs. Add just enough water to make firm dough.

Turnover

> 1 cup dry pastry mix
> 3 teaspoons freshly chopped sorrel leaves
> 2 teaspoons dried sweet cicely
> 1 teaspoon lemon juice
> 2 tablespoons brown sugar
> A few raisins

Add water to the pastry mix and make firm dough. Roll out and cut into two rounds the size of your baking dish. Mix dried sweet cicely with the lemon juice. Add the sorrel leaves and brown sugar and spread it on one pastry disk. Scatter the raisins on top. Wet the edges of the pastry and place the second disk on top and press down lightly. Place it in the dish and bake at 350°C for about 15 minutes or until golden.

If you prefer, you can make small individual turnovers.

GREEN SALAD WITH NASTURTIUM DRESSING

1 head lettuce

1 tomato (chopped)

1 small cucumber (chopped)

1 cup boiled corn kernels (optional)

$1/4$ teaspoon sugar

10-15 nasturtium flowers

Juice of 2 lemons

3 tablespoons salad oil

2 teaspoons chopped nasturtium leaves

$1/4$ teaspoon thyme

$1/4$ onion (finely chopped), or 1 spring onion

20g bean sprouts

Shred lettuce leaves into large bits and mix with tomatoes, bean sprouts, onion, cucumber and corn, and place in a bowl. (Do not use a metal bowl.) In a separate bowl or cup, mix the lemon juice and salad oil, stirring well. Add nasturtium leaves, thyme, salt and sugar, and mix. Place the nasturtium flowers on the green vegetables, and pour the dressing over the salad. Toss and serve immediately. Chopped crisply fried bacon—sausages will make it even more interesting.

CURLY KALE SOUP

250g curly kale leaves

1 large onion (finely chopped)

2 tomatoes (pureed)

$1^1/2$ litres stock (meat or vegetable)

$1/2$ kg potatoes

1 carrot (diced)

1 teaspoon chopped basil leaves or $1/2$ teaspoon dry basil

2 tablespoons butter

Pepper and salt to taste

$1/4$ teaspoon dried thyme

10 French beans (stringed and halved)

Strip the leaves off the stalks; wash and drain in a colander. Put the leaves in a vessel with half the stock and cook for five minutes.

Remove the leaves and chop finely and return to the stock. Sauté the onions, carrots, and tomato puree in a pan, in butter. Add to the kale and stock, and cook until tender. When cooked, turn off the heat and add the basil, thyme, pepper and salt, and let it stand for 15 minutes. Serve garnished with a ball of butter.

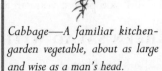

Cabbage—A familiar kitchen-garden vegetable, about as large and wise as a man's head.
—The Devil's Bedside Book

KALE AND POTATO SAUTÉ

  1 onion (chopped)
  10 basil leaves
  3 tablespoons vegetable oil
  500g potatoes (diced)
  500g kale leaves (coarsely chopped)
  Salt and pepper to taste
  Pinch of sugar

Sauté the onions in a frying pan until golden brown. Add the potatoes, kale, salt, sugar, basil and pepper, and sauté for 5 minutes. Cover and simmer until the potatoes are tender. When done, sprinkle a little thyme.

DUTCH KALE AND POTATO SOUP

The Dutch call this stew 'Stampot'.

  500 g kale leaves (washed and finely chopped)
  500 g potatoes (peeled and chopped)
  250 g frankfurters
  1 teaspoon salt
  50 g butter
  Pepper to taste or a few green chillies

Boil kale in water until tender, and drain, keeping the water. Arrange the potatoes in a pan and add the kale water until the potatoes are half covered. Chop the frankfurters into large pieces and add to the pan along with the cooked kale. Add salt, pepper or green chillies and cook over a low heat until the potatoes are very tender and the water has all but evaporated. Now add the butter and mix well. Serve hot with buttered toast.

COLCANNON

This is a dish traditionally served on Halloween in Scotland and Ireland. There is a ring hidden in it, predicting marriage for the maiden who finds it.

> *Did you ever eat Colcannon when*
> *it was made with yellow cream,*
> *And kale and praties blended*
> *like the picture in a dream?*
> *Did you ever take a forkful and*
> *dip it in the lake*
> *Of the clove-flavoured butter that*
> *your mother used to make?*
> *Did you ever eat and eat, afraid*
> *you'd let the ring go past,*
> *And some old married sourpuss*
> *would get it at the last?*
> Traditional Scottish Poem

$^1/_2$ kg potatoes (peeled and diced)

3 spring onions (finely sliced)

$^1/_2$ kg kale (washed and chopped)

150 ml milk

1 teaspoon salt, or to taste

25 g butter

Boil potatoes and kale separately. Drain the potatoes and mash in a pan until smooth. In a separate pan, simmer the spring onions in milk until soft, and add the mixture to the potatoes, beating well. Add the boiled, drained, kale. Season with salt and pepper, and stir over low heat. When the mixture is smooth and hot, add the butter and mix thoroughly. Serve hot and garnish with more butter.

GRILLED MACKEREL WITH FENNEL

4 mackerels (about 300 g each)

8 sprigs fennel leaves

Salt to taste

Freshly ground pepper to taste

4 tablespoons coarsely chopped fennel bulb (optional)

2 tablespoons vegetable oil

Wash the fish and pat dry. Sprinkle the cavities with salt and pepper. Fill each with 1 tablespoon of chopped fennel and two sprigs of fennel leaves. Brush the outside of the fish with oil and grill until it is done. Garnish with lemon wedges and fennel sauce.

Fennel sauce (about 300 ml)

1 small fennel bulb (trimmed)

100 g butter

25 g flour

Salt to taste

1 tablespoon chopped fennel leaves

Boil salted water and drop the bulb into the boiling brine. Parboil for 3-4 minutes. Remove, drain and chop very fine. Melt butter in a pan over low heat and add flour, stirring until you have a smooth mixture. Add 150 ml of the salt water and continue stirring until the sauce has thickened. Add the chopped fennel and simmer for 10 minutes or until the fennel is soft. Stir in chopped fennel leaves and serve with grilled or steamed fish.

CREAM OF FENNEL SOUP

1 fennel bulb (trimmed and cut crosswise)
Salt to taste
2 egg yolks
4 tablespoons cream
50 g butter
15 g flour
1 litre clear chicken soup stock
Pepper to taste
Pinch of sugar

Sauté fennel slices in half the butter in a covered saucepan over medium heat for about 10 minutes. In a larger pan, melt the remaining butter and add flour, stirring constantly over low heat until well blended. Stirring all the while, add the stock slowly until the ingredients are well mixed. Bring to boil, add the fennel and simmer over low heat. Cover the pan.

When the fennel is soft, pour through a soup sieve. Discard any pulpy remains. Return the soup to the pan and re-heat. Add salt, sugar and pepper. Beat the egg yolks with the cream and add to the soup, stirring constantly. Heat till it thickens. Do not let it boil. Garnish with chopped fennel leaves and serve.

HERB SUGARS

Herb sugars are very simple to make and lend a charming old-world touch to your meal. They can be used to decorate cakes, sweeten cool drinks like fruit juices, or sprinkled on *barfis*, in *kheers* and *payasams*.

To make the sugar, simply add any sweetly scented leaves like rose-geranium, lemon grass, rose petals, whole violets or peppermint leaves to fine white sugar. Place the mixture in airtight jars and store for about three weeks before using.

HERB-FLAVOURED OIL

Salads which need an oil-based dressing are greatly enhanced by these oils.

Clean and dry a bottle and put a branch of any fresh herb—thyme, basil, dill seeds, coriander seeds, lemon balm etc., and pour safflower oil into the bottle until full. Garlic, peppercorns and whole dried chillies may be added if desired. Can be used after a month.

TURMERIC PICKLE

$1/2$ kg fresh turmeric roots
Freshly ground chilli powder to taste
A lump of palm sugar (the size of a lemon)
6 teaspoons salt
2 teaspoons mustard seeds
20-30 curry leaves
1 tablespoon vegetable oil
15 cloves garlic
Juice of 6 lemons

Clean and scrape the roots, and chop into small pieces. Peel garlic and put the two into a ceramic or glass bowl. Add salt and set aside. Heat the oil in a pan, sputter the mustard seeds and add the curry leaves. Turn the flame down and add the palm sugar, stirring till it dissolves. Turn off the heat and add the chilli powder and lemon juice. When it has cooled, add the turmeric and garlic. Mix thoroughly and bottle in an airtight jar and refrigerate.

BAUHINIA SABZI

250 g Bauhinia buds
1 teaspoon cumin seeds
6 green chillies
A little turmeric power
Salt to taste
1 onion (finely chopped)
6 cloves garlic (crushed)
Half-inch piece of ginger (crushed)

Soak Bauhinia buds in boiling hot water and drain after 3 minutes. Remove the stems and chop in two. Sputter the cumin seeds in a pan and add onions, garlic, ginger, salt and turmeric. Sauté for 3-5 minutes till the onions brown a bit. Add the chopped buds and lower the flame. Cover and steam for 5-10 minutes till cooked. Remove the lid, and stir-fry for 2 minutes. Garnish with chopped coriander leaves.

Small Trees and Shrubs

You have a very difficult task ahead if you are planning to plant just one or two trees—there is so much to choose from, and tree lovers end up wanting far more than they can have. You cannot have a big tree in a small garden—there's simply no space for it. You'll have to restrain yourself to small trees whose branches won't be cut off because they are blocking out the sunlight or because they are crowding a wall or window or because the electric cables are being caught in the branches. Half the beauty of a tree is its form, and to mutilate a tree is an act of sheer vandalism. So avoid large trees if you are ultimately going to lop off its branches or crown. Instead, plant a small tree which can grow to its full height and spread to its fullest.

MANDARIN ORANGE (*Citrus japonica*)

> Granted that I
> No longer please you,
> But the flowering orange
> That grows by my dwelling
> Will you not come to see it?
>
> —Anon

Oranges have been grown by man for thousands of years. There is a theory that the apple in the Garden of Eden was actually an orange. The first we read of oranges and pomelos is in the ancient Chinese text, *Yu Kung* or *Tribute to Yu*, in connection with an emperor who reigned in 2000 BC. Oranges are said to have travelled to Europe through Persia along the old caravan route. By 300 BC, Theophrastus of Greece was describing lemons and oranges in his writings. Most species of citrus—oranges, lemons, grapefruit—are natives of east Asia; a few are native to South Africa.

The mandarin orange or China orange is a small tree which produces small, bitterish fruit that makes excellent marmalade. The best thing about it is that it bears flowers and fruit when very young, quickly providing the garden with scent and colour, and taking away the raw look of a new garden. It flowers and fruits almost throughout the year. It is a very satisfying tree to grow and it pots very well. The flowers are sweetly scented. In the nineteenth century, English brides wore wreaths of orange blossom on their hair, though not of mandarin orange.

This is a marvellous tree for a tiny garden. It is hardy, puts on a show very quickly, and has a neat growing habit. If grown in a large pot, it can grow upto 5 ft, but in the ground, it grows upto a height of 15 ft. It also makes a very good bonsai.

Mandarin oranges need well-drained soil which is moderately rich. Water sparingly during the growing period, just enough to keep the soil moist, and let the soil dry out between waterings. Reduce water to a minimum once the fruiting season is over. Begin feeding the plant when it begins to bear fruit. Feed it with an organic fertilizer rich in potash, every two weeks. The plant likes the full sun; but if potted, can be brought indoors when flowering and when the fruits have ripened. Don't let it go without direct sunlight for more than a couple of days. The flowers are small, white and perfumed, and the fruit is orange-gold. The tree is propagated by cuttings. If planted in the ground, the tree should receive a yearly dose of well-rotted cattle manure.

CORAL JASMINE (*Nycanthes arbortristis*)

> Redolent with the fragrance of sephalika blossoms resonant with bird
> song in undisturbed quietness,
> groves with lotus-eyed gazelles wandering in the glades.
>
> —Kalidasa

The Sanskrit name of the Coral Tree is Parijat which means 'arisen from the sea'. This was one of the five wish-fulfilling trees in heaven which emerged when the gods churned the ocean. Indra thought it was much too good for the earth and took it to Amravati where he planted it in his garden. One day, Narada gave Krishna a blossom of the Parijat and he in turn gave it to Rukmini. Satyabhama grew jealous and Krishna went to Amravati and stole the tree, but he couldn't give it to Satyabhama without arousing Rukmini's ire. Supreme diplomat that he was, he planted the tree in such a position, that while the trunk grew in Satyabhama's garden, many of the branches drooped into Rukmini's garden. That's how, as legend would have it, the Parijat came to earth.

The Latin name means 'night flower' and 'sad tree', the former for obvious reasons (the flower blooms at night), and the latter because of its drooping branches.

The Coral Tree is a small, quick-growing, deciduous tree with weeping branches. The tree can grow to a height of 15 ft or more. It is a free-flowering tree; the flowers appear throughout autumn and winter. They are pearly white with deep orange tubes which were used to dye the robes of Buddhist monks more than 2000 years ago. The flowers have a heady fragrance and fall as soon as the first rays of the sun touch them.

The Coral Tree needs semi-shade and likes well-drained soil not too rich in humus. Feed the plant just before the flowering season with well-rotted manure. The tree can be propagated by seed or cuttings.

HIBISCUS (*Malvaceae*)

> Then bathed in evening's glow red as fresh china rose flowers
> When the lord of Beings commences His Cosmic Dance . . .
>
> —Kalidasa

Most members of the hibiscus family are native to the warm tropical parts of the world. The China rose, *H. rosa-sinensis*, is also called the 'shoe flower' because the leaves were used to polish shoes. A native of China, this plant, if left unpruned, can grow to height of 15 ft. It is hardy, flowers profusely, and has large, showy flowers.

Okra or Lady's Fingers, a favourite vegetable in India, belongs to the hibiscus family. The hibiscus is found in India, China, Africa, North America and Hawaii. There's a variety that grows in the Galapagos where it thrives on lava and coral! In Sanskrit, the plant is called Japa (prayer). The Bluebird (*H. syriacus*), is a native of India and not Syria as the specific name suggests.

Hibiscus in general require porous, loamy soil rich in nutrients. The soil must be dug deep when planting as water-logging seriously affects the plant. If grown in a pot, the soil must be well drained. For the less hardy varieties, prepare the pit and raise the bed. The soil should be mixed with well-rotted animal manure, leaf mould, bone-meal and some blood-meal. The last is especially good for the red varieties. Most varieties of hibiscus thrive in the full sun but some, like the white hibiscus, blue hibisus and some of the yellow varieties, need partial shade.

Hibiscus come in many colours—white, blue (though not a true blue), mauve, crimson, red, flame, yellow, salmon pink and apricot. The plants usually have attractive foliage and even when not in flower, can be effectively used in a small garden.

There is a charming tale about why the red hibiscus is offered to Kali (Durga). When the gods begged Durga to deal with Raktabija, the *rakshasa*, she took the awful form of Kali, the Black One. Her terrifying appearance was augmented by a skull necklace and earrings made of corpses. But the final touch was given by Japa, the hibiscus who was an ardent devotee of hers. She gave Kali the redness from her flowers which the goddess smeared into her eyes to make them appear more fearful. Kali, pleased with the gift, said, 'Whoever gives me an offering of your flowers shall be blessed by me.' That is why even today, the red hibiscus is offered to Kali.

POMEGRANATE

> Behold, thou art fair, my love . . .
> Thy lips are like a thread of scarlet, and thy speech
> is comely: thy temples are like a piece of pomegranate within thy locks.
> —The Bible ('Song of Solomon')

The pomegranate grows in the wild from Iran to the Balkans but was naturalized more than 2000 years ago, from China to the Mediterranean. The Chinese have cultivated it for centuries and even developed a dwarf variety. The finest pomegranates come from Iran and Afghanistan. Babur, when describing Marghinan in Ferghana, says: 'Its apricots and pomegranates are most excellent. One sort of pomegranate they call the Great Seed (*Dana— i-kalan*); its sweetness has a little of the pleasant flavour of the small apricot and it may be thought better than the Semnan pomegranate.' Pomegranates were cultivated in West Asia more than 2000 years ago. Ancient coins from Jerusalem bear engravings of the fruit. In the West, there is an old belief that the devil lived

Pomegranate

in the pomegranate tree and that only a good whipping could drive him out.

The pomegranate is a small tree and rarely grows more than 12 ft tall. The flowers are a brilliant orange with a thick, fleshy calyx. There are many varieties available in the market. The fruit can be from dark red to pink-white, depending upon the variety. The fruits have a tough, leathery rind and ripen in September/October.

The plants grow well in porous soil rich in nutrients but not too rich in humus. It needs to be fed regularly during the fruiting period with bone-meal and a potash-enriched manure. Don't overwater the plant—it does not like too much water. Let the soil dry out between waterings. Plants from cuttings or air-layerings bear fruit quickly—within a couple of years. Sometimes they bear fruit the following year. The only serious pest is the caterpillar. Spray with a solution of turmeric, soap

> **Why there is Winter**
>
> *Proserpine, daughter of Ceres (goddess of agriculture) and Jupiter, was kidnapped by Pluto and taken to Tartarus, the underworld. Jupiter told Ceres that Proserpine could be restored to her if no food had passed her lips. But as Proserpine had already eaten six pomegranate seeds, she could spend only six months on earth. The other six she would have to spend in the underworld. Ceres mourns the six months her daughter spends in Hades, and that is when desolate winter takes over the earth.*

> *Pliny called the pomegranate the Apple of Carthage. The word 'pomegranate' comes from the French, meaning 'apple-seed'. In the ancient world, the pomegranate was a symbol of fertility and prosperity. The whole plant has medicinal properties.*

and neem extracts to keep them away. Pomegranates should be grown in the full sun. Two varieties of pomegranates bear white flowers—the single 'Albescens', and double 'Albo Plena'. Either would make an impressive addition to the garden. Pomegranates can be grown in large pots and thrive with very little care after the initial potting. But if you want edible fruits, the flowers must removed, leaving only two or three to mature; otherwise the plant will produce small, inedible fruit. Plants in pots must be fed more frequently than those in the ground. Feed only during the growing period.

CUSTARD APPLE (*Annona squamosa*)

This is a small, pretty tree with neat habits. Its flowers resemble pear blossoms. It bears fruit from September to November. The green fruits are about the size of a large apple. The rind is segmented and lumpy, and the fruits have a delicious fragrance and flavour.

When planting, choose a large fruited variety, one that has more pulp than seeds. The segments break open when the fruit is ripe, to reveal the sweet, white pulp in which the seeds

Citrus fruits were domesticated in Indo-China around 6000 BC.

are buried. The tree grows best in comparatively dry regions but can be grown in wetter areas if the ground is well drained. Feed when the tree begins to fruit and water frequently during this period, particularly if the weather is dry.

The tree can be easily propagated from seeds or cuttings and bears fruit within four to six years. The mammoth variety cultivated in many places has very tasty fruits.

LIME (*Citrus medice*) AND LEMON (*Citrus limon risso*)

Citrus is an important genus which has about 12 species and innumerable hybrids which include limes, oranges, lemons, tangerines, sweet limes and grapefruit. Quite a few of these have been cultivated in China since very early times. Christopher Columbus is credited with taking lemon and bitter orange seeds to the New World during his second voyage. The Dutch introduced lemons and oranges to the Cape of South Africa in the seventeenth century.

Some varieties of limes and lemons grow into very fine small trees. The trees should be shaped when young. Remove all branches from the base and the surplus ones above. The plant should not have more than four main branches.

Lemons like rich, well-drained soil. Some varieties will grow very well in moist areas, others do better in dry districts. Choose a plant suitable for the area you live in.

Babur's Garden in Kabul
Of the fruits of the hot climate people bring into the town—from Lamghanat the orang and citron . . . I laid out the Four Gardens . . . there oranges, citrons and pomegranates grow in abundance.
—Memoirs of Babur

AUSTRALIAN BOTTLEBRUSH
(*Callistemon lanceolata*)

This is a very graceful, small tree with a rather delicate appearance. The small leaves appear in stiff whorls on very slender branches which, in the weeping varieties, droop wistfully. The scarlet, pendulous flower-heads consist of fluffy stamens which grow on the ends of the branches. The flower-heads can be upto 8 inches long.

The tree grows well in dry and semi-dry regions. When full-grown, the bark develops fissures, giving it an interesting texture. The tree is easily grown from seed and cuttings.

CASSIA

Cassia is a genus of 500 trees belonging to the Leguminosae family, the third-largest family of flowering trees, which includes climbers, shrubs, trees and even water plants. Cassias are native to both hemispheres and grow in the tropical and warm temperate regions of the world. Some of the loveliest of all flowering trees such as the Javanese Pink cassia and Golden Shower tree belong to this family.

Pink Cassia (*C. javanica*)—This is a small to medium-sized tree with a graceful spreading habit. The light, feathery leaflets are rounded and the flowers, which grow in clusters, come in shades of pink, from strawbery to deep rose. The flowers appear from April to June. A native of Malaya and Java, this tree likes a humid climate but can be grown successfully in some dry areas. Though the flowering period is short, the loose clusters of flowers are an exquisite sight and the tree is well worth planting. The leaflets, when they appear, are a vivid green which deepens with age. The deep-pink buds appear on the ends of the branches along with new flush of leaves. The tree must be planted in a sheltered spot as it is not too hardy, especially when young. The wood is brittle and branches can snap off in a violent wind.

Amaltas/Shower of Gold (*C. fistula*)—This is one of the most popular garden trees in India and abroad, especially England. Also called Shower of Gold, it gets this name because of the long racemes of flowers which can be over a foot long. The flowers, seed pods and bark all have medicinal value. According to the English naturalist Hans Sloane (1660-1753), an extract of the pods 'helps mad people to sleep'! Various parts are used as an insecticide, as a cure for ringworm, and in cough medicines. In ayurveda, parts of the bark and fruit are used to cleanse the body of waste matter, and to treat heart diseases and other ailments.

This is a tree that does exceptionally well in dry and semi-dry regions. It will grow in moister areas provided the soil is well drained and there is no fear of water-logging. In deciduous trees, the leaflets, when they appear are a clear, fresh green. The canary-gold flowers which stream down from the branches, appear in May and June. The tree is bare for a very short while and the new growth appears quickly after leaf-fall. The tree is a slow grower but begins flowering when fairly young.

C. renigera—This is a small, quick-flowering tree native to Burma. It bears pale rose-pink flowers, from May to July. It is easily grown from seed or cuttings and flowers in three to four years. This species does better in dry regions than in moist ones.

BAUHINIA

All bauhinias are small to medium-sized trees with sweetly-scented flowers. *B. variegata* is a small tree and is seen lining many avenues in the cities. In Florida and Trinidad, it is often

Bauhinia

called the Orchid Tree as the flowers resemble an orchid. This tropical tree is native to India and grows in the plains and foothills. Villagers make a tasty vegetable curry out of the young flower-buds. Bauhinias are named after two sixteenth century botanists, Jean and Gaspard Bauhin. It is also called the Camel-foot Tree because the deeply-notched leaves resemble a camel's hoof print. Kalidasa, the great Indian poet-dramatist sings praises of this tree in many of his poems and plays.

The bi-lobed leaves are split in the centre and are fairly large, making it easy to recognize the tree. The flowers may be pink, purple-magenta, or white, depending upon the variety. *B. candia* has white flowers and *B. purpurea* has purple-magenta flowers. The flowers are large and showy, with claw-like petals. Some varieties flower in November/December; others in March, often before the leaves appear.

Bauhinias grow easily from seed or cuttings. Plants from cuttings are immensely satisfying as they flower in the following season. Bauhinias like well-drained, fairly rich soil, but will grow in poor soil as well. Young saplings can be affected by the cold, so in the northern plains, it is advisable to mulch the young saplings during winter. Excellent for a garden which can accommodate both summer- and winter-flowering trees. It adds colour to gardens in the north, when most other shrubs and trees are bereft of flowers.

Its topmost twigs are tangled by a gentle breeze, sprays of blossoms rise out of delicate leaf crowns;
bees are whirling drunk on honey trickling down;
whose mind is not ripped by the beauty of this Kovidara tree?
    —Kalidasa

TEMPLE TREE FRANGIPANI (*Plumeria*)

This is one of the best-loved trees of the tropics, and widely cultivated in many parts of India. It was grown in temple courtyards, both Buddhist and Hindu, in ancient India, Burma and Thailand, and the flowers were offered to the gods (hence the name Temple Tree). It is also called the Pagoda Tree as it is grown near the burial grounds in Burma where pagodas mark the graves. In the East, it is associated with the continuity of life for it has the ability to burst into flower, even when lifted from the ground.

Plumerias are small trees whose stubby, thick branches taper smoothly. The broad leaves are lanceolate, with a fine point. They grow at the ends of branches in crowded whorls. The five-petalled flowers may be pink, white, creamy-white with a yellow heart, or a deep pink-red, depending upon the variety. The flowers have a waxy texture and are very fragrant. The tree usually flowers twice a year—once in March/April when it blooms freely and once again in September/October. In the right conditions (warm, moist climate), a full-grown tree will bloom almost throughout the year. The tree loses leaves in winter as it grows older. Young trees remain green all the year round. When wounded, the branches exude a milky sap which is poisonous but has medicinal uses. In South America and India, people use the sap to treat inflammation and fevers. In Java, the flowers are used to make a sweet dish which is very popular.

The tree is easily propagated from cuttings, but one should remove its leaves and let the cutting dry before planting, especially in the northern plains which have extreme climates. This hardens the latex which makes for better rooting. In warm, moist regions, the cutting can be put directly into the ground. Though the tree grows best in humus-rich soil, it will grow perfectly well in fairly poor soil, just the thing for a gardener who does not have the time to enrich the land before planting. Plumerias do extremely well in large pots and can make an exotic feature in a small pot garden.

CRAPE MYRTLE (*Lagerstroemia indica*)

This small tree is not indigenous to India but to China. It has small, oval leaves which may be arranged opposite each other or in whorls. The flowers which appear on the tips of the twigs, have a delicate crepe-like crinkley texture. The fruit has a woody shell.

This tree does very well in the northern plains where the summers are hot and dry. It has a long flowering period—from May until the beginning of the cold season. It is not a very pretty sight in winter, when it sheds its leaves, but that is more than compensated for by its long flowering season and free-flowering habit. The plant needs severe pruning which is best done in winter, when it is resting.

L. lancasteri is a small tree, with leaves larger than those of *L.indica* but its clusters of flowers are just as spectacular.

Crape myrtles, if shrubs, look their best when grown in groups. The shrubs can also be trained as tall hedges. The tree variety can be used to line a small path or grown singly, and can make the vertical feature in a small garden. Grow a Coral Tree or abauhinia nearby to provide the focal point in winter when the crape myrtle is bare.

The flowers may be mauve, white, salmon pink or pale lilac. The tree is easily propagated from seed and cuttings, and begins flowering within a couple of seasons.

BRUNFELSIA

This is a small, slow-growing shrub. *B.americana* has white flowers which turn a pale yellow as they age and *B. calycina* has sweetly-scented purple flowers which also change colour as they age, to pale mauve and then white. This trait has given them the sobriquet 'Yesterday, Today and Tomorrow'. The plant has neatly-shaped leaves and interesting, crooked branches.

Brunfelsias are a great favourite in the tropics where the weather is warm and moist. The full-grown shrub has a long flowering period—from spring to the onset of the colder season. In the northern plains with its extreme climate, it has a brief flowering period, but the shrub is attractive even when not in flower. It may flower again for a short spell after the rains.

In hot, dry regions, the plant should be sheltered. The plant requires some pruning, but drastic pruning is not advised. It is easily propagated by cuttings. Brunfelsias do well in pots. There is a free-flowering dwarf variety available in nurseries which has deep violet flowers.

DURANTA/PIGEON BERRY/SKY FLOWER (*Plumieri*)

This plant from tropical America is commonly used as a hedge plant, but can be very ornamental if planted singly. *D. variegata* has pretty, green and cream foliage, and the plant looks charming even when not in flower. Durantas have long sprays of small mauve flowers which appear only on the top of the stems, and are a great favourite with bees. The flowers, though not dramatic, are lovely, and the orange-gold berries which hang in long bunches are truly striking. Durantas are hardy and easy to grow. The branches are sturdy and the slender twigs have a drooping habit.

LANTANA

This hardy shrub is from tropical America but has been naturalized in India. In fact, in many areas the plant has become an absolute nuisance. The hybrid varieties have large heads of flowers in mauve, bright golden-yellow, white and orange-red. The plant flowers profusely for a long period. Lantanas have prickly stems; the leaves are rough-textured and toothed, and have a slightly unpleasant smell.

Lantanas will thrive even in the poorest of soils and need very little attention, but they will not grow in clayey, soggy soil. The seeds have a habit of spreading and germinating in the most annoying way, and in a small garden, this can be disastrous. Be vigilant and remove all seedlings as they appear. The best way to prevent this is by not allowing the plant to seed. Remove the flower-heads as they begin to wither. The hybrids are not quite as prolific as the old varieties. *L. sellowiana* is a trailing variety with pretty, mauve, verbena-like flowers. It is a useful plant for growing in tubs and urns and is very effective in hanging baskets. It can also be trained up a pipe, draped on a fence, or used to cover any unsightly patch.

HYDRANGEA

Like the last green in the palette's colours,
these leaves are without lustre, rough and dry
under umbelled flowers that were duller
but for a blue reflected from the sky.

—Rilke

These are bushy shrubs, and some may have a climbing habit. The flowers are borne on short stems and the inflorescence is large. The flowers are often sterile like those of the Hortensia group. The origins of this plant are a little convoluted but most are from China and Japan.

There are many garden hybrids available in the nurseries—some are hardy, others delicate. Some like growing in the full sun while others need to be partially shaded. The flowers come in shades of blue, purple and pink, and there is also a snow-white variety, *H. paniculata*, though sadly, it is not easily procured.

The nature of the soil affects the colour of the flower. If grown in alkaline soil, the flowers will be pink or red, and if grown in acidic soil, they will be blue or purple.

The young leaves of a particular variety, H. thunbergii, are used in Japan to make a sweet tea called Amacha. On Buddha's birthday, a decoction made from the leaves is used to wash his images.

All hydrangeas like a cool climate, rich soil and a regular mulching with leaf compost. They will not grow in the northern plains but do very well in the hills and cooler regions. The bush should be thinned out when new shoots appear in spring so that the remaining branches receive enough light and air to ripen the wood. If this is not done, the blooms are usually small and the flower- heads scanty. Remove dead wood in winter. A variety called 'Blue wave', if grown in acidic soil, has flowers that are a deep Gentian-blue. The Lacecaps can have blue, white or pink flowers which are fragrant.

The plant can be used to fringe a shrubbery, placed in key positions in lawns and borders or grown against a wall. They can also be grown in large tubs. If the garden is infomal and natural in style, hydrangeas make a charming feature in a woodland setting.

Cuttings made in summer will root easily and soon grow into sturdy plants.

FUCHSIA

This is a very important plant from an ornamental point of view. There are some 100 species, mostly native to Central and South America, though there are a few found in New Zealand and Tahiti. The stems are woody and the pendant flowers look like a ballerina's tutu. The sepals and petals are usually in different colours—red/white, purple/red, pink/white. There are countless cultivars with long, flying sepals and frilled petals. The small leaves are smooth, and the juicy berries edible. Maori women used the blue pollen of *F. excorticata* to paint their faces.

Fuchsias like a moderate climate; they will not grow in very hot or very cold places. They like soil rich in humus. Drooping fuchsias look very attractive in window-boxes or hanging baskets.

Nature's Super Cleaners

Clean the air! Clean the sky! Wash the wind.

—T.S. Eliot

Modern human beings, especially those of us who live in cities and towns, breathe the most filthy, noxious air, and we have no one to blame but ourselves. We decimate the forests, kill the earth and pollute the air and oceans, all for the sake of some paltry comforts and in our arrogant belief that everything in this world is there solely for our benefit. We are not only arrogant, we are stupid as well, for although we know that a pollution-free world is what we need, we will not give up the polluting agents (automobiles, synthetic fabrics, gas stoves, cosmetics etc.) we want so badly. Forests, oceans and clean air can all go to the devil with our blessings.

Man needs air even more than food, clothing and shelter. No air, no homo sapien. The earth was inhabitable until plants made it possible for higher life forms to exist by converting the highly toxic atmosphere into one conducive to life. Rainforests are the lungs of the world, releasing oxygen and removing carbon-dioxide, and the wetlands with their aquatic plants are the kidneys that remove toxic wastes from the water. We moronic humans are doing our best to eradicate them, forgetting that without plants, neither man, nor woman, nor child could exist, leave alone the denizens of the forest or air. We are dependent on them not only for food, clothing and medicine, but also for the very air we breathe. If we insist on using polluting agents in addition to the noxious substances we release, the least we can do is grow plants which will rid us of the toxins.

Carbon-dioxide, carbon-monoxide, methane and ammonia are among the 150 toxic substances that human beings release. With 6 billion humans on this planet, that's a formidable amount of toxic substances!

All plants are eco-friendly, but some are more efficient at cleaning up our messes than others. With the right plants, we can create an environment that mimics the way nature cleans up the earth's atmosphere.

Modern city-dwellers spend almost 90 per cent of their time indoors where the air is no cleaner than the air outside. The main cause of pollution is automobile emissions. But the air is also polluted—by chlorinated water which releases chloroform, gas stoves, grocery bags, face tissues and synthetic fabrics which release formaldehyde; cleaning agents which release ammonia; duplicating machines which release trichloroethylene; cosmetics which release acetone and alcohol; and adhesives, stains, varnishes and tobacco smoke which release benzene. These polluting agents cause diseases which range from nervous disorders and asthma to allergies and ENT infections. Scary, isn't it? But nature has the solution. Scientists at the NASA Research Centre discovered that houseplants could remove volatile organic chemicals from sealed test chambers, and in 1984, demonstrated the ability of plants to remove formaldehyde.

American plantscapers and houseplant growers quickly caught on, and the Associated Landscape contractors of America jointly landed a two-year study with NASA to evaluate the ability of twelve common houseplants to remove the most common toxins—formaldehyde, benzene and trichloroethylene—from the air. To date, fifty houseplants have been tested for their ability to remove various toxic gases. And interestingly, there is no apparent damage to the plants. Some are good at removing formaldehyde, others xylene and toluene, some ammonia, and some remove more than one toxic substance. Plants also release phytochemicals which supress mould, spores and bacteria found in the ambient air. Reason enough for keeping indoor plants, not to mention that they will make your living space more attractive.

The plants mentioned below rate high on the list of air-purifiers.

Dendrobium orchid—The name comes from the Greek word meaning 'tree of life'. An epiphyte, it belongs to that group of plants (cacti, orchids, bromeliads) that release oxygen even at night, the opposite of most plants. This tropical orchid is native to many countries including India and is very tolerant of indoor air. Its exotic white flowers are sweetly scented. Keep the plant in semi-shade, check the plant regularly and remove all insects that will harm it. Water frequently during spring and summer, sparingly during the rains. The soil mixture should be rich in leaf mould and peat manure. (*See* 'Orchids and Other Exotica'.)

King of Hearts (*Homalomena wallisii*)—This attractive plant is the best remover of ammonia in the air. It needs a certain amount of care if it is to grow healthily. It likes an airy but shady spot, though dappled sunlight will do it no harm. It likes a warm, humid climate. Spray the leaves frequently during the hot, dry summers. Keep the soil moist and feed with a liquid fertilizer during the growing period (March to October). Use fairly rich, well-drained soil.

Dumb cane (*Diffenbachia*)—This plant is neither a cane nor a bamboo but belongs to the arum family. (For care *see* 'House Plants'.)

Dragon Tree (*Dracaena marginata*)—This is one of the best-known and easy-to-grow of all dracaenas. It is very happy in indoor conditions. The leaves do not turn yellow when indoors, and the plant tolerates low light levels and dry air. The glossy leaves are edged with red. Originally from Madagascar, the plant needs semi-shade. It can also tolerate low temperature. The soil should be moist but not soggy. Feed all through summer at regular intervals; twice a month will do. Stop feeding in winter. When the older leaves begin to yellow, remove immediately. It grows well in standard soil mixture. It is an efficient remover of xylene and trichloroethylene.

Gerbera

Gerbera (*Gerbra jamesonii*)—This South African plant has large, attractive, daisy-like flowers. The hybrid varieties come in a range of colours—yellow, red, pinks and orange. The flower-heads are borne on long sturdy stems and the large leaves are a little leathery. Gerberas, named after an eighteenth century German physician, like a cool climate, and in the right conditions, will keep flowering for months. They don't do well in the northern plains except in the cool months. Use good garden animal manure mixed generously with well-rotted compost. Do not overwater as the roots will rot. Feed during the growing season. Its ability to remove toxins makes it a valuable indoor plant even when not in flower.

Kimberly Queen (*Nephrolepis obliterate*)—This tropical fern is quite common in cities and towns as it does not need the high level of humidity that most ferns do. The tapering, long fronds grow freely and the plant has a lush growth even when potted. It is very highly rated as a toxin remover. Though the plant tolerates dry air, a regular misting of the leaves is beneficial. The soil mixture should consist of leaf mould mixed with a little sandy soil. It likes to remain where it is, so don't transplant or divide unless absolutely necessary. Keep the soil moist but not soggy. The root ball should not dry out. This fern increases the humidity in the air and removes alcohol and formaldehyde. It is a very well-behaved indoor plant. In dry areas, it should be grown near plants that need high levels of humidity, like orchids.

Peace Lily (*Spathiphyllum*)—This plant is in a class of its own when it comes to removing toxic substances from the air. It removes acetone, methyl alcohol, ethyl acetate, ammonia *and* benzene! To a lesser degree, it also removes trichloro- ethylene, formaldehyde and xylene. A native of Columbia and Venezuela, it has elegant foliage and produces milky-white spathes which are borne on long, stiff stalks. The spathes are green when they open, turn pure white as they mature, and become green again when they begin to age. They stay on the plant for a long time. The plant likes a moderately warm climate and is best grown

Peace Lily

in semi-shade. The leaves are prone to attacks from scale insects, and snails can decimate the leaves. The soil mixture should be well drained, and rich in rotting organic material. Keep the soil moist. The plant is suited to hydro-culture.

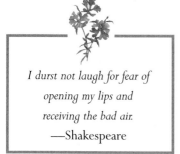

I durst not laugh for fear of opening my lips and receiving the bad air.
—Shakespeare

Dwarf date palm/Phoenix Palm (*Phoenix roebelenii*)—This small, delicate palm is a native of North Africa and sub-tropical Asia. A slow grower, it makes an excellent pot plant. The long fronds are almost horizontal to the stem and droop gracefully. It does exceptionally well indoors as long as it is placed in an airy, well-lit spot. The phoenix palm is sensitive to hard water and overwatering. The root ball should be kept evenly moist. Reduce watering during the winter months. Mist the leaves frequently during the dry weather—it loves attention and fuss. Feed regularly in summer. The soil mixture should be rich in compost and humus.

Bamboo palm (*Chamaedirea seifrizii*)—This is an extremely elegant palm from Mexico and is very easy to grow. It requires no fuss and will grow well in almost any indoor situation. Like other palms, it is rated high on the list of eco-friendly plants. The fans, which are a rich green, grow on the crown, and the slender canes grow in clusters. It likes being potted and is resistant to pests. If kept too dry, it can be attacked by mites and scale insects. It does not like direct sunlight. A cool, partially sunny situation is ideal. Water copiously in summer; in winter, just enough to keep the root ball moist. Do not cut the tips of the fans as that will retard the growth and new shoots will not appear. The soil mixture should consist of good garden soil mixed with well-rotted compost. Make sure the drainage is good.

Spider Plant (*Chlorophytum cosmosium*)—This plant from South Africa rates high on the list of air-purifiers. (*See* 'Potted Plants and Indoor Gardens'.)

Schefflera/Umbrella Tree (*Brassaia actinophylla*)—This hardy evergreen is from Indonesia and Australia and is a trouble-free indoor plant. It is a slow grower and excellent for pot cultivation. If in the ground, it can reach upto a height of 6 ft. The glossy, oval leaflets grow in radiating groups at the end of the leaf stem.

The Umbrella Tree, as it is often called, is very hardy and easy to grow. It does well in dappled sunlight. Water thoroughly but let the soil dry out between waterings. Increase watering in summer and reduce in winter. Pot in soil rich in organic nutrients. If the air is too dry, mist the leaves as it likes a high level of humidity.

Dracaena warneckii and *D. fragrans* belong to a large group of palm-like plants. The arching, lance-shaped leaves grow in rosettes. Both are highly-rated air-purifiers. They like a well-lit, semi-shaded position. Though the plants like to be watered thoroughly, they will not stand waterlogging. *D. warneckii* develops root-rot if kept too damp or cold. To stimulate new growth in *D. fragrans*, cut back to about 20 inches. Grow in rich, loamy soil. Young plants should be repotted each year at the same time till they mature. Mist the leaves during hot, dry weather conditions.

Boston Fern (*Nephrolepis exaltata*)—This native of the tropics, though a common houseplant now, was popularized by the Victorians who prized it for its foliage. The tapering fronds have a cascading habit and can grow upto 3 ft in length in the right conditions. This is a good fern for hanging baskets. As an air-purifier it has few rivals but will need some attention when grown indoors, if it is to thrive. Water regularly and mist the leaves. It likes a light, airy position and does not like the hot sun.

Ferns grow best in an almost soil-less mixture consisting of well-rotted leaf compost and a little sandy soil. Make sure the pot has a good drainage hole, and place a layer of dry moss over the pot shards. Ferns are propagated by division.

Ficus alii—This variety of ficus comes from Thailand and resembles *F. benjamina*, but is much hardier. In some gardening books in the West, it is called a 'new' ficus only because it became popular there as recently as in the 1980s. A Japanese plant collector imported it from Thailand and first sold it commercially in Florida. Though it likes the full sun, it will grow in partial shade. Grow in normal soil mixture and do not overwater. It increases the humidity level and is rated high as a toxin remover.

Areca Palm (*Chrysalidocarpus lutescens*)—This delicate palm is often called the Butterfly Palm as the long fronds have the same fragile beauty and the leaflets spread out on either sides of the rib like butterfly wings. It comes from Mauritius and the tropics. The foliage is composed of long fans with narrow leaflets. It makes a good pot plant, though it can grow up to a height of 20 ft. It is very tolerant of indoor conditions and releases enormous amounts of moisture into the air. It is eminently suited to dry conditions and removes toxins at an astonishing rate. It likes rich, loamy soil and regular watering and feeding. Grow in partial sunlight.

Others—Lady Palm (*Rhapis excelsa*), Rubber Plant (*Ficus robusta*), *Dracaena deremensis,* English Ivy (*Hedera helix*), Golden Pothos (*Epipremnum aureum*), Chrysanthemum, *Philodendron erubescens,* Syngonium, Parlour Palm (*Chamaedorea elegans*), Weeping Fig (*Ficus benjamina*), Wax Begonia (*Begonia semperflorens*), *Philodendron selloum,* Heart-leaf Philodendron (*P. oxycardium*), Mother-in-law's Tongue (*Sansevieria trifasciata*), Maranta, Dwarf Banana (*Musa cavendishii*) Christmas Cactus (*Schlumbergera*) Oakleaf Ivy (*Cissus rhombifolia*) *Aglaonema crispum,* Anthurium, Croton, Poinsettia, Dwarf Azalea, Peacock Plant (*Calathea makoyana*), Cyclamen (*Aloe vera*), *Achemea fasciata*, Tulips (*Tulipa*).

Plants which Remove Ammonia
Lady Palm
King of Hearts
Anthurium
Chrysanthemum
Dendrobium Orchid
Tulip
Ficus benjamina

Plants which Remove Xylene and Toluene
Dwarf Date Palm
Areca Palm
Moth Orchid
Dumb Cane
Dendrobium Orchid
Kimberly Queen

Plants which Remove Formaldehyde
Boston Fern
Chrysanthemum
Gerbera
Dwarf Date Palm
Bamboo Palm
Kimberly Queen
Rubber Plant

Select Bibliography

Angel, Marie, *Cottage Flowers* (London: Pelham Books, 1980).

Archer, W.G. (ed.), trans. Rehatsek, Edward, *The Gulistan or Rose Garden of Sa'di* (London: George Allen & Unwin Ltd., 1964).

Beilenson, Peter and Behn, Harry (translated by), *Haiku Harvest* (New York: The Peter Pauper Press, 1962).

Beri, S.N., *The Houseplant Guidebook* (Delhi: Hind Pocketbooks, 1987).

Bianchini, Francesco and Corbetta, Francesco, *Health Plants of the World* (New York: Atlas of Medicinal Plants, Newsweek Books).

Boyle, John A. (ed.), *Persia History and Heritage* (London: Henry Melland, 1978).

Chiej, Roberto, *The Macdonald Encyclopedia of Medicinal Plants* (London: Macdonald, 1984).

Conran, Shirley, *The Magic Garden* (London: Macdonald & Co., 1983).

Cooper, Cathy, *Aromatherapy* (London: Sunburst Books, 1995).

Dang, Rupin, *Flowers of the Western Himalayas* (New Delhi: Indus, 1993).

Evans, Hazel, *The Patio Garden* (New York: Penguin Books, 1985).

Fitzgerald, Scott (translated by), *Rubaiyat of Omar Khayyam* (London: Penguin Books Ltd., UK).

Fletcher, W.W., *The Pest War* (Oxford: Basil Blackwell & Mott Ltd., 1974).

Ghazi, Zahiru'd-din Muhammad Babur Padshah, trans. Annette Swannah Beveridge, *Babur-Nama* (*Memoirs of Babur*) (Delhi: Low Price Publications, 1997).

Gibson, Michael, *The Rose Gardens of England* (London: Collins, 1988).

Gorer, Richard, *The Growth of Gardens* (London: Faber and Faber, 1978).

Graves, Robert, *Collected Poems* (Doubelday & Company, Inc., 1955).

Griffith, Ralph T.H., *Hymns of the Rigveda* Vol III (Munshiram Manoharlal Publsihers Pvt. Ltd., 1987).

Harler, Agnes W., *The Garden in the Plains* (London: Oxford University Press, 1948).

Harris, John (compiled by), *A Garden Alphabet* (London: Octopus Books Limited, 1979).

Hellyer, Arthur, *Practical Gardening* (England: Hamlyn, Middlesex, 1984).

Hicks, David, *Garden Design* (London: Routledge, Kegan & Paul, 1982).

Hrdlicka, Zdenek and Hrdlickova, Venceslava, *The Art of Japanese Gardening* (London: Hamlyn, 1981).

Hunt, Peter (ed.), *The Marshall Cavendish Encyclopedia of Gardening* (London: Paul Hamlyn, 1969).

Huxley, Anthony (ed.), *Evergreen Garden Trees & Shrubs* (London: Blandford Press, 1975).

Jaggi, O.P., *Scientists of Ancient India and Their Achievements* (Delhi: Atma Ram & Sons, 1991).

Jekyll, Gertrude, *Wood and Garden* (Longman Group Ltd.)

Keene, Donald (compiled by), *Anthology of Japanese Literature* (London: Penguin Books Ltd., UK, 1955).

Kerrod, Robin, *Trees* (Bristol: Purnell, 1985).

Lancaster, Late S. Percy, revised by Bose, T.K. and Mukherjee, D., 'An Amateur in an Indian Garden', *Gardening in India* (New Delhi: Oxford and IBH Publishing Company Co. Pvt. Ltd., 1989).

Lesniewicz, Paul, trans. Simpson, Susan, *Bonsai: The Complete Guide to Art and Technique* (Dorset: Blandford Press, Poole, 1985).

Lunardi, Costanza, *Simon & Schuster's Guide to Shrubs and Vines* (New York: Simon & Schuster Inc., 1988).

Milner-Gulland, Robin and Levi, Peter (ed.), *Penguin Modern European Poets* (1962).

Morris, Ivan, Court Life in Ancient Japan, *The World of the Shining Prince* (Penguin Books, 1964).

Nichols, Beverly, *Down the Garden Path* (Antique Collectors' Club, 1997).

Nicholson, Reynold A., *Rumi, Poet and Mystic* (One World Publications, UK).

Perry, Frances, *Flowers of the World* (England: Optimum Books, Middlesex, 1972).

Phillips, C.E. Lucas, *Roses for Small Gardens* (London: Pan Books, 1972).

Polunin, Oleg, and Stainton, Adam, *Concise Flowers of the Himalaya* (New Delhi: Oxford India Paperbacks, 1997).

Randhawa, M.S., *Flowering Trees* (New Delhi: National Book Trust, 1983).

Rayzer, G., *Flowering Cacti: A Colour Guide* (London: David & Charles, 1984).

Richardson, Rosamond, *Roses: A Celebration* (London: Piatkus, 1984).

Rose, Graham, *The Romantic Garden* (London: Penguin Books, 1996).

Scholes, Robert; Comey, Nancy R.; Klaus, Carl H.; and Silverman, Michael (ed.), *Elements of Literature* (Oxford: Oxford University Press, 1975).

Seymour, Jacqueline, *Trees*, Nature Series (Great Britain: Colour Library International, 1978).

Shewell-Cooper, W.E., *Enjoy Your Gardening* (London: Pan Books Ltd., 1957).

Smith, Geoffrey, *Shrubs & Small Trees* (Middlesex: Hamlyn, 1985).

Stryk, Lucien and Ikemoto, Takashi (translated by), *The Penguin Book of Zen Poetry* (Penguin Books Ltd., UK).

Swarup, Vishnu, *Garden Flowers* (New Delhi: National Books Trust, 1995).

The Cambridge History of English and American Literature (18 volumes).

The Complete Works of Shakespeare (Collins' Clear-Type Press, 1923).

The Concise Oxford Dictionary of Quotations (Oxford University Press, 1981).

The Reader's Digest Complete Library of The Garden (three volumes), (London: The Reader's Digest Association, 1963).

Tillotson, G.H.R., *Architectural Guide for Travellers,* Mughal India (London: Viking, 1990).

Titley, Norah, and Wood, Frances, *Oriental Gardens* (London: The British Library, 1991).

Verey, Rosemary, *The Scented Garden* (London: Michael Joseph Limited, 1981).

Warren, William, *Tropical Flowers of India & Sri Lanka* (Hong Kong: Periplus Editions, 1998).

Weiss, Gaea and Shandor, *Growing and Using the Health Herbs* (New Jersey: Wing Books).

Wickham, Cynthia, *The Houseplant Book: A Complete Guide to Creative Indoor Gardening* (London: Marshall Cavendish Editions, 1979).

Wolverton, B.C., *Eco-Friendly House Plants* (George Weidenfeld & Nicholson Ltd., 1996).

Xenophon, trans. Rex Warner, *A History of My Times* (Hellenica: Penguin Books, 1979).

Index